IMAGES
of America

BUILDING THE NATCHEZ TRACE PARKWAY

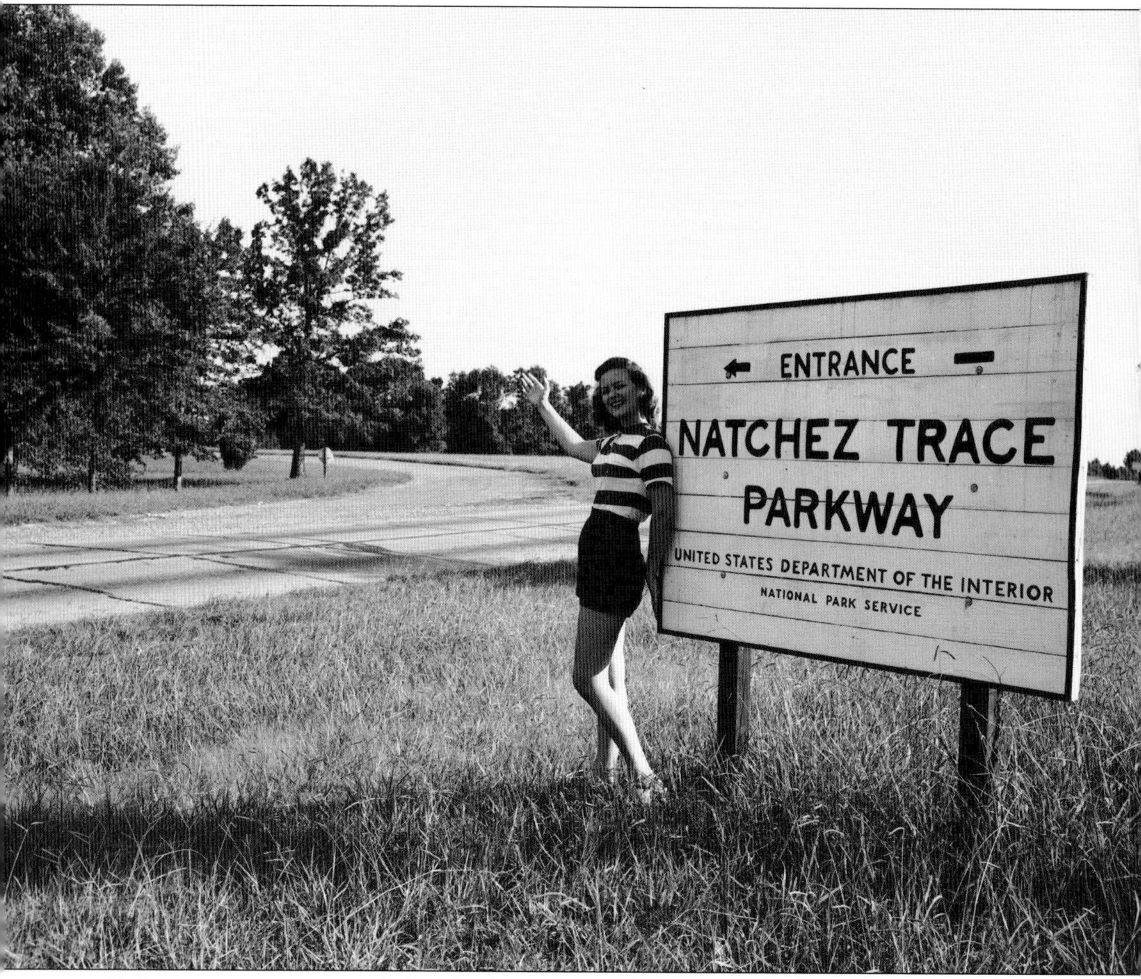

Early promoters envisioned the Natchez Trace Parkway in part as a gateway for travelers from the North to explore Southern historic sites. Mississippi governor Fielding L. Wright's daughter appeared in this promotional photograph to highlight the parkway as a new attraction. Governor Wright was Strom Thurmond's vice presidential running mate on the Dixiecrat ticket in 1948. The parkway national park image is not yet defined on the temporary entrance sign. (Courtesy of Godwin Advertising Collection, Special Collections Department, Mitchell Memorial Library, Mississippi State University.)

On the Cover: Until the recent development of convenience markets, automobile travelers had to be concerned about where fresh drinking water could be found along the route. Parkway designers highlighted access to springs where travelers could stop and use their own cups to drink water flowing out of the hillsides. Located at the Meriwether Lewis site, Old Springs became an attraction that merited its own sign, loop, and picnic area. (TSLA.)

IMAGES
of America

BUILDING THE NATCHEZ TRACE PARKWAY

Natchez Trace Parkway Association

ARCADIA PUBLISHING

ISBN 978-0-7385-9153-7

Published by Arcadia Publishing
Charleston, South Carolina

Printed in the United States of America

Library of Congress Control Number: 2011940458

For all general information, please contact Arcadia Publishing:
Telephone 843-853-2070
Fax 843-853-0044
E-mail sales@arcadiapublishing.com
For customer service and orders:
Toll-Free 1-888-313-2665

Visit us on the Internet at www.arcadiapublishing.com

This book is dedicated to the early Natchez Trace Parkway Association leaders who envisioned the Natchez Trace Parkway and who sacrificed time and resources to make it a reality.

CONTENTS

FOREWORD

The Natchez Trace Parkway is the latest chapter in the story of one of America's oldest roads. Centuries of struggle for human survival played out on its winding path through the Southern wilderness. The earliest peoples built giant ceremonial mounds, Indian tribes battled for territory, French and Spanish explorers established outposts, American settlers helped forge their independence, explorer Meriwether Lewis's life ended in mystery, international spies plotted treason under the Spanish moss, and cutthroat bandits and ingenious swindlers preyed on travelers. The hardy and clever survived, settlements became towns, and elements of the culture of the Deep South emerged.

The 20th-century creation of a tristate national park from little more than faded accounts of the old Natchez Trace required imagination, ingenuity, and political savvy. The Natchez Trace Parkway Association's vision to preserve sites important to the Southwest Territory was first presented through an artist's colorful renderings of the experience of historic sites from Natchez to Nashville. A road commemorating the old Natchez Trace was proposed to connect those experiences. Drawing upon the colorful stories of authors and journalists such as Eudora Welty and Jonathan Daniels, early association leaders wove tales of the history and lore of the old Natchez Trace so vividly that the public could imagine a ride along the historic road before the first section of parkway opened. The organization's stately ceremonies gave substance to a park that was little more than a dream. The leaders' larger-than-life personalities drew attention to the cause. Their infectious enthusiasm sold the vision first to local communities, then to governors, and finally to federal legislators. Their chameleonlike ability to adjust methods to gain support kept the project alive during periods of changing national priorities. Fittingly, the Southern charm and inventiveness that successfully maneuvered the project through the halls of Congress and the labyrinth of bureaucracy were, to some extent, a product of the survival skills developed by early settlers on the old Natchez Trace and passed down to their descendants.

The 75th anniversary of the Natchez Trace Parkway is an important benchmark to recall the vision of the association founders and to celebrate the association's productive partnership with the National Park Service and the states. Each contributed its own unique perspective and set of skills to give birth to one of our nation's great national parks.

—Tony L. Turnbow
President of the Natchez Trace Parkway Association

ACKNOWLEDGMENTS

A photograph history book can be limited by availability of photographs. Some events and people important to the parkway story are absent from this book only because no photographs of them could be obtained. The association thanks Pat Green; George Herron; Harry Martin; Nancy Conway; Dot Ward; Wendell Simpson; Dan Brown; Calvin Lehew; Katie Watson; Rick Warwick and the Williamson County Archives (WCA); the State of Tennessee Department of Tourist Development (TN); Permanent Collection, Belle Meade Plantation; and Rebecca Garber of Brandon Hall (BH) for providing photographs and information from their collections, and Eudora Welty, LLC, for permission to use a photograph. Thanks also go to the staffs at Mississippi State University (MSU), the University of Mississippi at Oxford (UMO), the Mississippi Department of Archives and History (MDAH), the Tennessee State Library and Archives (TSLA), the Memphis *Commercial Appeal*, the New Orleans *Times-Picayune*, and the Nashville Public Library, which houses the Nashville Banner Collection (Nashville Public Library, Special Collections). Photographs courtesy of those contributors will be referenced by the abbreviations following their names. This book would have been impossible without the help of parkway superintendent Cam Sholly, Christina Smith, Marty Owens, Terry Wildy, Tom Berryhill, and the excellent Natchez Trace Parkway staff. Also, thanks go to Dr. Elbert Hilliard, Susann Hamlin, Emma Crisler, Clay Williams, and Matt Milligan for their assistance in reviewing the materials and for their good suggestions for both content and form.

Introduction

Although the Natchez Trace is one of the oldest trails in North America, by 1900 it was fading from the public's memory. Much of the road was still being used as part of state and county road systems at the dawn of the 20th century; the Natchez Trace, however, had lost its identity as a national road. Relics of its historic significance to the development of the United States still existed, but they lacked a practical link that could be used to tell the story.

Mississippi regent of the Daughters of the American Revolution (DAR) Elizabeth Jones recalled accounts of the old Natchez Trace and suggested protecting its memory by erecting historical markers along the route. The first marker for the state society was set on the bluff overlooking the Mississippi River at Natchez in 1909. Lucille Mayfield, whose husband's ancestor was a member of John Gordon's Company of Spies in the War of 1812, placed several markers as chair of the Natchez Trace Society. Within a few years, DAR markers had been placed from Natchez to Tishomingo County. In Tennessee, the DAR dedicated two markers on the centennial of the declaration of the War of 1812. Daughters of the War of 1812 also placed bronze markers along the old Natchez Trace at locations significant to the march of Andrew Jackson's troops.

The markers and their dedication ceremonies sparked discussions of paving the old road and preserving associated historic sites. The Natchez Trace Parkway was first proposed as a military road. The Natchez Trace Military Highway Association was formed in 1932, and flamboyant newspaper contributor and self-appointed Civil War colonel Jim Walton traveled throughout Mississippi promoting the project with tall-tale lectures of Natchez Trace history. He called himself the "knight of the Natchez Trace." The DAR welcomed the interest "Colonel" Walton generated, even if his facts could not always be substantiated.

A meeting of all interested groups was called for July 18, 1934, at the Edwards Hotel in Jackson, Mississippi. The suggestion was made that various supporters pool their efforts around a new organization, thus the Natchez Trace Parkway Association was born. Lucille Mayfield was elected president, and it was assumed that the DAR would continue to lead the effort. Natchez Trace committees were formed in each county along the old Natchez Trace from Natchez to Nashville. Though the association generated local support, at first it was unable to attract the support of government leaders outside Mississippi, particularly in Washington, DC, where federal support would prove crucial.

Four events changed everything. Lucille Mayfield moved to Washington, DC, to become an assistant to the director of the Works Progress Administration, Secretary of the Interior Harold Ickes. In her new position, Mayfield was able to make contacts inside the executive branch to promote the parkway. Mississippi congressman Jeff Busby adopted the project and worked to secure funding through his position on the powerful House Committee on Appropriations. Mississippi senator Pat Harrison drew on his personal relationship with Pres. Franklin Delano Roosevelt to make the project a New Deal parkway, and Roane Fleming Byrnes was persuaded to become the new president of the association. Byrnes proved to be a fearless human dynamo, whose 35-year commitment to completing the parkway was later credited by Congressman Busby as making the difference. The timing was perfect in the early 1930s to initiate a new federal road project as the Roosevelt Administration had adopted the then novel concept of national parkways to provide Depression-era jobs. The people were in place to turn the idea of building a Natchez Trace commemorative road into reality.

Preserving the history of the old Natchez Trace was paramount for the supporters from the beginning, but generating support from the three states and from federal legislators required proponents to piggyback various projects and programs most likely to attract political support. During the Great Depression, political leaders supported the idea of building a superhighway through the South to create construction jobs. During World War II, the parkway was touted as an important military route to transport troops from Fort Knox to the Gulf Coast without interfering with civilian traffic. Supporters later accepted the National Park Service (NPS) Mission 66 plan to make the parkway a modern recreational experience, because the plan spurred funding for additional construction and visitor amenities. The 1976 American bicentennial provided incentive to build more miles of road to connect historic sites. In the late 1970s and 1980s, promoting tourism development was used to gain the support of businesses.

Obtaining and maintaining political support over seven decades took unprecedented persistence. The Natchez Trace Parkway Association's request for funds competed not only within the National Park Service, but also with every other federal agency and need. The long lag time (up to a decade) between obtaining the right-of-way and cutting a ribbon to open a new section also made it more difficult to maintain public interest. More than two decades elapsed between the initial survey and the opening of the first paved section. National political interests constantly changed, federal officials came and went, and the construction process was slow. The federal government twice considered abandoning the project altogether. In 1955, a newspaper referred to the spotty areas of completed sections as a "motorist's mirage." Selling the vision of the parkway became more difficult the longer the completion was delayed from the government's announced date of 1966, almost 40 years before the final section opened. The association kept a tenacious hold on its dream and continued to push.

The National Park Service at first struggled with the new parkway concept of combining a modern road with the preservation and interpretation of historic sites. The new road could not be built entirely on the old Natchez Trace, because construction would destroy the historic character of a road that the park service was obligated to protect. Conversely, if the parkway were not to be located on the old road, how did it fit into the preservation mission of NPS? Adding to the uncertainty was the discovery that the original courses of Indian trails, the 1798 mail route, and the 1801 and 1807 military roads had changed through the years—each improvement had straightened portions of the road to lessen the distances between various points. NPS resolved the dilemma by determining that its mission was to memorialize the old road by providing a scenic parklike link between historic sites running generally along the routes of the old Natchez Trace.

Creating a park to commemorate the Natchez Trace required more than building a road. Trees were planted in some locations to create and shield a scenic corridor. Wooden way-finding signs were erected not only to direct visitors but also to unify the visitor experience. Wayside stops and interpretive markers were created to highlight and elucidate prehistoric and historic treasures of the Southwest Territory. A visitor center and some visitor amenities were built. Gradually, a national parkway began to take shape.

When Roane Fleming Byrnes died in 1970, Harry Martin, director of the Community Development Foundation (CDF) of Tupelo, assumed the role of parkway lightning rod. The parkway had not been completed by 1966 as promised by Mission 66; funding for construction lagged; and there was no similar program on the horizon. Martin saw the completion of the parkway as an economic benefit for the entire region, and he began a 30-year effort (often behind the scenes) to forge the association's state committees into a unified force to promote completion. With funding from the CDF, the association hired part-time executive director Jim Ballard. A new generation of leaders stepped forward in all three states and concentrated the efforts to "Finish the Trace."

The new leaders succeeded by focusing on the singular mission of completing the road. The northern section of the roadway in Nashville neared completion in time for the Tennessee state bicentennial in 1996. The final sections in Jackson and Natchez opened simultaneously in 2005. Roane Fleming Byrnes had said that she hoped to ride on the parkway from Natchez to Nashville before she traveled above on the streets of gold. She was remembered in the 2005 ceremony in Natchez when the ribbon was cut to open the last section of the road and a granite DAR marker bearing her name was dedicated.

Historic Natchez Trace

The old Natchez Trace emerged from a system of paths created by early peoples on the North American continent. The trails connected their settlements and helped establish a system of trade. Though most of the trail known as the Natchez Trace ran from present-day Natchez to Nashville, the trail system may have extended north to present-day Canada and south into South America. When the federal government authorized construction of a federal road along the old trails, it was first named the Columbian Highway.

As the early peoples formed into tribes or migrated to the area, the trails became more distinct. The Chickasaw Nation was centered near present-day Tupelo. Both Chickasaw and Cherokee tribes used the northern portion of the old Natchez Trace as hunting grounds. The Choctaw Nation was established farther south in the central Mississippi area. Until it was almost eliminated by French military forces following the tribe's capture of Fort Rosalie in Natchez in 1729, the Natchez tribe lived in the Natchez area. Remnants assimilated with the Chickasaw and the Natchez are now a treaty tribe under the Cherokee Nation.

Britain, France, and Spain all vied for land along the old Natchez Trace. Spanish explorer Hernando de Soto is believed to have traveled the Old Trace as far north as southern Tennessee. After the Revolutionary War, Spain controlled settlements at Natchez and what became Memphis to further protect its interests to the west in Mexico and to the east in Florida. France alternately controlled Natchez and attempted to establish outposts northward to present-day Nashville; however, in the 1736 Battle of Ackia, the Chickasaw decisively removed the French from their territory. After the French and Indian War, Britain attempted to prevent its colonists from moving west of the Appalachians, but more than 5,000 crossed the mountains. Some settlers moved to the area and married Chickasaw and Choctaw women before the area was legally opened for settlement.

Pres. Thomas Jefferson recognized that the ability to control access to ports at Natchez and New Orleans would be crucial for the westward expansion of the United States. In 1801, he negotiated treaties with the Chickasaw and Choctaw to build a road along the Indian paths from Nashville to Natchez. Ostensibly, the purpose of the road was to provide an improved route for the delivery of mail between the two cities and for the return of Mississippi River boatmen selling crops and other goods at the ports. But Gen. James Wilkinson revealed its military purpose in his notations on the Natchez Road survey. President Jefferson ordered the US Army to begin construction in 1801, and in 1803 he dispatched companies of troops down the road to Natchez to defend the Louisiana Purchase. In some respects, the Natchez Trace as a federally improved road is a monument to President Jefferson's vision of westward expansion.

American settlers had moved south into Tennessee in the late 1700s. Subsequent treaties with the Chickasaw and Cherokee gradually allowed settlement farther south. Settlers moving to the new territories traveled on the military route, first banding together in Nashville for safety and then moving to new towns along the Old Trace. When the northern Mississippi Territory near present-day Huntsville was opened for settlement about 1809, the movement of hundreds of settlers at Gordon's Ferry would be compared to the later Oklahoma land rush.

As one of the first federally improved roads, the Natchez Road had much in common with modern roads. The Army was ordered to build it eight feet wide to accommodate wagons and carriages, and an additional four feet were cleared on either side. Bridges were built over small streams, and ferries were established at the Duck and Tennessee Rivers. Men ordered to maintain the road were required to erect mile markers at each mile and to place directional signs at intersections to point toward the nearest settlements. Though the Chickasaw and Choctaw retained the right to operate inns for travelers, President Jefferson implemented a program to encourage the building of accommodations about every 20 miles, or the distance travelers could cover in a day. The inns, often called taverns, provided food, drink, stables for horses, and space where travelers could spend the night. Some innkeepers also operated trading posts to provide supplies for travelers. The word *stand* became a common term used to describe a Natchez Trace inn. Stone-lined wells located along the Old Trace may have been dug by the Army to supply water for travelers on ridges. Settlements that would become significant Southern towns sprang up along the road.

When Britain threatened to invade New Orleans in 1813, Gen. Andrew Jackson's cavalry marched south on the Old Trace to Natchez. Inns along the road provided food, forage, and services to the troops. On the return march, Jackson earned the nickname "Old Hickory" when he ignored a War Department order to dismiss his troops before he had led them back home. Like his troops, General Jackson walked most of the distance. In 1814, as the Battle of New Orleans neared, Jackson ordered that thousands of new recruits march down the Old Trace to join his forces at New Orleans. However, only a portion of those men were sent down the old Natchez Trace—General Jackson's aide-de-camp disobeyed the order and sent many of the soldiers south by river. More men died on the perilous marches than died on the battlefield at Chalmette. Stands served as hospitals, and many soldiers who did not survive the marches are buried along the old Natchez Trace. Jackson told his troops that at New Orleans they had "conquered the conquerors of Europe," defeating the British in the victory that put Jackson on the path to the presidency. Jackson returned on the old Natchez Trace in a carriage accompanied by his wife, Rachel, and his son. The couple was welcomed with victory celebrations in settlements as they proceeded northward. The general told assembled crowds his view of the effect of the war efforts on American independence when he said, "henceforth our rights will be respected."

The road became known as a haven for notorious bandits, who often robbed and killed unsuspecting travelers. Some bandits pretended to be gentlemen to win the confidence of travelers before robbing them. Others disguised themselves as American Indians. Robbers were so brazen that victims included soldiers returning from the Battle of New Orleans and Chickasaw chief Tuscumbia.

Religious circuit riders rode along the old Natchez Trace evangelizing the new settlements as part of the Great Awakening Movement. It was said that they were also motivated to eradicate the influence of the earlier French settlers, whose lifestyle differed from the Puritan influences of the eastern settlements.

By 1830, old Natchez Trace began to lose its prominence as a national highway. Andrew Jackson, who had proved the importance of the road, hastened its decline by building a more direct route to New Orleans in 1817. To the west, the invention of the steamboat made travel up the Mississippi River more convenient and safer than traveling on the Old Trace. Nevertheless, communities continued to use the Old Trace for local travel, and much of it was absorbed into local road systems. The Old Trace proved its military use again during the Texas War for Independence as volunteers traveled to Texas. Portions were also used during the Civil War by both Union and Confederate forces.

Even today, abandoned sections of the old Natchez Trace remain identifiable as deep ruts running through the forests. Those well-worn paths preserve a moment in time when the footsteps of thousands of settlers and the wheels of their wagons and carriages hewed the soil and when men such as Meriwether Lewis, Andrew Jackson, Davy Crockett, Piomingo, Pushmataha, Sam Houston, James Audubon, Zachary Taylor, Ulysses Grant, Jefferson Davis, Henry Clay, and possibly even Abraham Lincoln joined them as fellow travelers on the narrow road through the Southern wilderness.

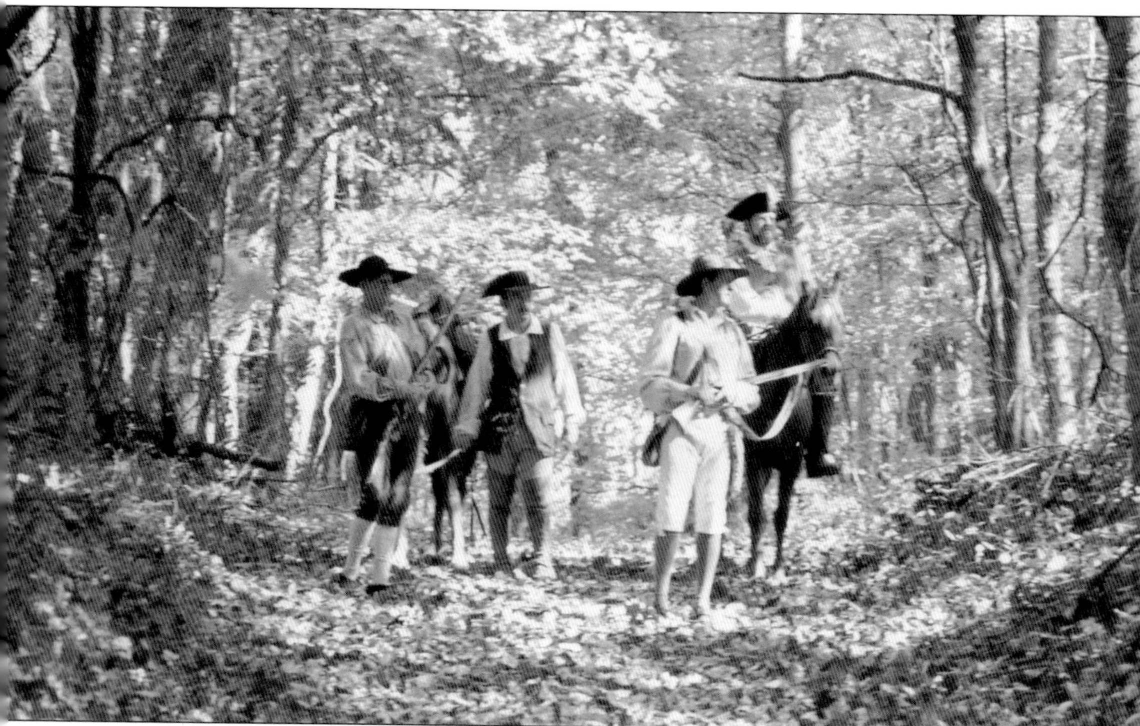

Travelers on the old Natchez Trace encountered numerous hardships and dangers. Boatmen returning to the Ohio Valley from Natchez or New Orleans passed settlers heading south on the road. Both groups met post riders, American Indians, and, occasionally, notorious bandits on the trail. This early-1980s Tennessee Department of Tourist Development photograph depicts the journey of travelers on an abandoned section of the Old Trace. Note the depression in the soil created by thousands of travelers in the early 1800s. (TN.)

One

Relics of the Past
"Pave the Trace"
1907–1934

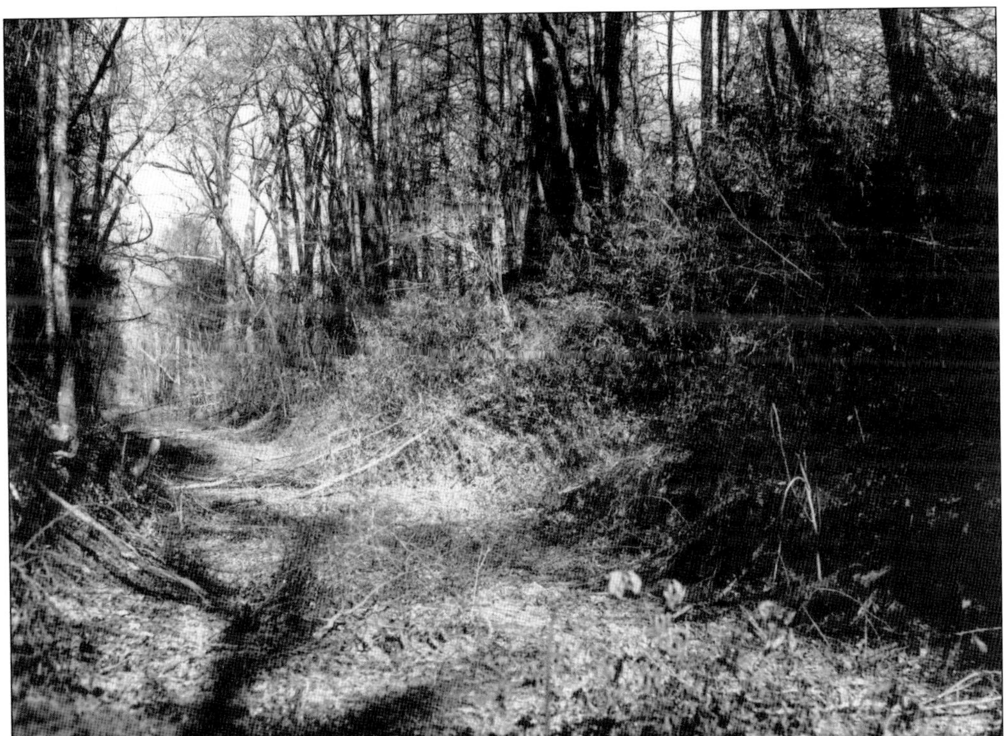

Abandoned portions of the old road, such as this one near Rocky Springs, Mississippi, remained discernible even though no one had traveled them for decades. Centuries of traffic from American Indians, early settlers, horses, wagons, and carriages had worn deep trenches into the terrain. Vegetation did not grow well in soil compacted by thousands of travelers. When surveyors searched for the old Natchez Trace in the 1930s, the barren areas of the roadbed were often distinguishable from the surrounding forest. (NPS.)

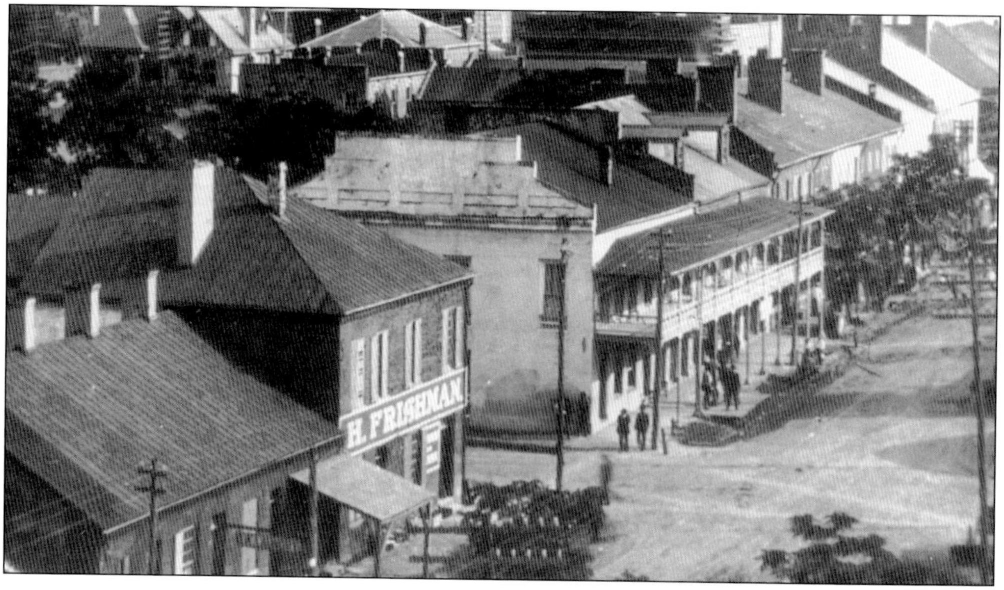

The old Natchez Trace served as an important transportation corridor for the settlement of the Southwest Territory. Settlers moving south into what was then the western frontier hoped to start new lives or make their fortunes in the new settlements. Land speculators fueled development. Occasionally, swindlers sold deeds to towns that did not exist. Settlements along the Natchez Road developed into towns in Mississippi such as Jackson, Mathiston, Iuka, French Camp, and Port Gibson (pictured above and below around 1905). Though sections of one of the first federally improved roads became so intertwined with new roads that it could no longer be distinguished, historic sites along the old Natchez Trace reminded the curious of the important events that had occurred along the road. Unfortunately, some of the sites no longer exist. (Both, MDAH.)

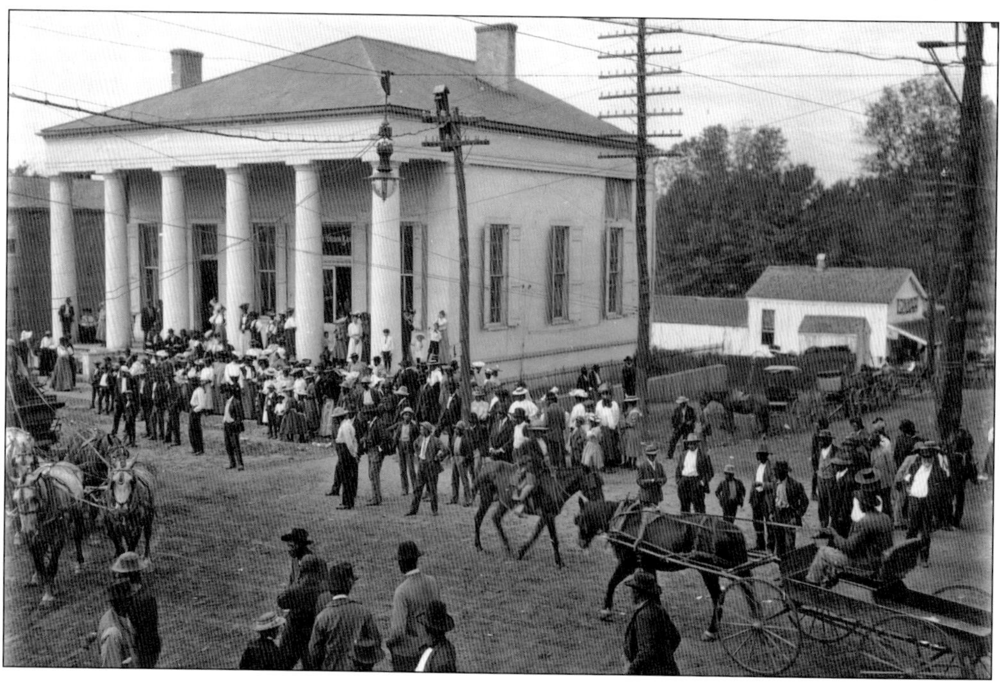

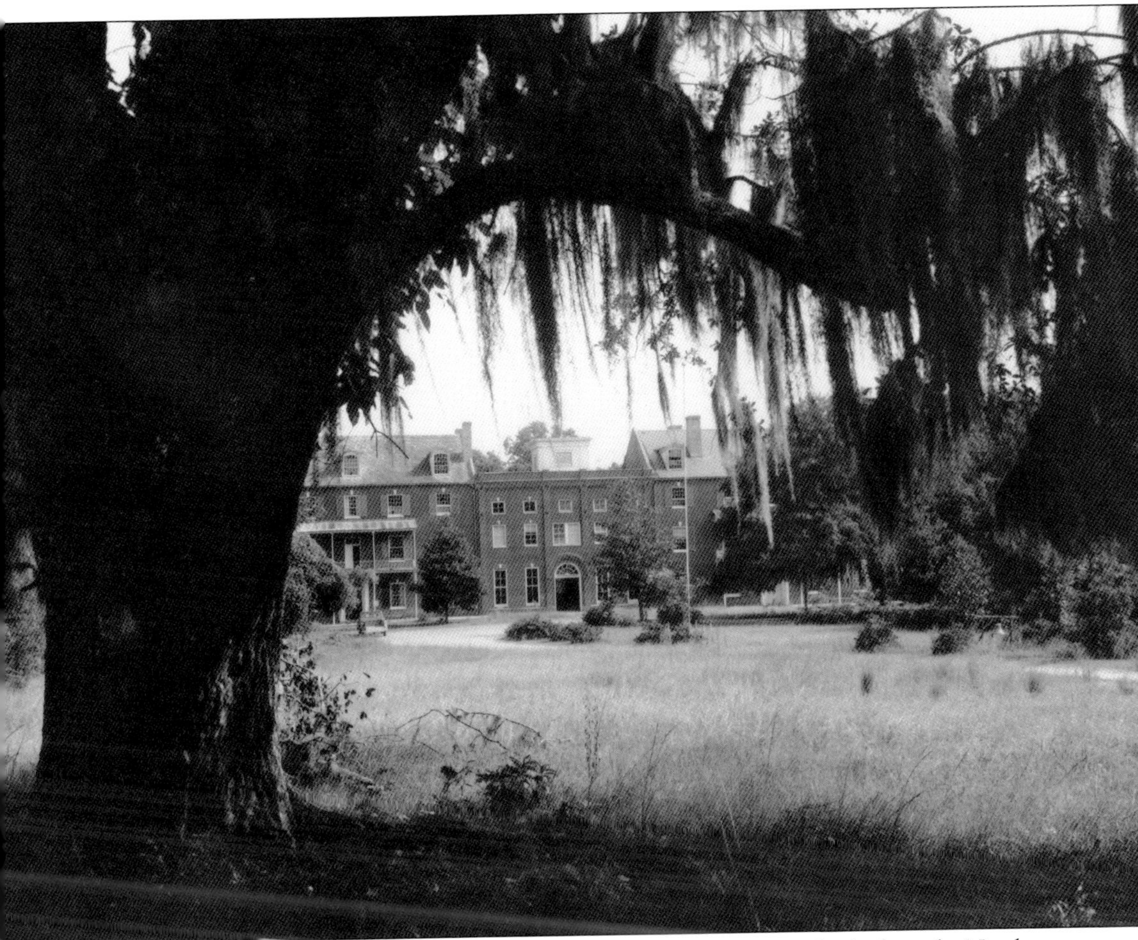

In 1802, Jefferson College was established near one of the Army cantonments built along the Natchez Road. The cantonment area, later Fort Dearborn, developed into Washington, Mississippi, the second capital of the Mississippi Territory. In February 1807, the town witnessed the preliminary hearing of former vice president Aaron Burr, who had previously traveled the Old Trace to generate support for his plan to invade Mexican territory. President Jefferson ordered Burr arrested for attempting to foment a rebellion in the Southwest Territory. Gen. Andrew Jackson's troops camped nearby during the War of 1812, and several of the houses served as hospitals during the war. Following Jackson's victory at the Battle of New Orleans, the town honored the general and his family with a victory celebration just before they began their return up the Old Trace. Jefferson Davis, the future president of the Confederacy, was a student at Jefferson College. (NPS.)

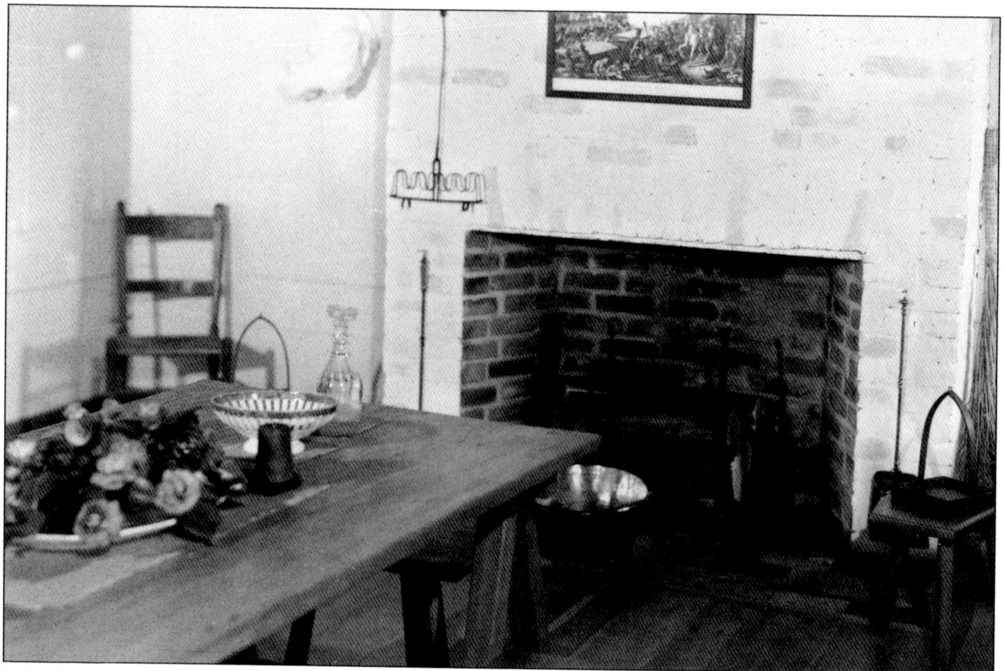

The Ferguson house, known as Mount Locust, was built when the area was Spanish West Florida and it is one of the oldest houses in Mississippi. Both Indians and settlers offered hospitality to travelers, as there were no other shelters along the road in that area. So many travelers expected overnight accommodations at the Ferguson house that William Ferguson built four additional cabins just for guests. (NPS.)

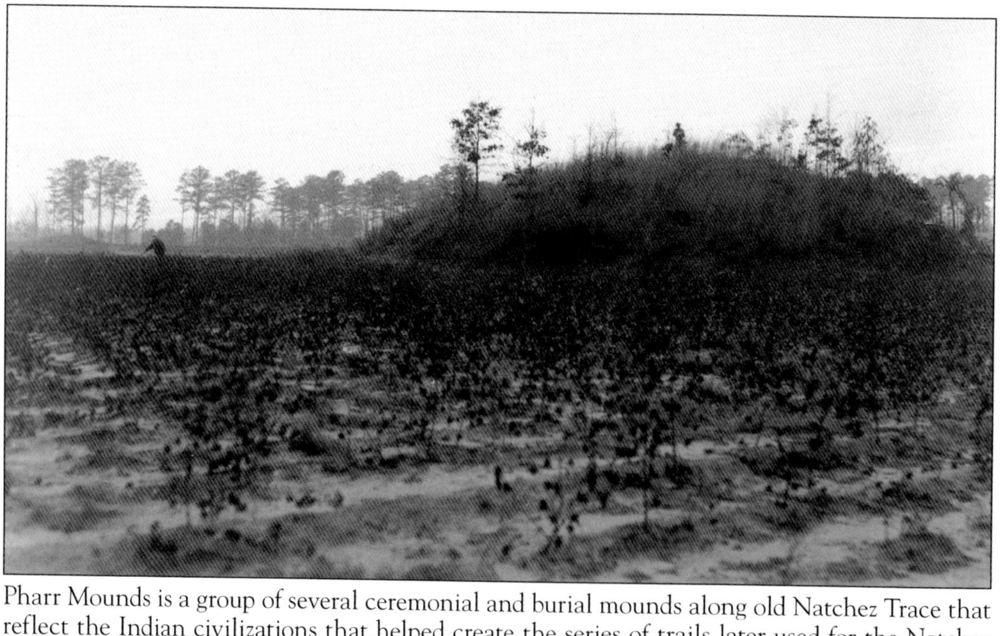

Pharr Mounds is a group of several ceremonial and burial mounds along old Natchez Trace that reflect the Indian civilizations that helped create the series of trails later used for the Natchez Road. The Chickasaw, Choctaw, and Natchez were the most prominent recent tribes along the trails. The Choctaw and Chickasaw generally cooperated with the settlers—and even saved some of them from starvation. (NPS.)

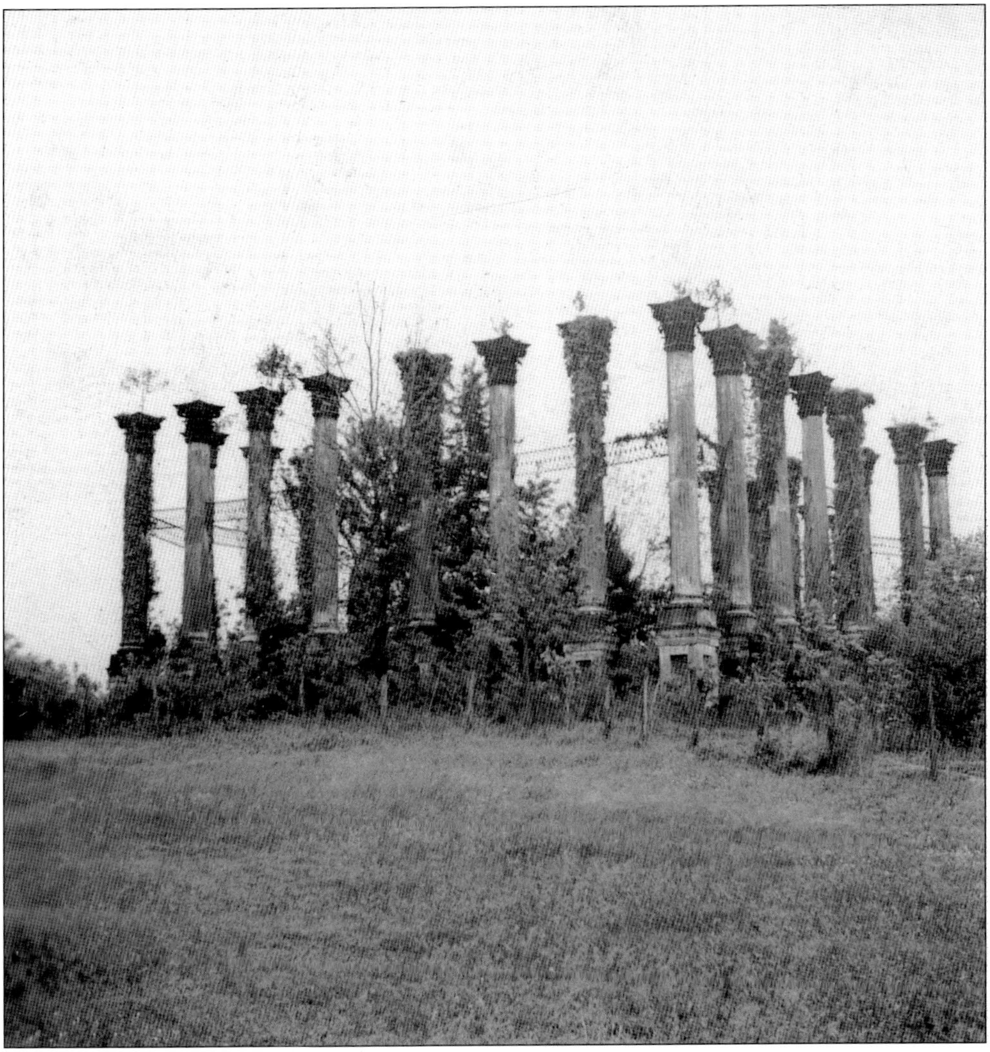

The ruins of Windsor, which burned in 1890, have become an iconic symbol of Mississippi's antebellum architecture and the shattered Old South cotton kingdom. Windsor's ghostly columns once surrounded a plantation house built by Mississippi planter Smith Coffee Daniel II. The house was used as a hospital during the Civil War and survived the conflict. (NPS.)

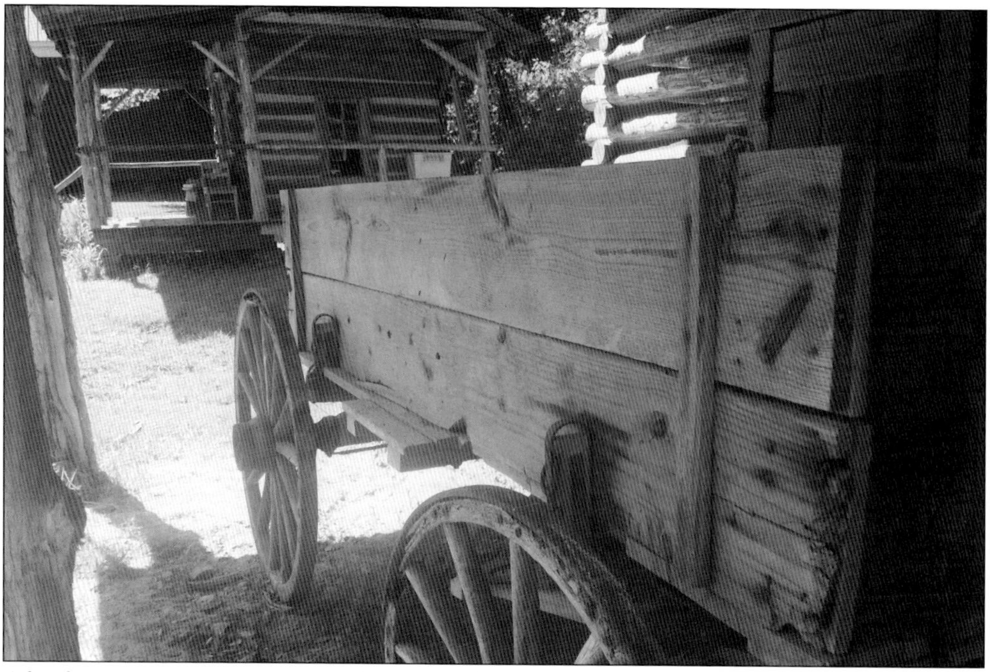

After first operating a trading post called Lefleur's Bluff, French settler Louis Lefleur and his Choctaw wife, Rebecca, moved north from Jackson, Mississippi, where they opened and operated a tavern and trading post. Travelers called it "French Camp." A former slave said that a young Abraham Lincoln spent the evening there when returning from one of his two trips down the Mississippi River. General Jackson's soldiers also camped nearby, and some are buried there. (Author.)

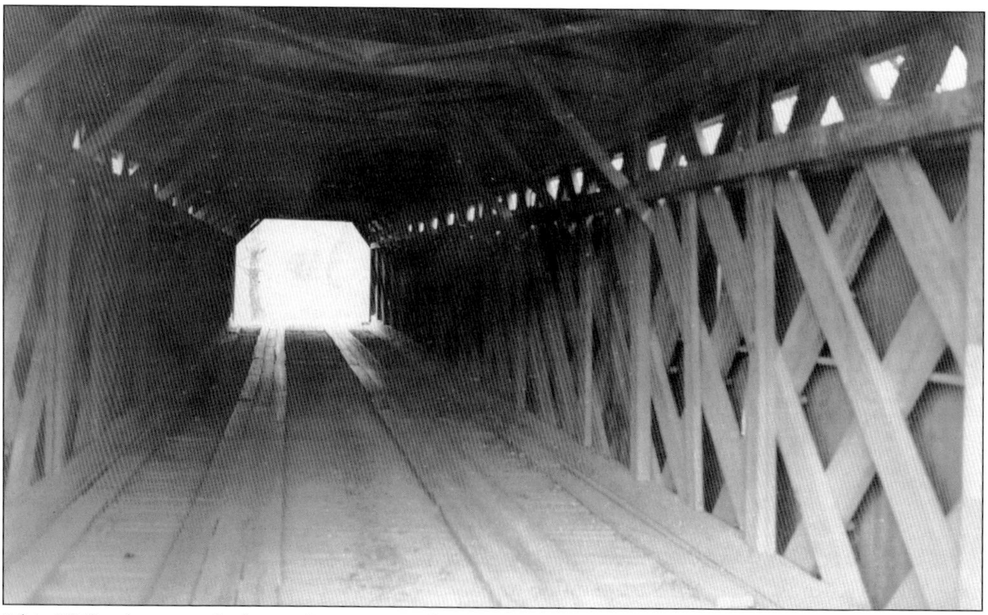

This 1940s photograph shows the interior of a covered bridge near the Buzzard Roost stand, operated by Levi Colbert. This is the view travelers would have seen riding through the long wooden structures as the sound of horses' hooves and wagon wheels reverberated around them. (NPS.)

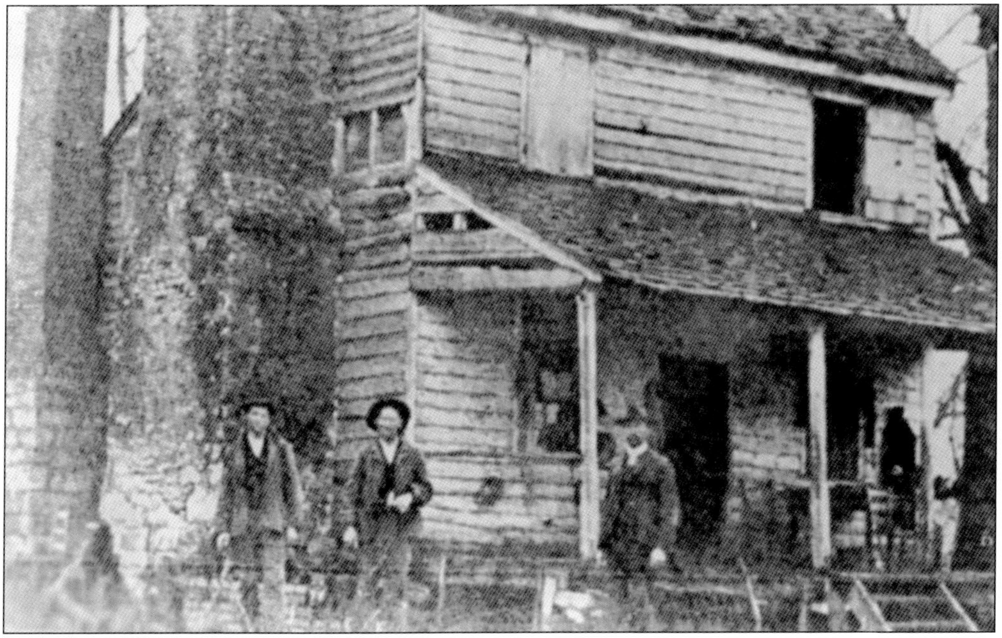

Chickasaw chief George Colbert's house was one of the structures built in 1802 by the Army for troops constructing the Natchez Road. It was subsequently conveyed to Colbert to operate a ferry and inn for travelers at the Tennessee River crossing. Travelers approaching the river yelled to get the attention of the ferry operator, whose crew of five men pulled travelers across the water on floating platforms. (NPS.)

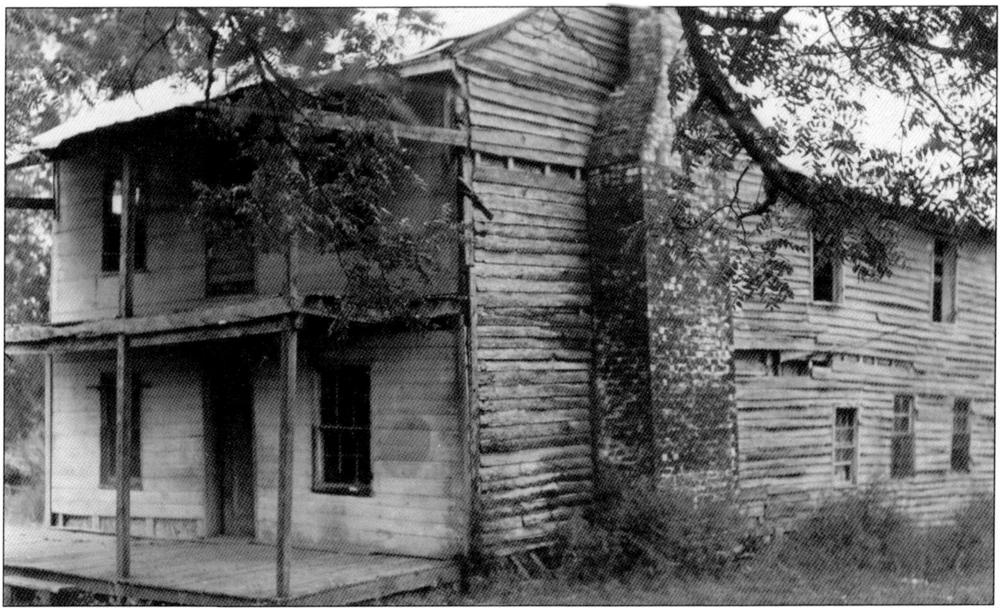

The Buffalo River iron ore mining operation was one of the first nonagricultural industries along the old Natchez Trace. Alternately owned by a US Supreme Court justice, Pres. James K. Polk's father, and Chickasaw agent James Robertson's son-in-law George Napier, the business supplied iron for horseshoes, cookware, and farm implements that new settlers needed. The Napier building also served as a trading post, which sold food and supplies to travelers. (NPS.)

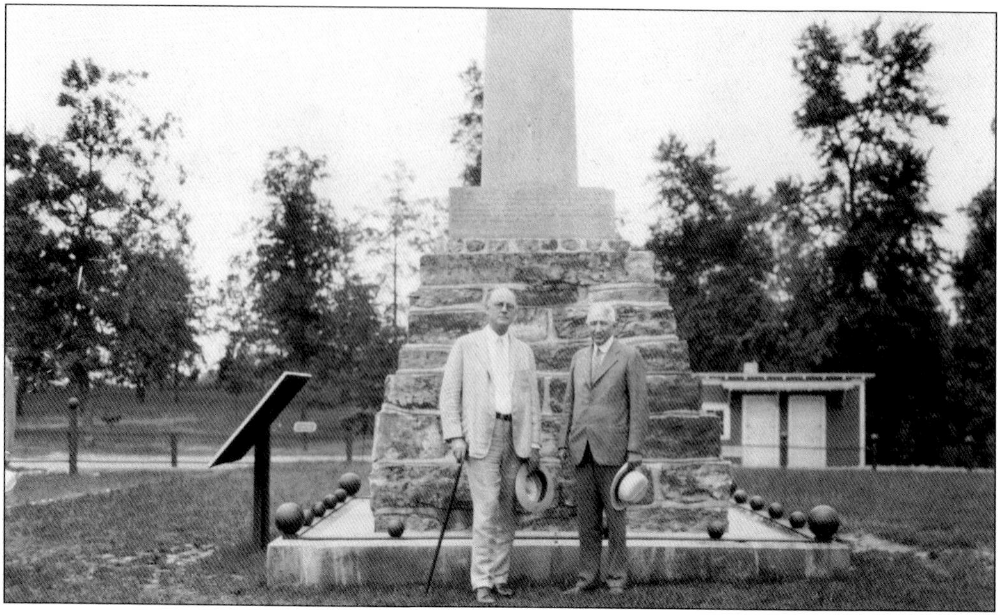

Meriwether Lewis, leader of the Lewis and Clark Expedition, died on the old Natchez Trace at Grinder's Stand in 1809, only three years after returning from his famous expedition. The cause of his death is still debated among historians. The State of Tennessee erected a monument over his grave in 1848. The Meriwether Lewis Monument Association held large meetings on the grounds and successfully encouraged Pres. Calvin Coolidge to declare the site a national monument in 1925. The first superintendent of the national monument was a descendant of Lewis's only sister, Jane. The Meriwether Lewis Monument Association provided a Tennessee base of support for the later formation of the Natchez Trace Parkway Association. These photographs were taken at the 1926 Meriwether Lewis National Monument dedication ceremony. (Both, TSLA.)

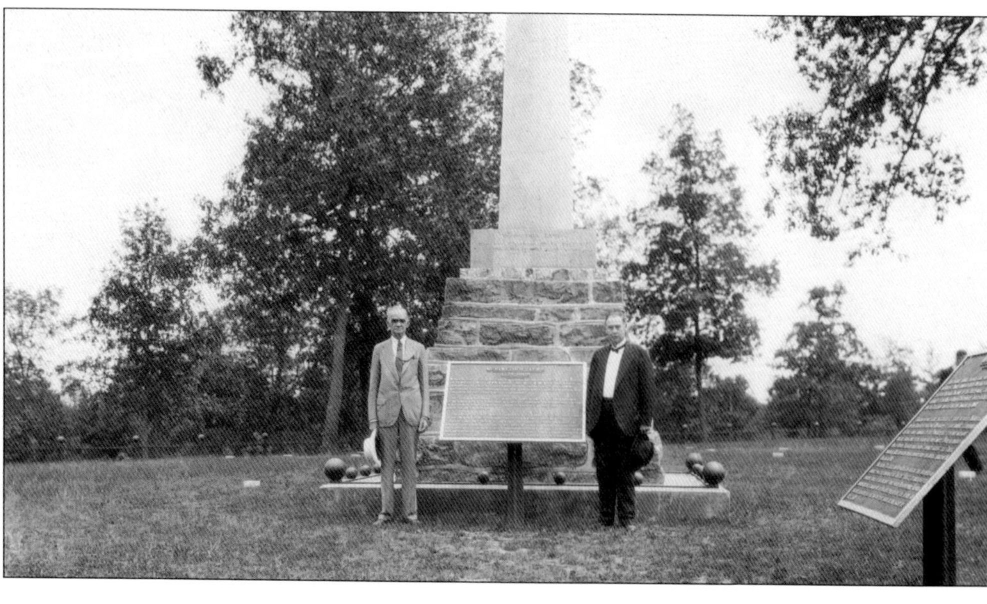

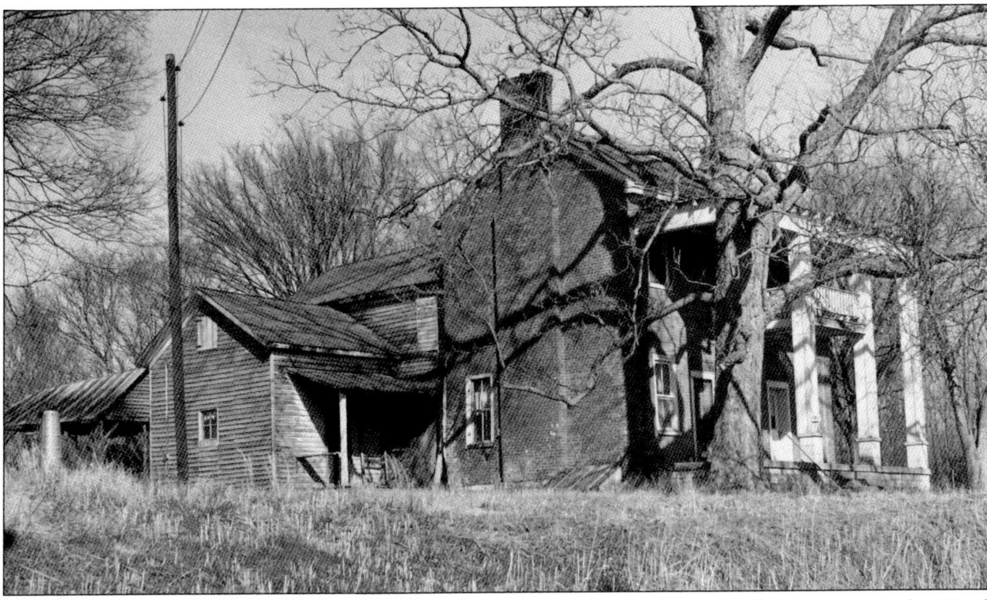

Capt. John Gordon operated this inn. He also ran a trading post and a ferry crossing the Duck River. The inn was one of the buildings constructed in 1801 by the Army as part of Gen. James Wilkinson's cantonment—a supply depot for soldiers building the Natchez Road. Chickasaw chief William Colbert was Gordon's original partner in the operation. Captain Gordon led Jackson's Company of Spies during the War of 1812. In 1818, Gordon added the Federalist brick structure to the wooden inn. (Nashville Public Library, Special Collections.)

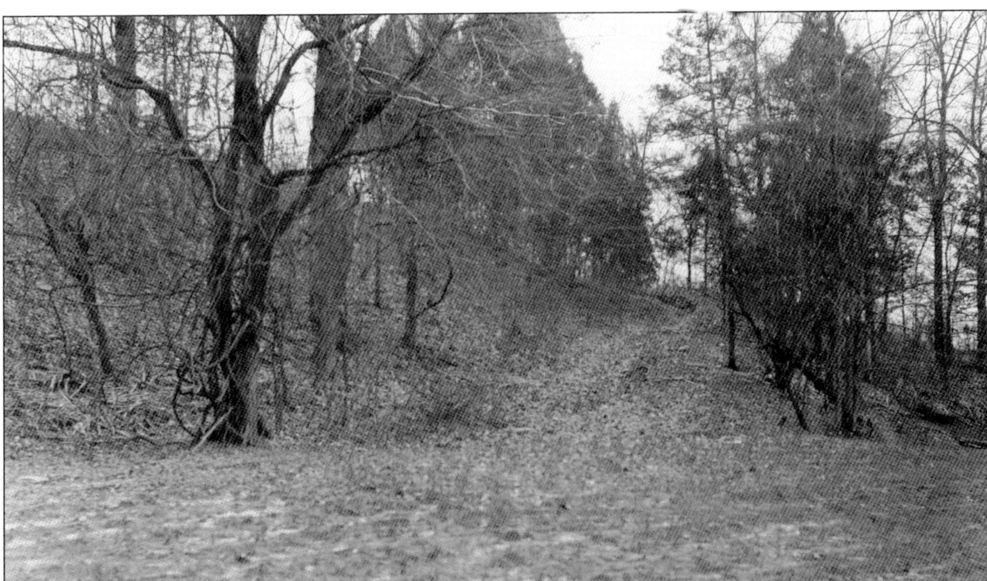

This 1940s photograph shows the old Natchez Road leading from the Duck River ferry to Gordon's inn. In the early 1800s, Gordon's Ferry was located at a critical intersection of the Natchez Road and the Duck River, both important transportation routes on the border of the US territory and the Chickasaw Nation. The military considered the importance of its strategic location during both the War of 1812 and the Civil War. (NPS.)

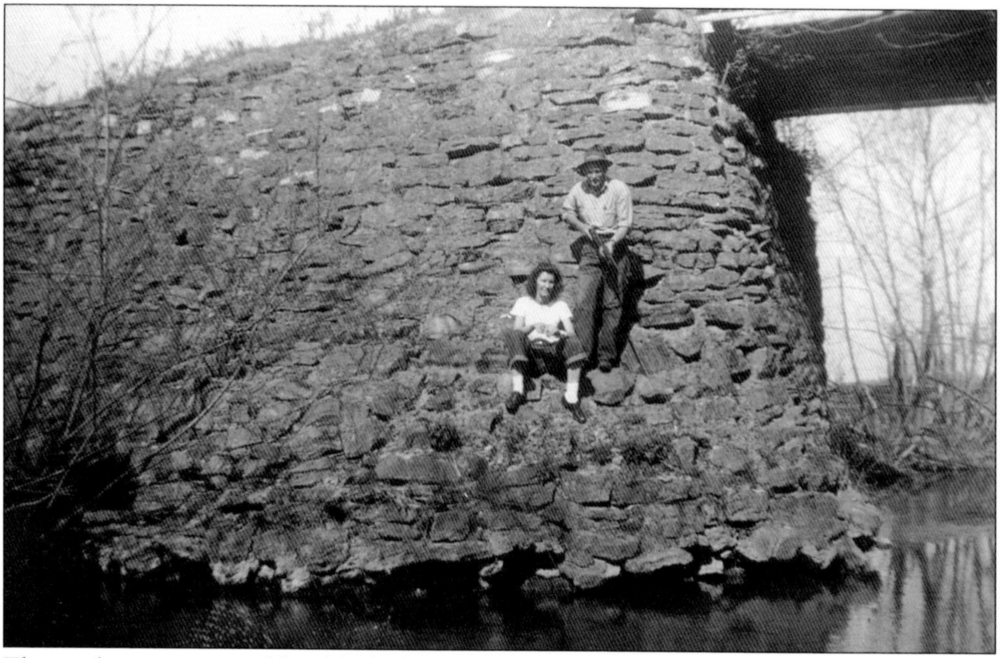

The northern terminus of the old Chickasaw trail was located at Cunningham Bridge. Virginian Robert Preston built the bridge across the Harpeth River to link the old Natchez Trace to several new roads leading to Franklin and Nashville. The bridge was to have been a for-profit toll bridge, but it did not make a profit. Preston's great-grandson Robert Preston became famous on Broadway and in the motion picture production of *The Music Man*. (WCA.)

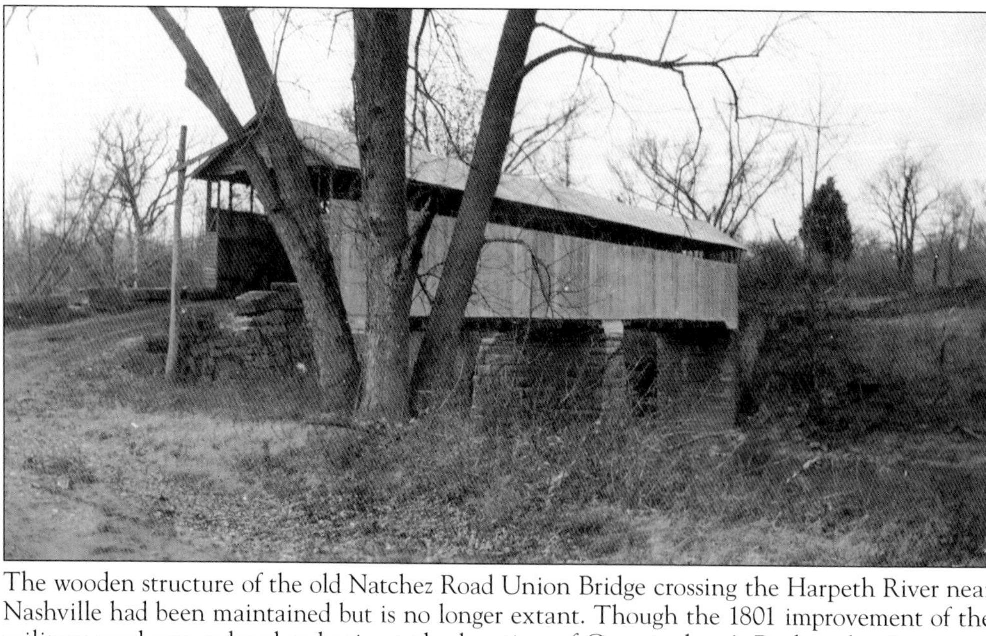

The wooden structure of the old Natchez Road Union Bridge crossing the Harpeth River near Nashville had been maintained but is no longer extant. Though the 1801 improvement of the military road was ordered to begin at the location of Cunningham's Bridge, the Army was persuaded to build roads to Franklin and toward Nashville. Both roads became known locally as the Natchez Road or Natchez Trace. Post riders had already established a trail from Nashville to the Chickasaw Trace. (NPS.)

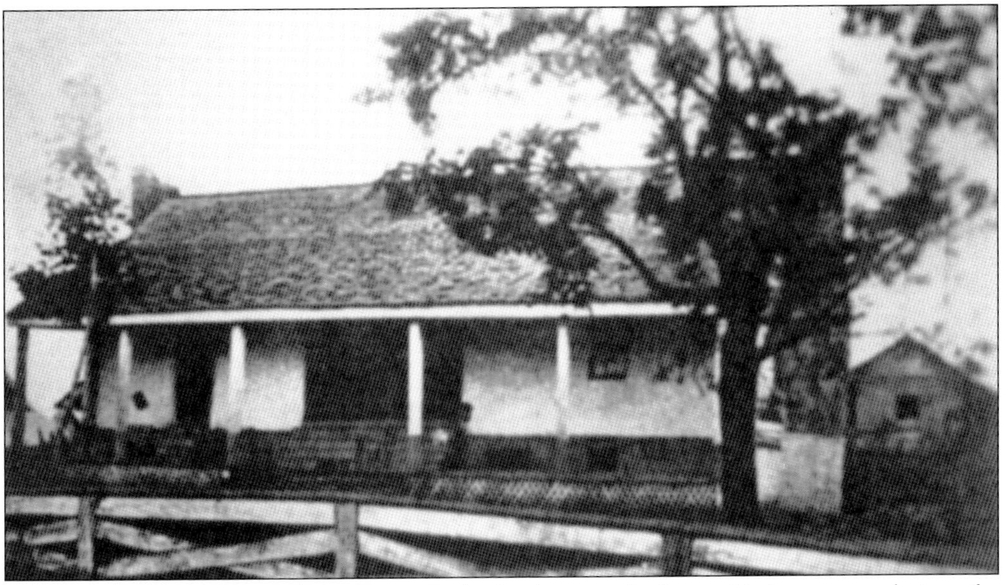

Thomas Hart Benton's mother, Nancy, built this house, which provided accommodations for Natchez Trace travelers. Though Benton served as Andrew Jackson's aide-de-camp during the 1813 Natchez Expedition, he shot Jackson during a brawl on the streets of Nashville. General Jackson still suffered the effects of the shooting during the Battle of New Orleans. Benton's great-nephew Thomas Hart Benton became an influential early-20th-century painter. (WCA.)

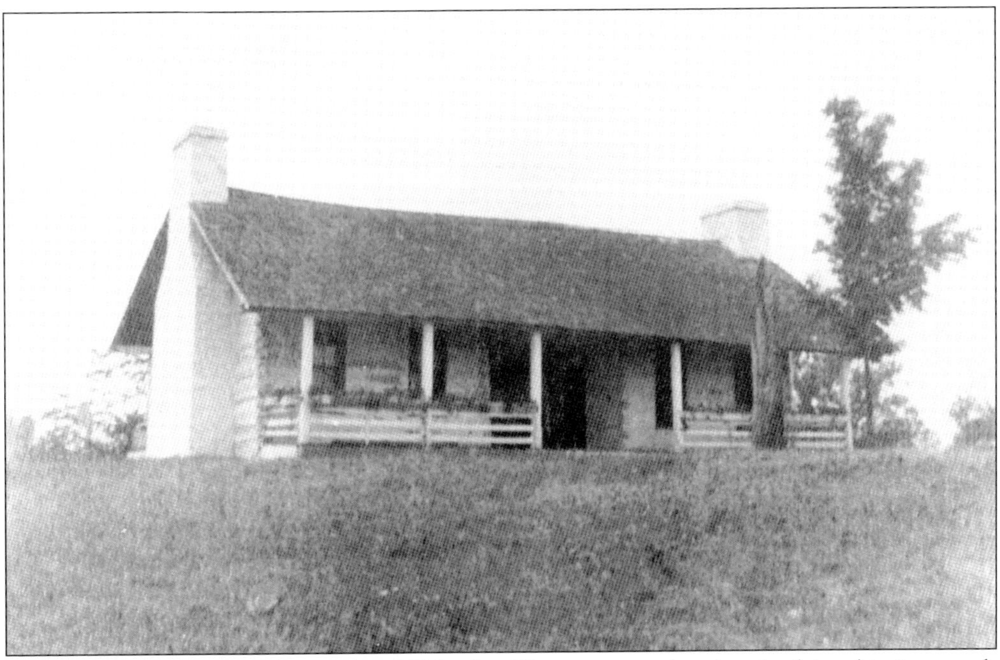

Benjamin Joslin, a post rider on the old Natchez Trace, operated an inn in this cabin just south of Nashville. The station was one of the first outposts on the road near Nashville. Joslin and his successor, John Harding, also operated a blacksmith shop for travelers. Andrew Jackson's cavalry officers, preparing to march on the old Natchez Trace during the War of 1812, stopped here to have their horses shod. (Courtesy of Permanent Collection, Belle Meade Plantation.)

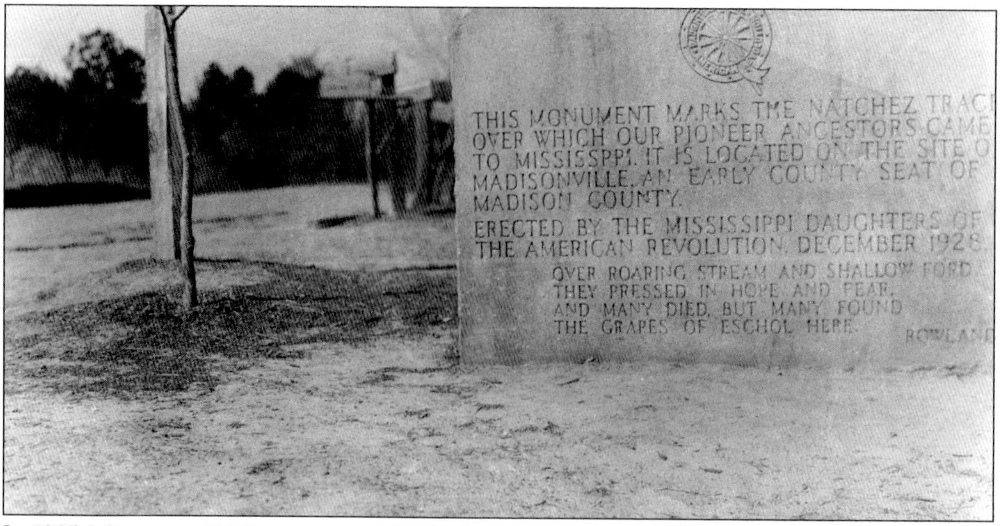

In 1905, Mississippi DAR vice regent Elizabeth Jones warned, "We are in danger of losing all signs . . . of our once famous military road." When Jones became state regent, she instituted a program to place granite monuments at points along the old Natchez Trace in Mississippi. (UMO.)

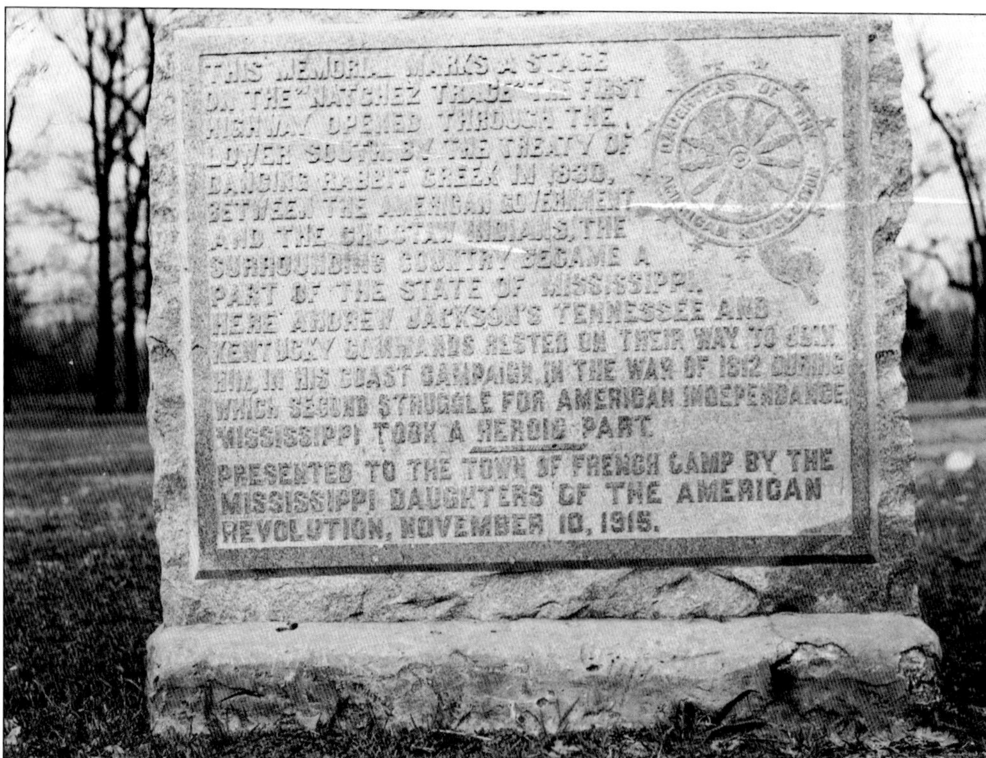

DAR member Lucille Mayfield supported Elizabeth Jones's work to place markers along the Old Trace. A.B. Mayfield, an ancestor of Mayfield's husband, served in John Gordon's Company of Spies during the War of 1812. In 1934, Lucille Mayfield became the first president of the association. (NPS.)

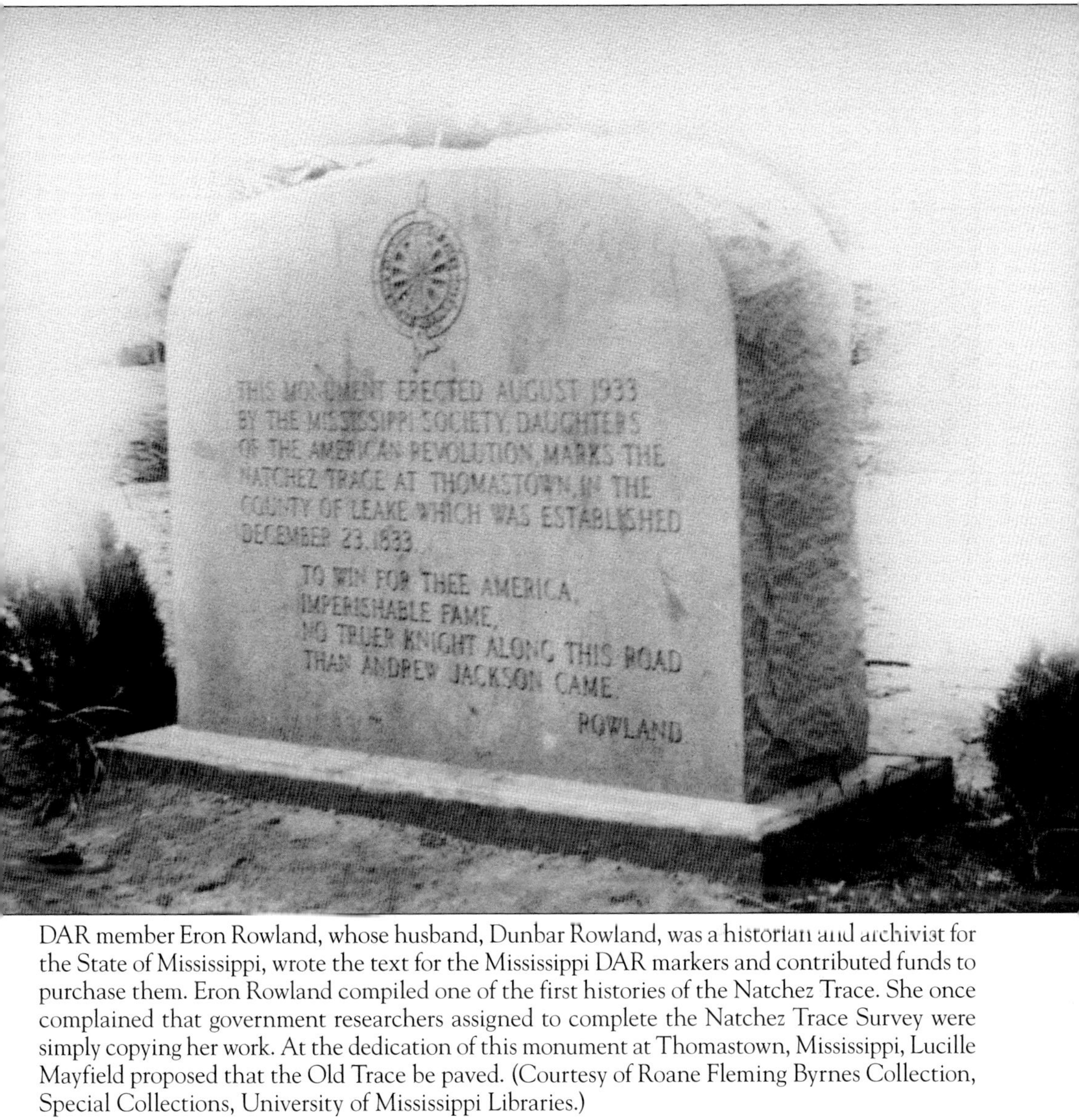

DAR member Eron Rowland, whose husband, Dunbar Rowland, was a historian and archivist for the State of Mississippi, wrote the text for the Mississippi DAR markers and contributed funds to purchase them. Eron Rowland compiled one of the first histories of the Natchez Trace. She once complained that government researchers assigned to complete the Natchez Trace Survey were simply copying her work. At the dedication of this monument at Thomastown, Mississippi, Lucille Mayfield proposed that the Old Trace be paved. (Courtesy of Roane Fleming Byrnes Collection, Special Collections, University of Mississippi Libraries.)

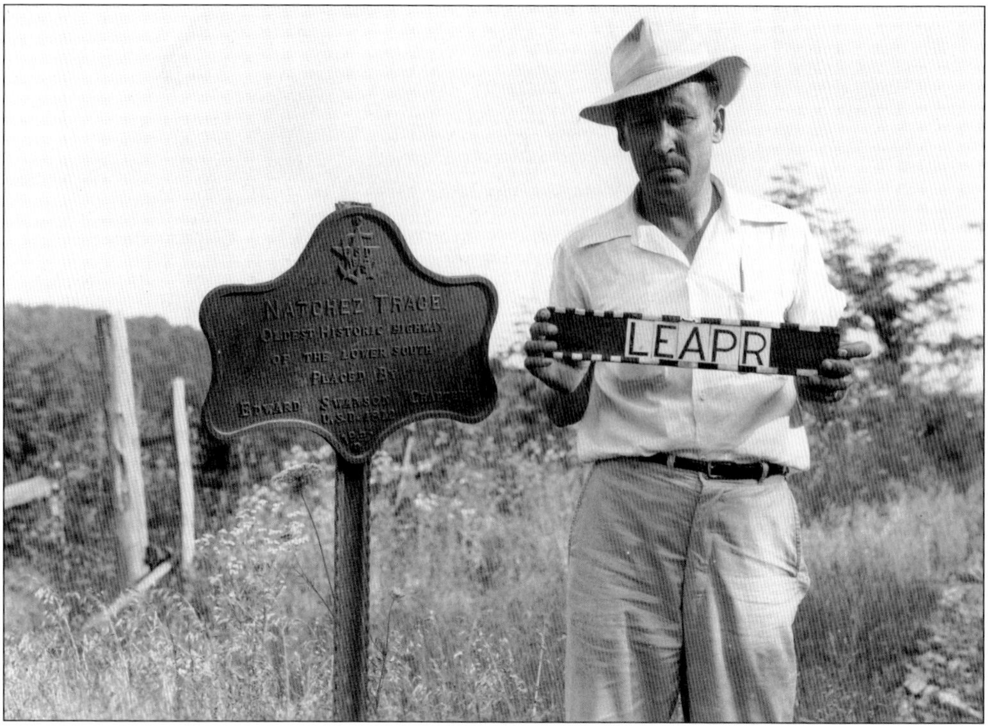

In 1914, Daughters of the War of 1812 Tennessee president Louise Spencer initiated the program to place 12 bronze markers along Old Trace at sites that had been significant to the march of Andrew Jackson's troops during the War of 1812. In 1931, Susie Anderson Glenn was appointed chair of the Tennessee State Committee for Marking the Old Natchez Trace. (NPS.)

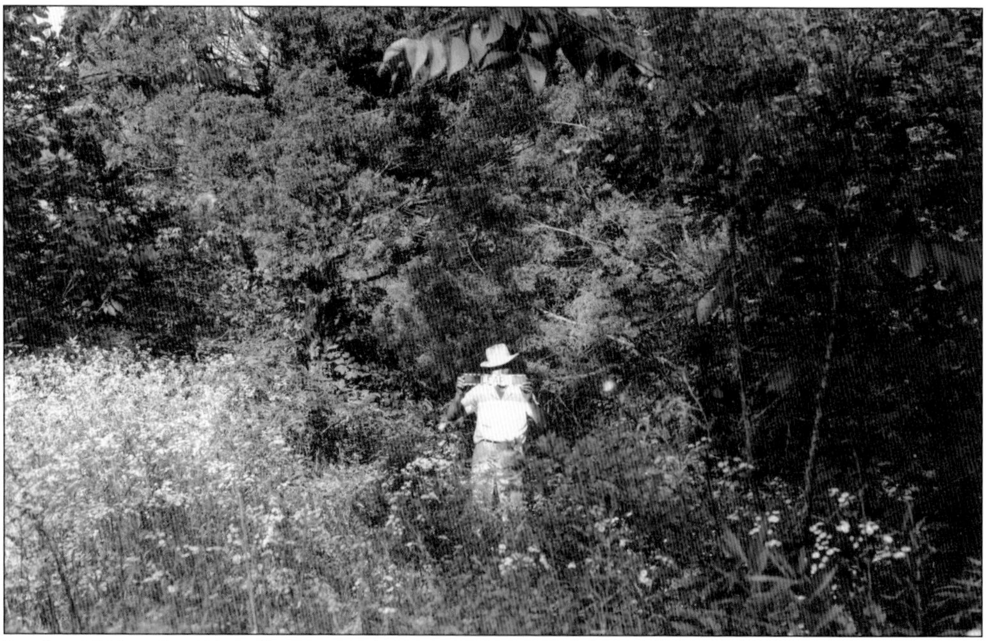
In the 1940s, the War of 1812 marker located just south of Leiper's Fork, Tennessee, helped surveyors verify the location of the old road for the future parkway. (NPS.)

Two

Moonshine and Meatloaf
The Road to Yesterday— The Parkway of Tomorrow 1934–1954

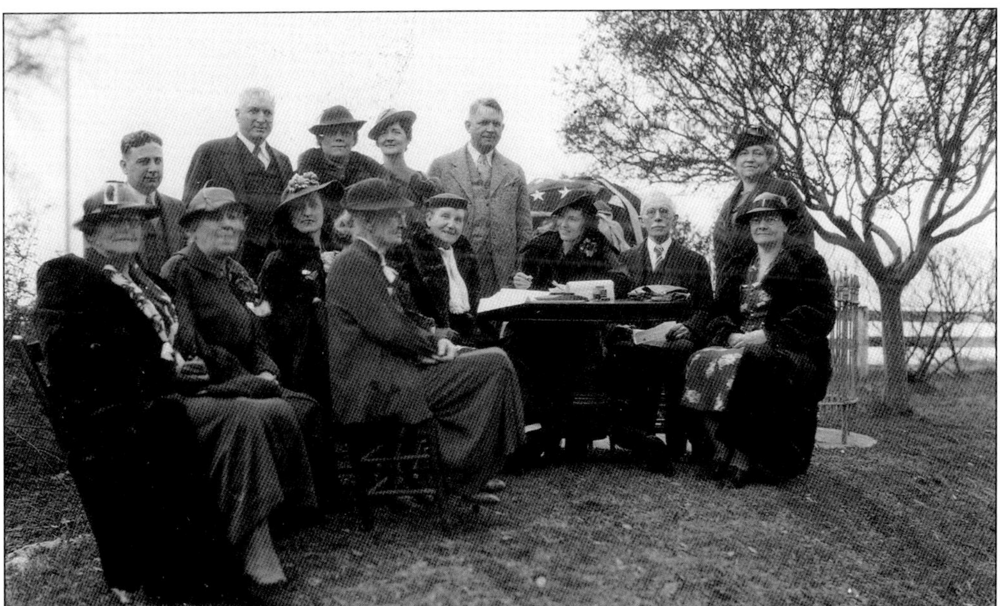

Roane Fleming Byrnes, the new association president, is shown seated in front of the flag-draped DAR monument in Natchez as she receives the first contribution to pave the Natchez Trace. Also pictured are, from left to right, (first row) Mrs. Murrell, Mrs. Ed Ratcliff, Mrs. Ben Cameron, Elizabeth Jones, Roane Fleming Byrnes, master of ceremonies Gerard Brandon, Mrs. Hugh Jenkin (standing), and Miss Charlie Compton; (second row, standing) Natchez mayor William Byrne, Charles Engle, two unidentified women, and future Natchez mayor Walter Abbott. The older woman in profile is Florence Sillers Ogden. (NPS.)

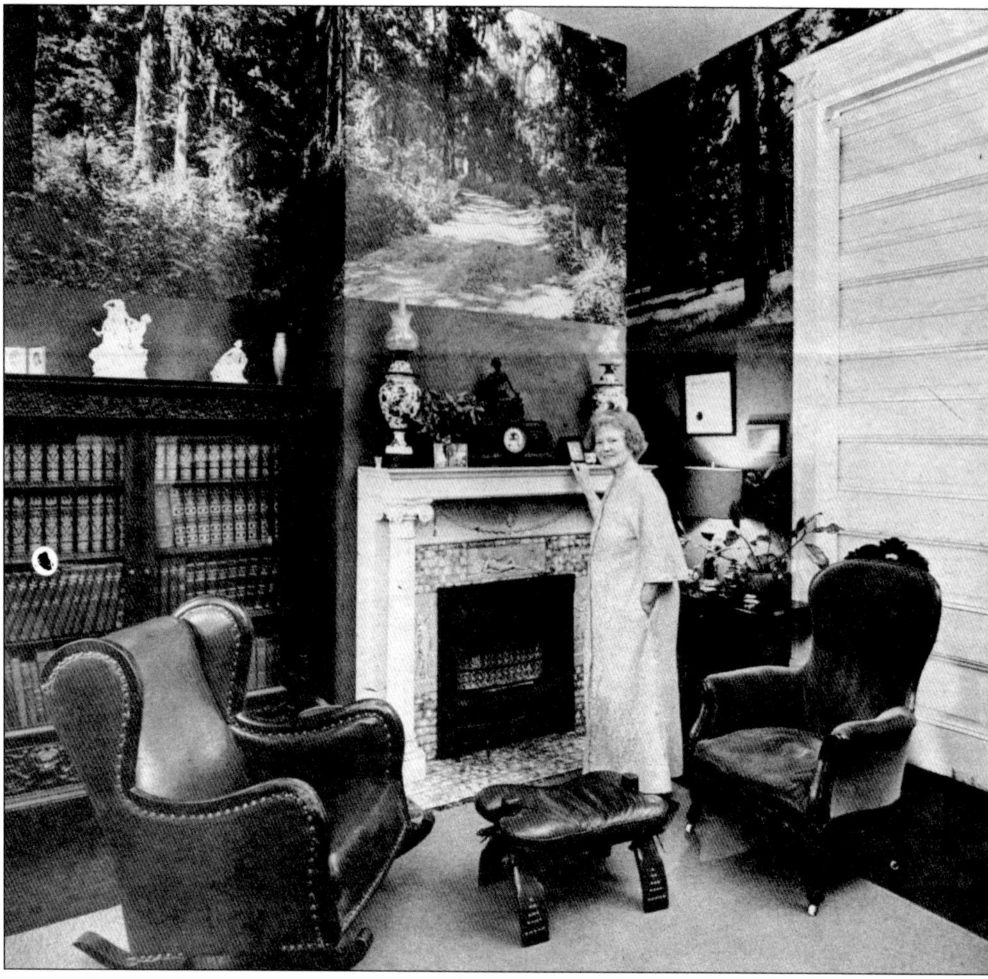

Roane Fleming Byrnes invited national leaders to her Natchez home Ravennaside for Southern hospitality. During dinner, she invariably turned the conversation to the parkway. Guests were then encouraged to tour her "war room" to view paintings of the completed parkway and progress maps. The leaders fell under the spell of her charm and left Ravennaside committed supporters. A friend commented that the Natchez Trace was paved with "moonshine and meatloaf." (Courtesy of *Commercial Appeal*.)

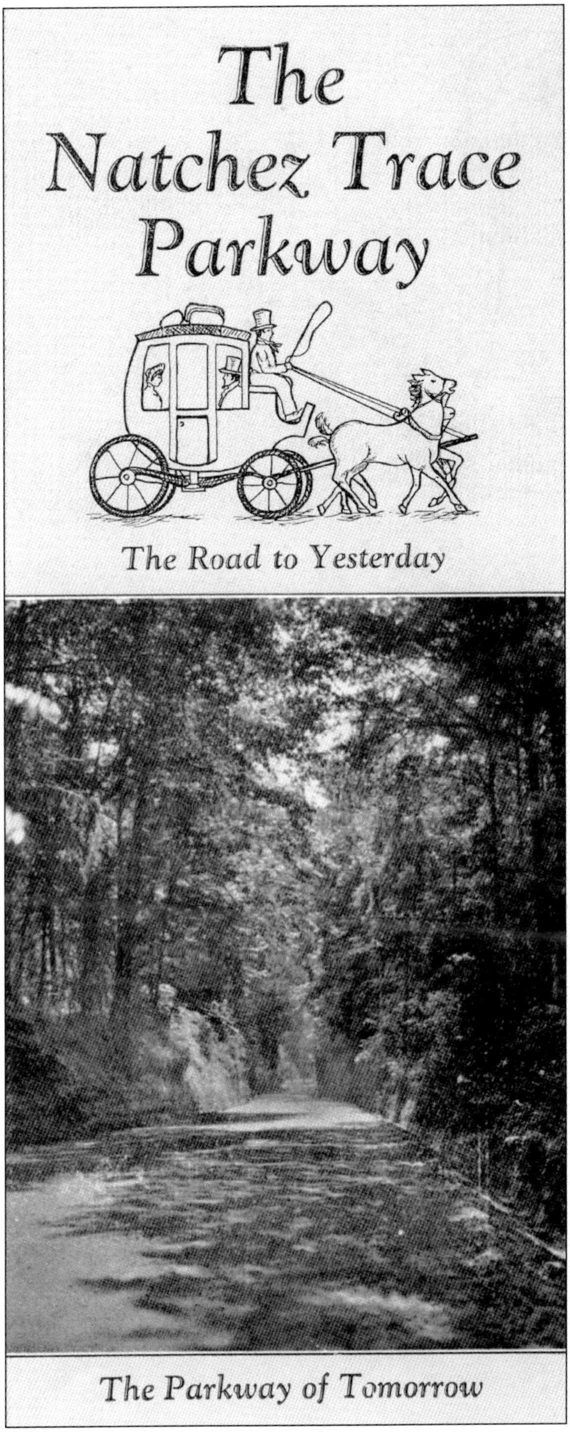

In 1934, the association's first promotional piece advocated its vision of the completed parkway as visitor experiences at historic sites from Andrew Jackson's Hermitage, through Chickasaw and Choctaw villages, to Natchez grand mansions—all linked by a modern highway along the old Natchez Trace. (NPS.)

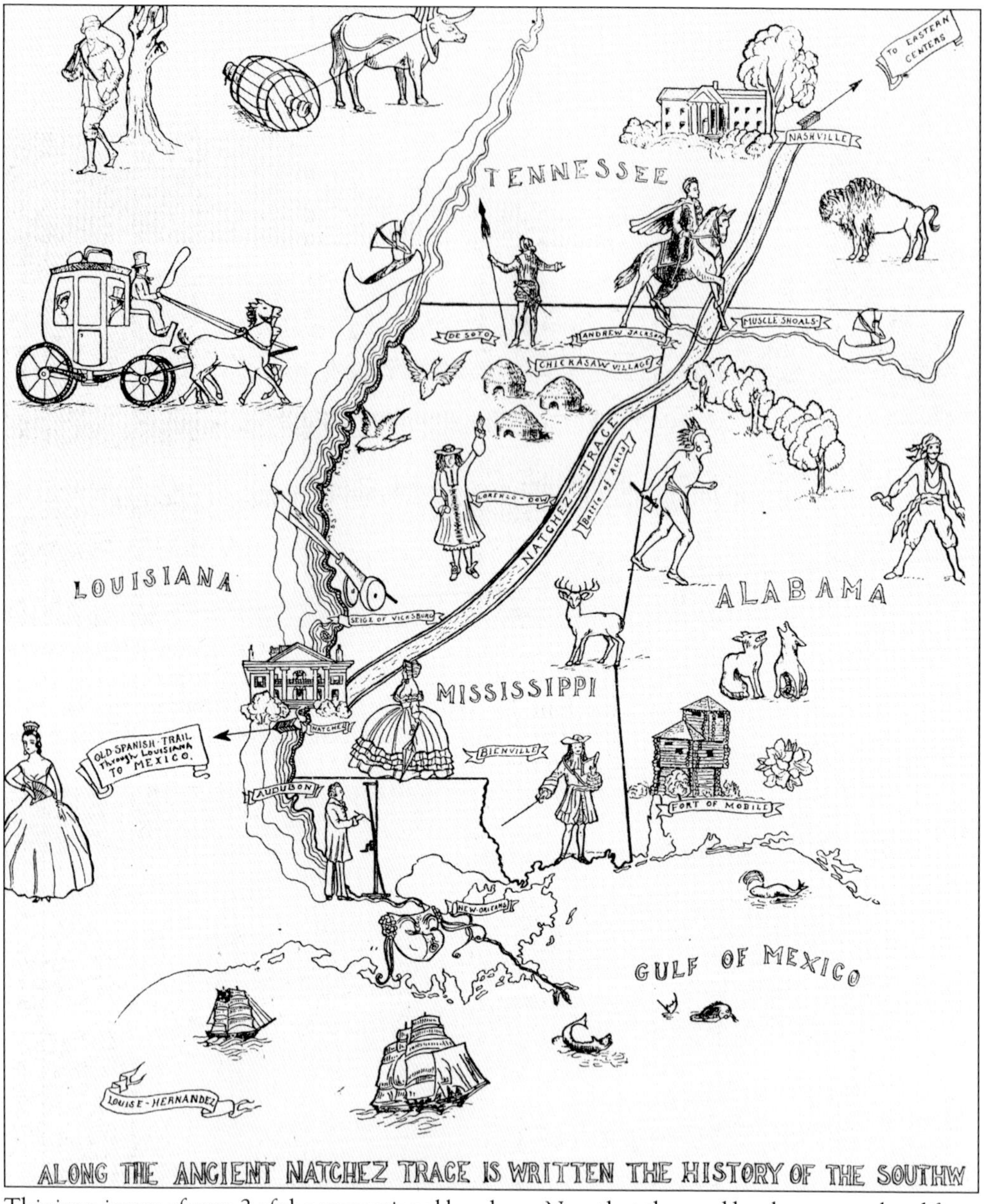

This is an image of page 2 of the promotional brochure. Now that the road has been completed from Natchez to Nashville, the Natchez Trace Parkway Association is working to support completion of the sites and interpretation to provide the experience originally envisioned. The sentence at the bottom of the piece reads: "Along the ancient Natchez Trace is written the history of the Southwest."

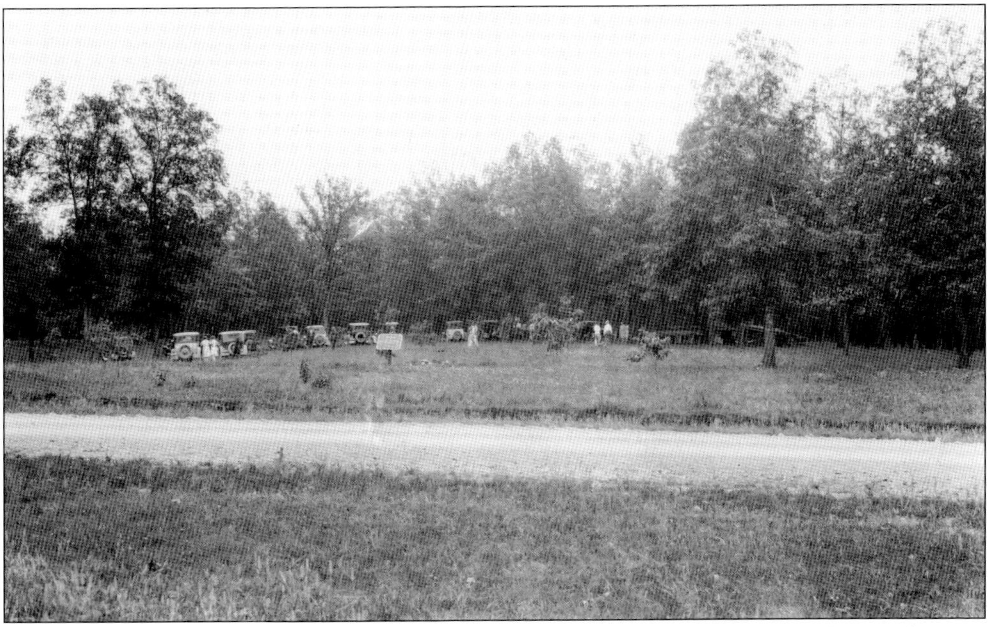

In addition to broadcasting over NBC-affiliated radio stations, the association and its predecessor association generated local public support by holding rallies in towns along the parkway. Mayfield spoke to a crowd of over 1,000 at the June 14, 1934, rally at the Meriwether Lewis National Monument. This photograph may show the Grinder's Stand location before the 1935 cabin was built. Note the temporary speaker's dais in the background. (TSLA.)

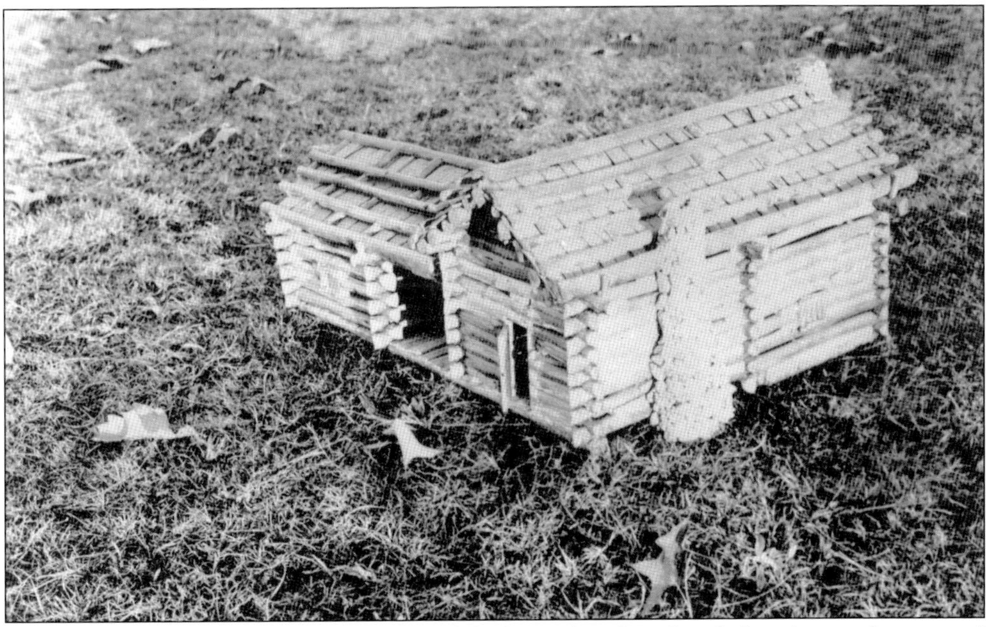

Someone at the rally had built a small model of Grinder's Stand and placed it on the original site to suggest that the government reconstruct the cabin. The park service attempted to obtain enough information to recreate the inn on the original foundation; however, when accurate details proved elusive, the decision was made to build a period cabin and locate it a few feet south of the original foundation. (NPS.)

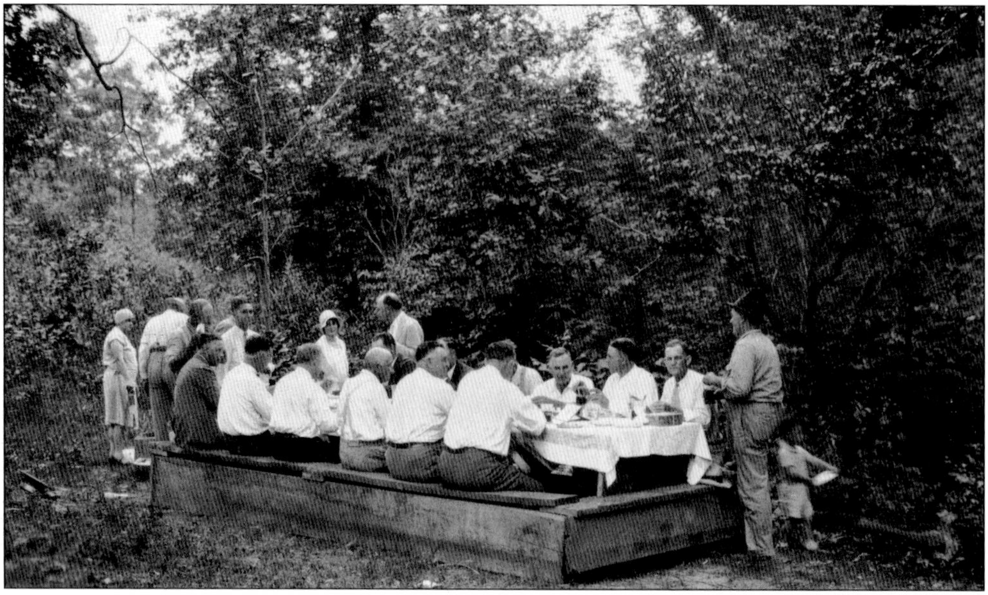

Public gatherings of Natchez Trace supporters often included meals for dignitaries and those who drove long distances. The makeshift wooden picnic tables provided a glimpse of the experience of a picnic in a future national park picnic area. Note the child on the right patiently waiting to eat. In those days, men ate first, and the children finished the food that remained after the women had taken their turn. (Both, TSLA.)

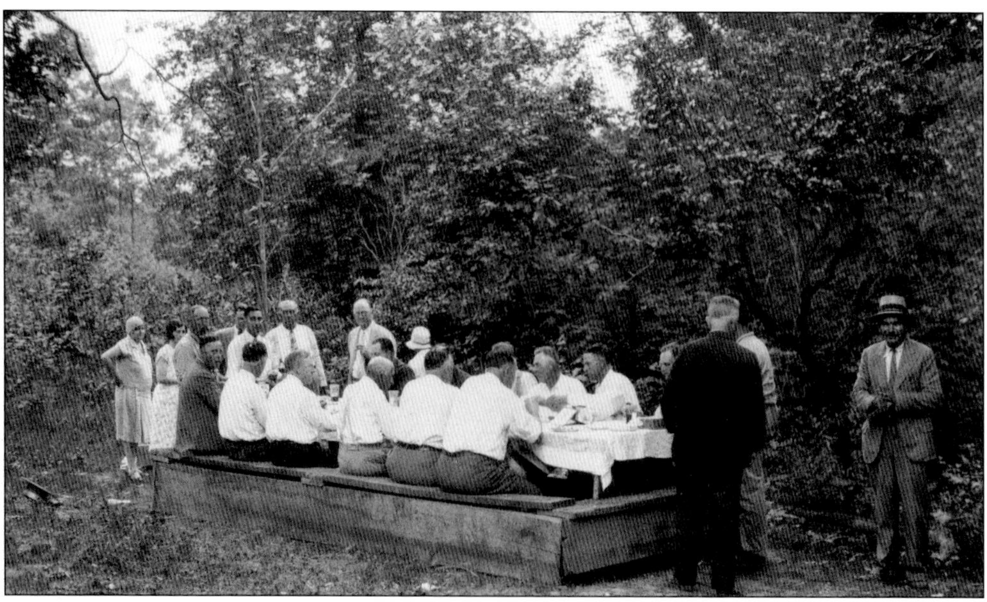

"Colonel" Jim Walton from Eupora, Mississippi, called on the young congressman Thomas Jefferson Busby (pictured) at his office in Houston, Mississippi, to present the idea that the federal government should pave the Natchez Trace. Busby immediately saw the value of the project. He told groups assembled in Mississippi that he would introduce a parkway bill in Congress, but he needed people to "whoop and holler" for the project. The association had its mission. (Courtesy of Houston, Mississippi, Historical Society.)

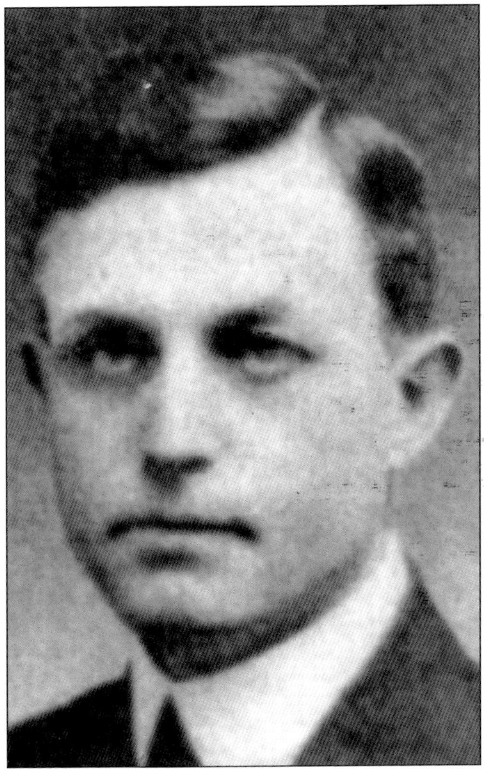

Mississippi senator Pat Harrison (in white suit to right of FDR) used his powerful position as chair of the Senate Finance Committee to push for funding. When appropriations for the initial survey hit a snag, Mayfield assured Byrnes that the senator was using several political tricks to overcome any challenges. Mayfield later said that while others had taken credit for the parkway appropriation, Harrison had worked behind the scenes to obtain the required funding. (Courtesy of Felton M. Johnston Collection, Archives & Special Collections, University of Mississippi.)

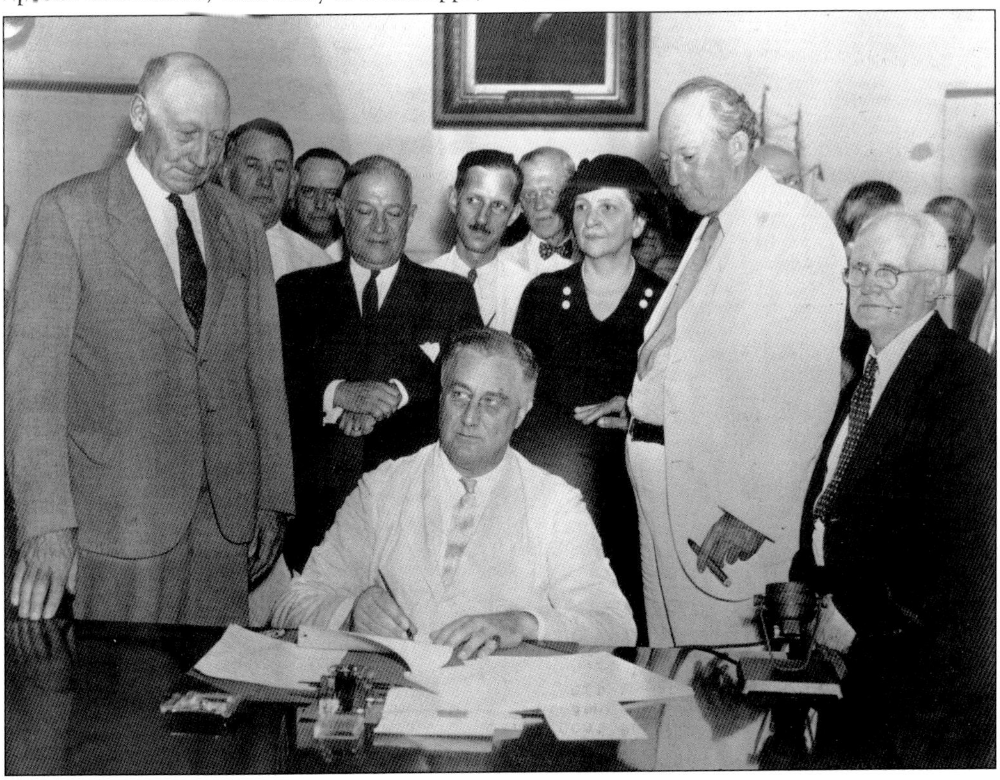

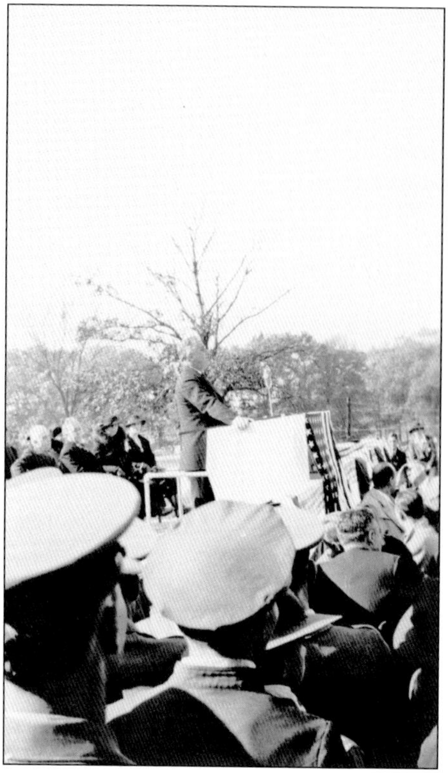

After Senator Harrison met with Pres. Franklin D. Roosevelt (pictured at left) at the White House, Mayfield wrote that the president "is intensely interested in the development of this historic old road and its association with General Andrew Jackson." Roosevelt told the senator that he would build the road to honor Jackson. Later when Harrison tried to talk to the president about other road projects, Roosevelt always asked, "What about the Natchez Trace?" (MDAH.)

President Roosevelt, Eleanor Roosevelt, and Secretary of the Interior Harold Ickes traveled to Tupelo on November 18, 1934 (pictured at left), to promote the Tennessee Valley Authority. During the trip, the Roosevelts visited this homestead house on the land that would become the future parkway visitor's center. Anticipating the visit, association secretary Ralph Landrum encouraged members that it would be a "splendid time to call his attention to the need for the Natchez Trace." (NPS.)

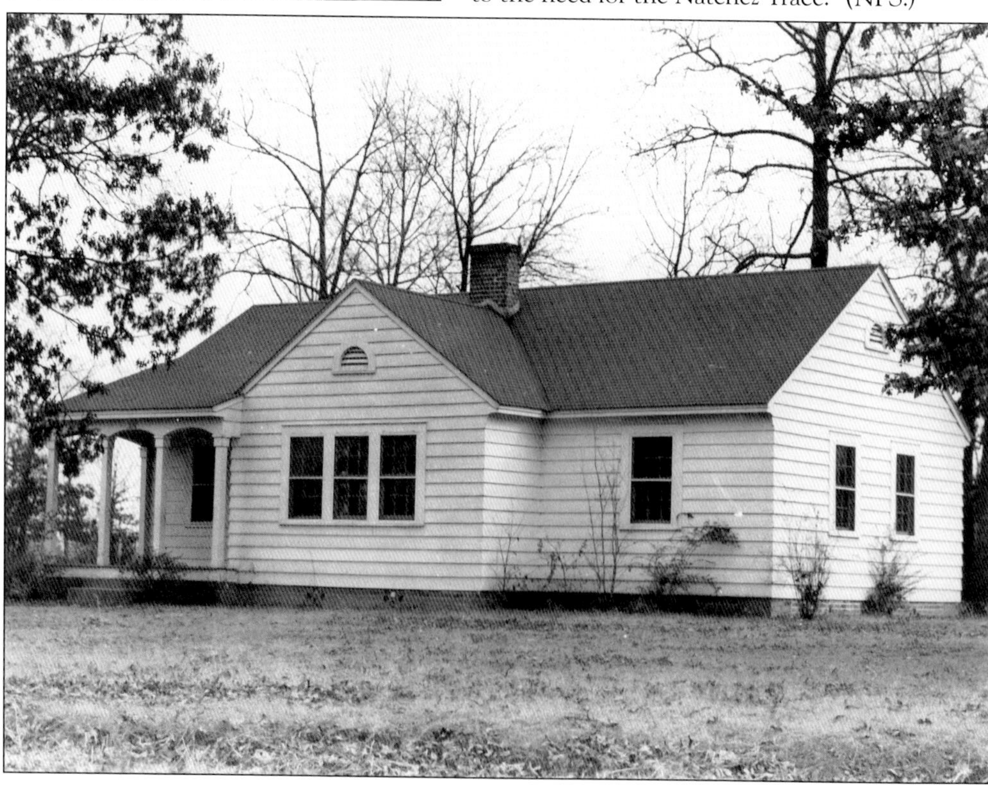

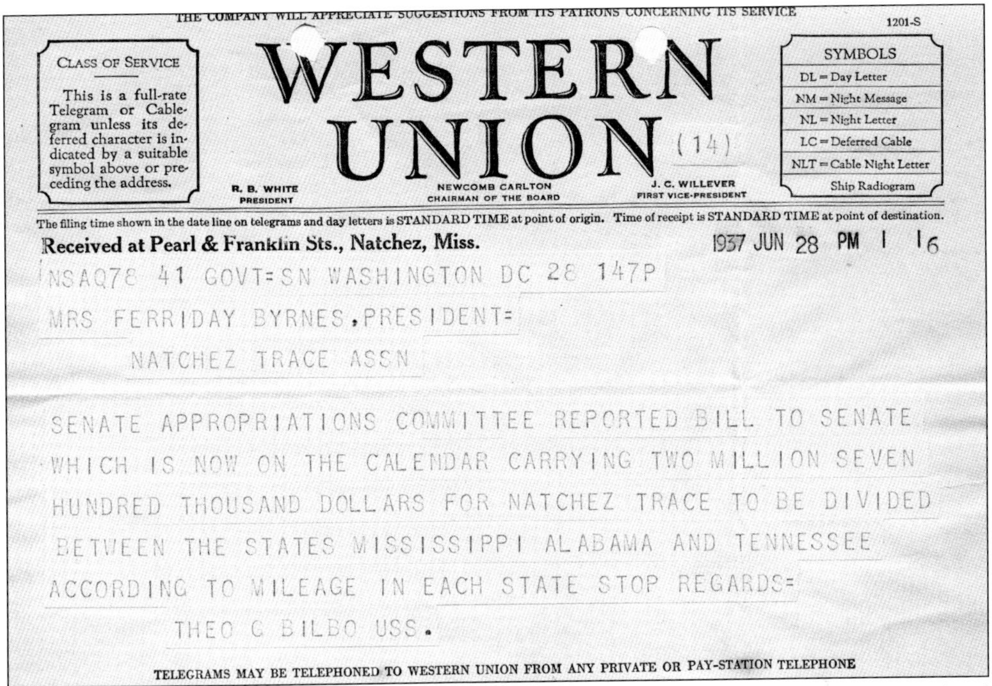
THE COMPANY WILL APPRECIATE SUGGESTIONS FROM ITS PATRONS CONCERNING ITS SERVICE

1201-S

CLASS OF SERVICE

This is a full-rate Telegram or Cablegram unless its deferred character is indicated by a suitable symbol above or preceding the address.

WESTERN UNION

(14)

R. B. WHITE, PRESIDENT — NEWCOMB CARLTON, CHAIRMAN OF THE BOARD — J. C. WILLEVER, FIRST VICE-PRESIDENT

SYMBOLS

DL = Day Letter

NM = Night Message

NL = Night Letter

LC = Deferred Cable

NLT = Cable Night Letter

Ship Radiogram

The filing time shown in the date line on telegrams and day letters is STANDARD TIME at point of origin. Time of receipt is STANDARD TIME at point of destination.

Received at Pearl & Franklin Sts., Natchez, Miss. 1937 JUN 28 PM 1 16

NSAQ78 41 GOVT=SN WASHINGTON DC 28 147P

MRS FERRIDAY BYRNES,PRESIDENT=

NATCHEZ TRACE ASSN

SENATE APPROPRIATIONS COMMITTEE REPORTED BILL TO SENATE WHICH IS NOW ON THE CALENDAR CARRYING TWO MILLION SEVEN HUNDRED THOUSAND DOLLARS FOR NATCHEZ TRACE TO BE DIVIDED BETWEEN THE STATES MISSISSIPPI ALABAMA AND TENNESSEE ACCORDING TO MILEAGE IN EACH STATE STOP REGARDS=

THEO G BILBO USS.

TELEGRAMS MAY BE TELEPHONED TO WESTERN UNION FROM ANY PRIVATE OR PAY-STATION TELEPHONE

Political leaders kept Roane Fleming Byrnes apprised of each victory or defeat. The federal government agreed to build the parkway if the states provided the land. Though states were reluctant to help fund a federal project, after much persuasion from Byrnes and the association, the states eventually agreed to pay for rights-of-way and scenic easements to encourage investment of federal dollars and the creation of construction jobs. (Courtesy of Roane Fleming Byrnes Collection, Special Collections, University of Mississippi Libraries.)

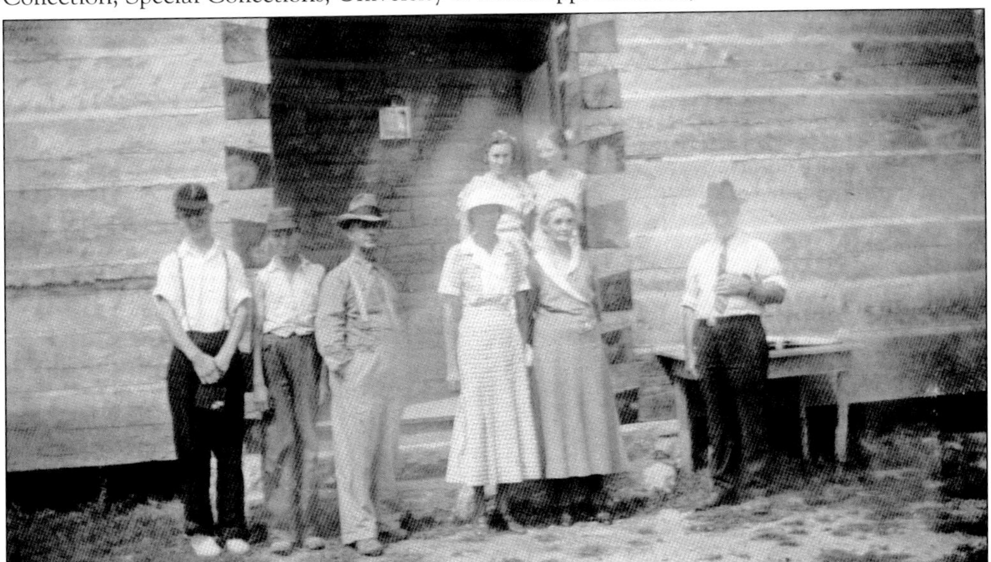

In the summer of 1935, Works Progress Administration workers built a period cabin at the Grinder's Stand site, as envisioned at the 1934 rally. Construction neared completion as the Fain family toured the new attraction. A superintendent's home and garages were also built. The superintendent of the national monument site coordinated closely with the parkway administration. (Author.)

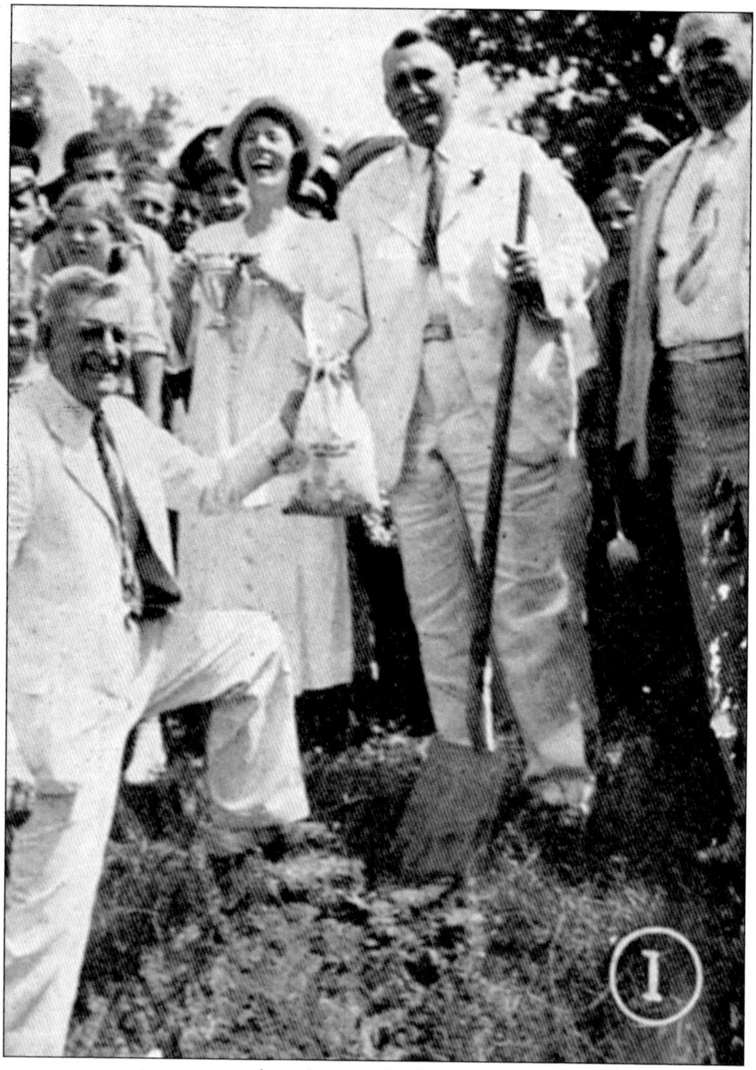

When parkway construction was ready to begin, the first of two inaugural ceremonies was held at the Galloway home in Madisonville on September 15, 1937. Mississippi governor Hugh L. White raised the first shovel of dirt. The dirt was placed in a silver urn and handed to Byrnes, who called it the most "valuable earth ever dug in Mississippi or perhaps the whole South" because it meant that "the ancient Natchez Trace is to be preserved as one of the greatest parkways in the United States." (NPS.)

Groups in Texas and Louisiana jumped on the bandwagon, forming Natchez Trace Associations. It was suggested that just as the old Natchez Trace had connected to El Camino Real in Texas, the parkway could be extended to Mexico City. Byrnes did not flinch from the challenge. With help from the Natchez newspaper editor, she immediately set out to make arrangements to meet with Mexican president Lazaro Cardenas. (Courtesy of *Commercial Appeal*.)

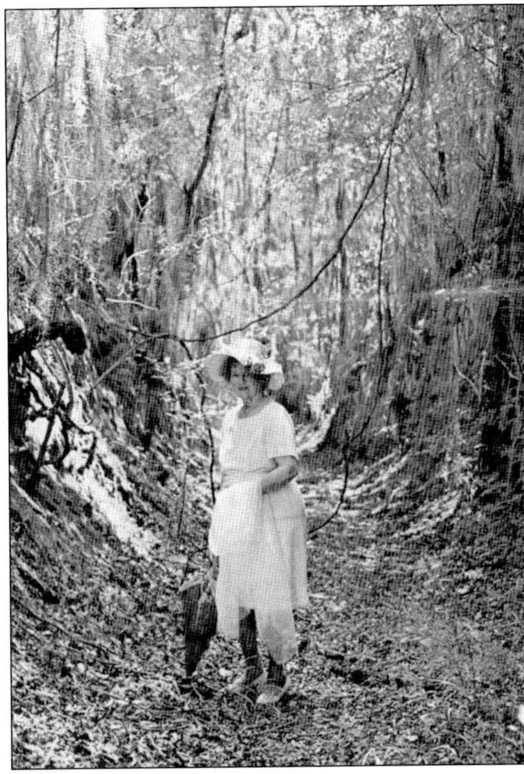

Byrnes's train trip to Mexico was scheduled to allow numerous stops and speaking engagements between Natchez and Los Angeles to promote the parkway. She used her Southern charm on Mexican communications minister Gen. Francisco Mugica and invited him to the inaugural ceremony for the parkway. The Mexican president returned the favor and invited her to bring Natchez Trace Association leaders to Mexico as guests of the Mexican government. (Courtesy of *Commercial Appeal*.)

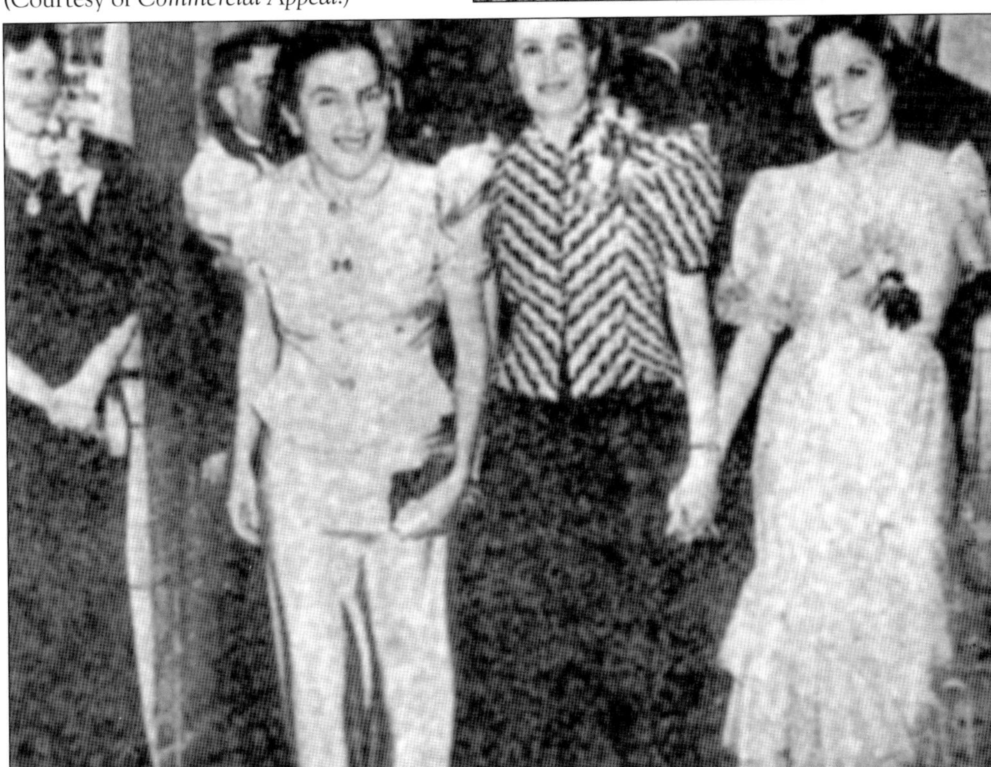

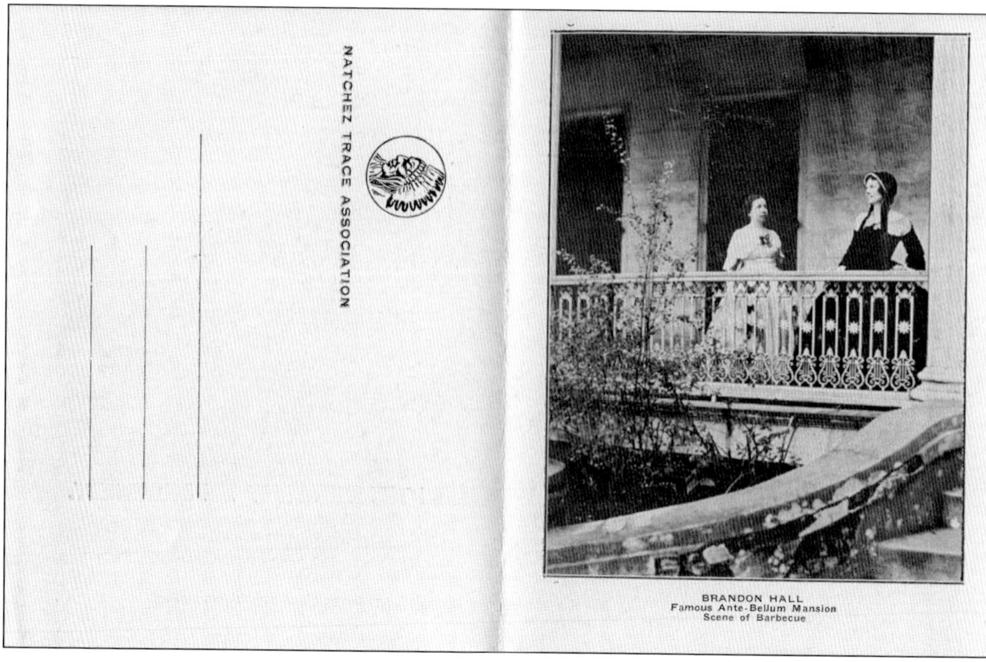

Reminiscent of the hospitality shown to visitors during the Natchez pilgrimages, Byrnes appeared in period dress at Brandon Hall in the photograph on the cover of the invitations for the inaugural event. She invited Paramount Pictures to film the gala for newsreels to be shown in theaters. (Both, NPS.)

The Adams County Unit

of the

Natchez Trace Association

invites you to be present at the

Inauguration of Construction on the Natchez Trace Parkway

in the Adams-Jefferson Unit

AT BRANDON HALL

NATCHEZ, MISSISSIPPI

on Thursday, October 28, 1937, 11:00 A. M.

THE FAVOR OF A REPLY IS REQUESTED

MRS. FERRIDAY BYRNES
PRESIDENT NATCHEZ TRACE ASSOCIATION OF MISSISSIPPI

MRS. HOBSON ALEXANDER,
PRESIDENT ADAMS COUNTY UNIT

PROGRAM

THURSDAY, OCTOBER 28th, 1937, At 11:00 A. M.

Military March .... Jefferson Military College Band
Invocation .... Rev. Stuart Henry
Memorial Tree Planting— By Representatives of Republics and States interested in the Natchez Trace.
Music .... Jefferson Military College Band
Welcome to Visitors .... Hon. W. J. Byrne, Mayor of Natchez
Hon. G. L. Powlett, President Adams Co. Board of Supervisors.
Address .... Hon. Hugh L. White, Gov. of Mississippi
Introduction of distinguished visitors. Officers of the Natchez Trace Association and Representatives from Tennessee, Alabama, Mississippi, Louisiana and Texas.
Remarks by visiting U. S. Senators and Governors.
Welcome to Senor General Francisco J. Mugica, Secretary of Communications, Mexico, D. F.
La Paloma .... Jefferson Military College Band
Address .... Hon. Dan R. McGehee, U. S. Congressman
Music by the Natchez School Band and Greetings from the Pep Squad
Address .... Hon. H. J. Patterson, Highway Commissioner
Address .... E. D. Kenna, Director, Mississippi Highway Department
Address .... Representative of the National Park Service
Address .... F. L. Brownell, Chief Engineer, Bureau of Public Roads
Address .... Hon. Theo. G. Bilbo, U. S. Senator
Benediction .... Rev. M. J. McCarthy
Reception and Barbecue Dinner

Natchez Trace Dance at Crystal Pool from 9 P. M. 'till (?)

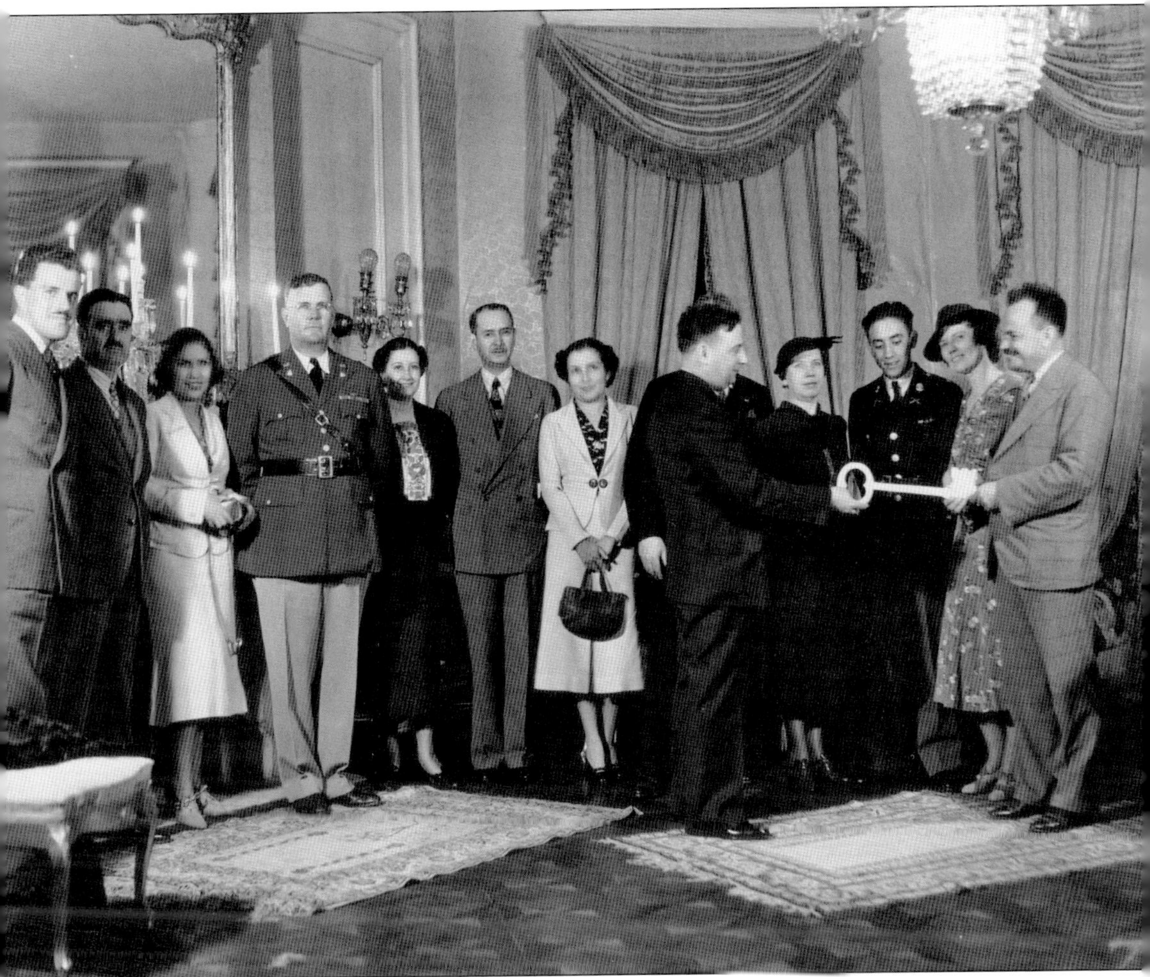

Mexican president Lazaro Cardenas sent a delegation to the inaugural Natchez ceremony in hopes that the parkway would eventually be extended to Mexico City. Mexico reportedly followed through on its commitment by paving a road from Mexico City to Laredo, Texas. Here, Natchez mayor William Byrne presents the key to the city to Mexican general Francisco Mugica. Roane Fleming Byrnes is standing to the general's right in the parlor at Ravennaside. (Courtesy of Roane Fleming Byrnes Collection, Special Collections, University of Mississippi Libraries.)

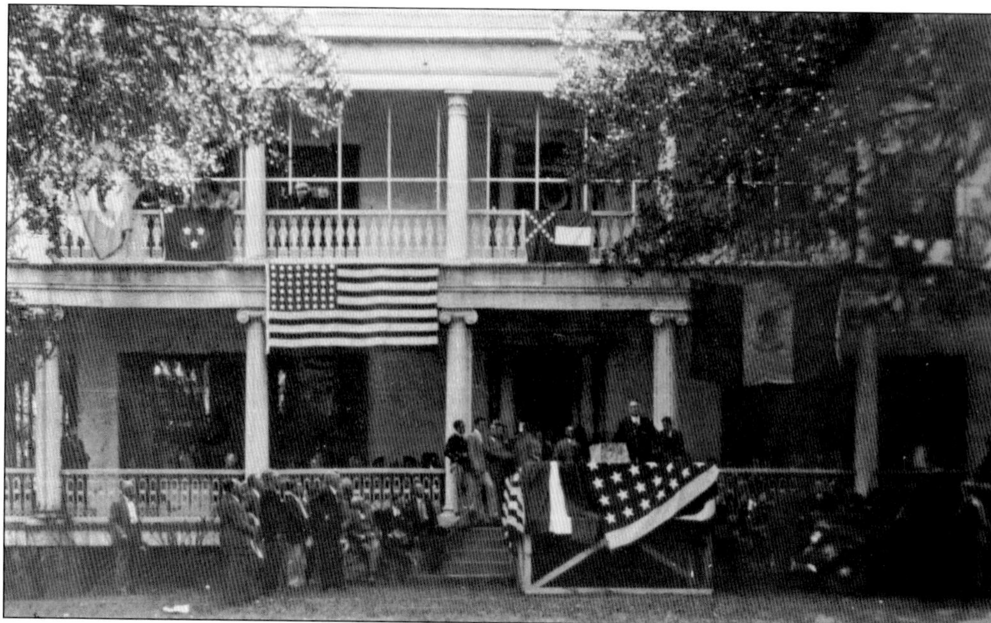

The stately Brandon Hall, located on the old Natchez Trace, hosted the grand inaugural. The Mexican flag hung from the railing along with those of the various states that were represented. President Roosevelt sent Undersecretary of the Interior Charles West as his representative. The association had gathered at the Natchez Eola Hotel. Marching bands led parades through the streets to a motorcade to Brandon Hall. (BH.)

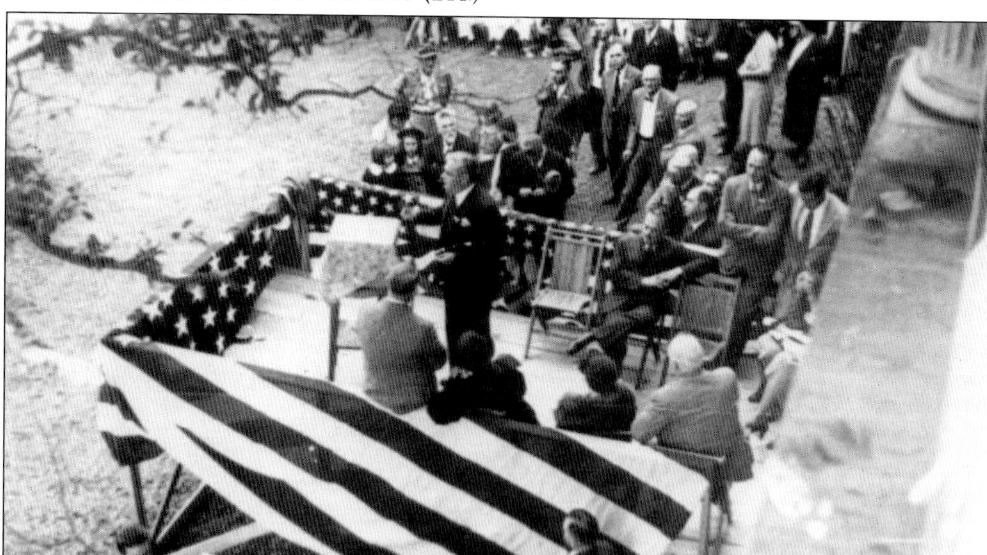

Mississippi governor Hugh White addresses the crowd at the inaugural ceremony. He is holding a small tree that is to have been planted to memorialize the event. The first Natchez Trace Association secretary/treasurer Ralph Landrum is sitting on the speaker's platform rail facing the governor. Byrnes is seated next to him. At the conclusion of the ceremony, a barbecue was held on the grounds of Brandon Hall. Rep. Ben Chase Callion capped off the day by holding a ball at Crystal Pool in honor of the Mexican delegation. (Courtesy of Roane Fleming Byrnes Collection, Special Collections, University of Mississippi Libraries.)

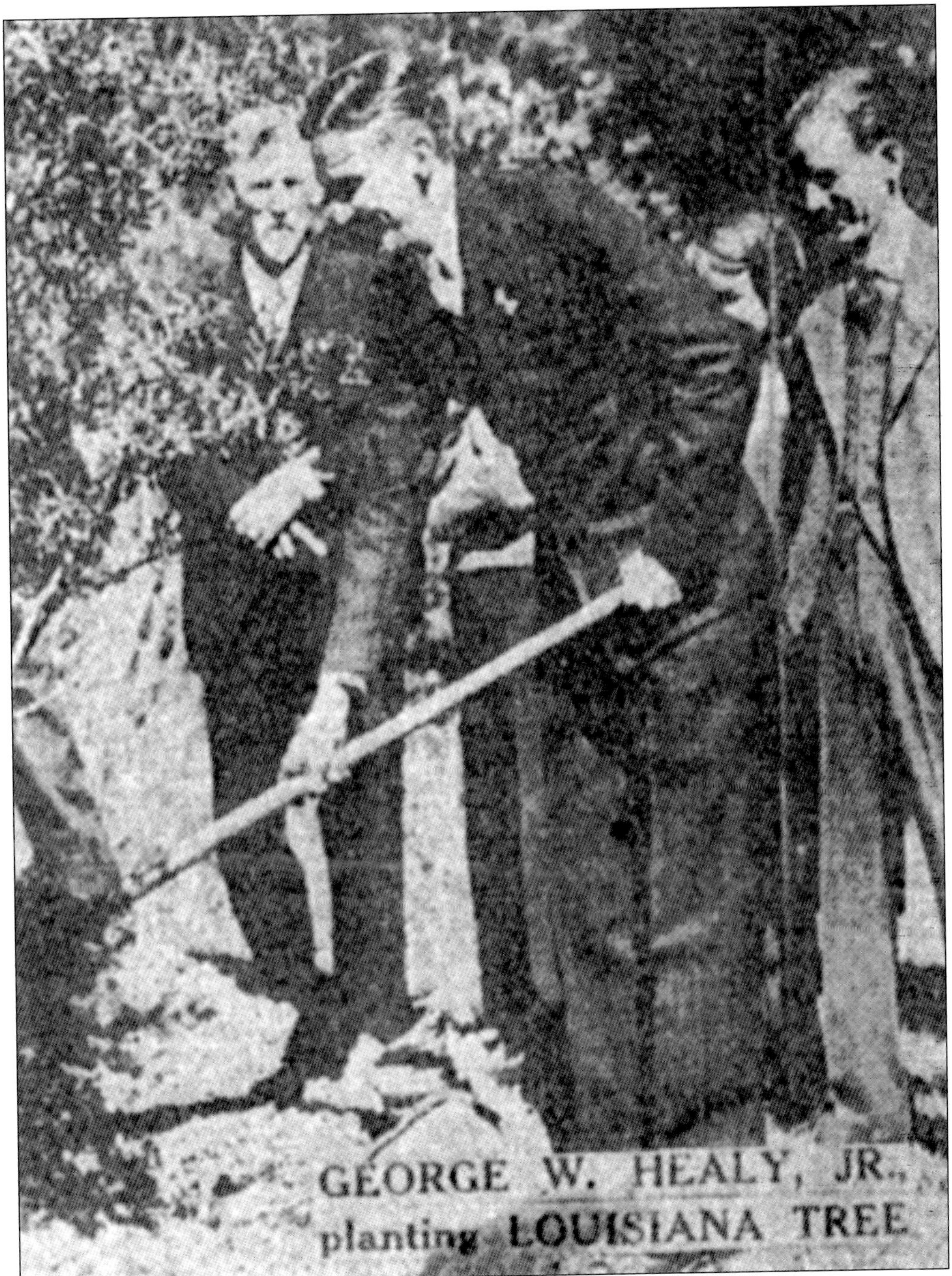

As part of the ceremony, representatives from the participating states, the federal government, and the government of Mexico planted trees along the future parkway. Texas supplied a pecan tree. New Orleans *Times-Picayune* editor George W. Healy Jr. planted the Louisiana tree. For years, the parkway marked the inaugural trees, which were located only a few feet from the pavement near mile-marker 9. (Courtesy of *Times-Picayune*.)

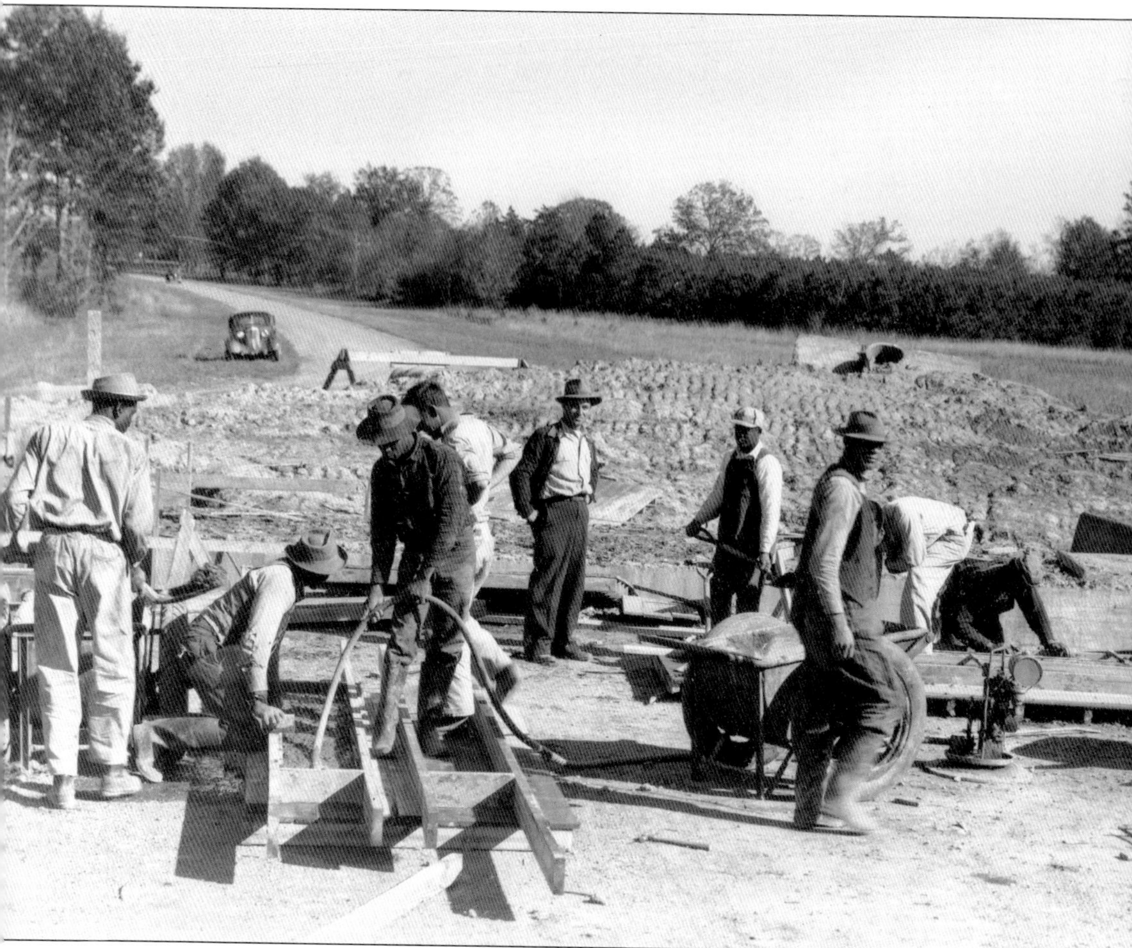

The construction crew is preparing to mix concrete by hand to build a culvert. This 1947 photograph reveals how much of the old Natchez Trace had been converted to local roads and no longer appeared to be different from numerous other local roads. It would take years before the parkway appearance would be established. (NPS.)

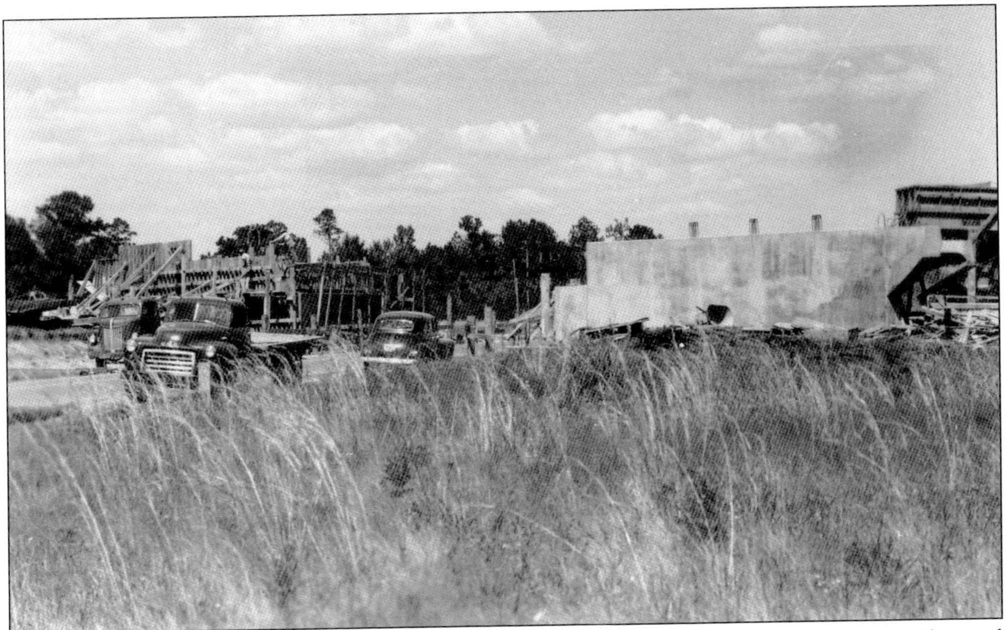

This photograph shows work beginning on the first section of road between Kosciusko and Ridgeland. Even as work started on one section, more land was needed for the next. The association appealed to the Mississippi State Legislature for support with the vision that "the Trace would not be just a road but a national park and would mean to the South what Yellowstone means to the West." (NPS.)

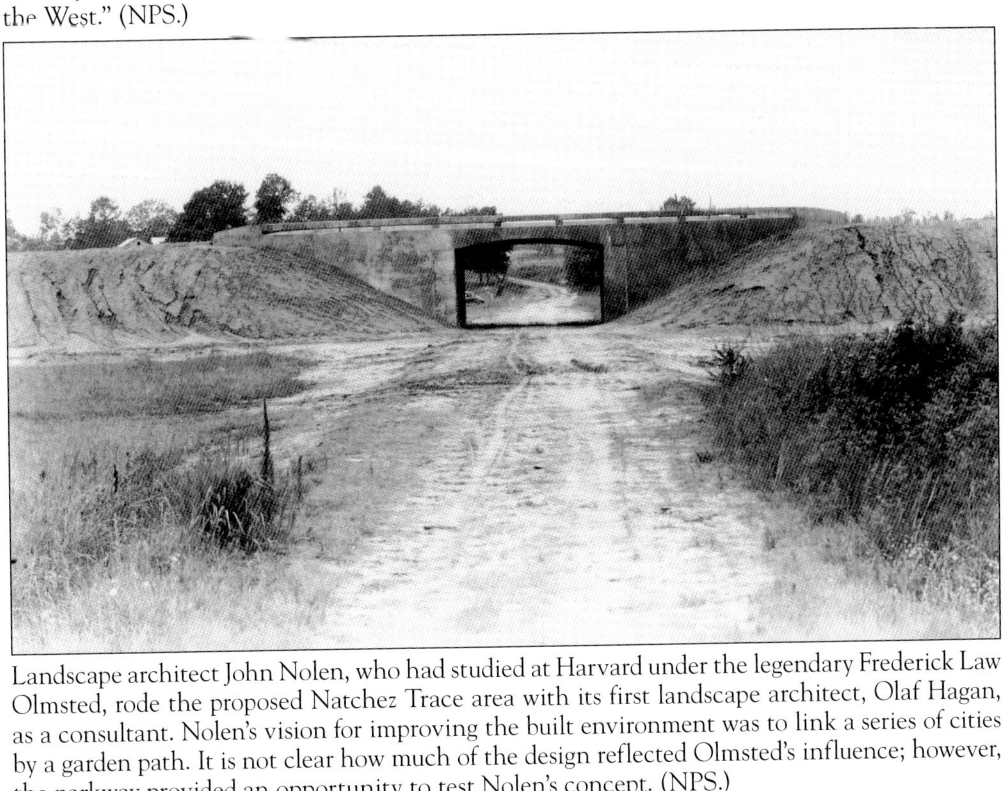

Landscape architect John Nolen, who had studied at Harvard under the legendary Frederick Law Olmsted, rode the proposed Natchez Trace area with its first landscape architect, Olaf Hagan, as a consultant. Nolen's vision for improving the built environment was to link a series of cities by a garden path. It is not clear how much of the design reflected Olmsted's influence; however, the parkway provided an opportunity to test Nolen's concept. (NPS.)

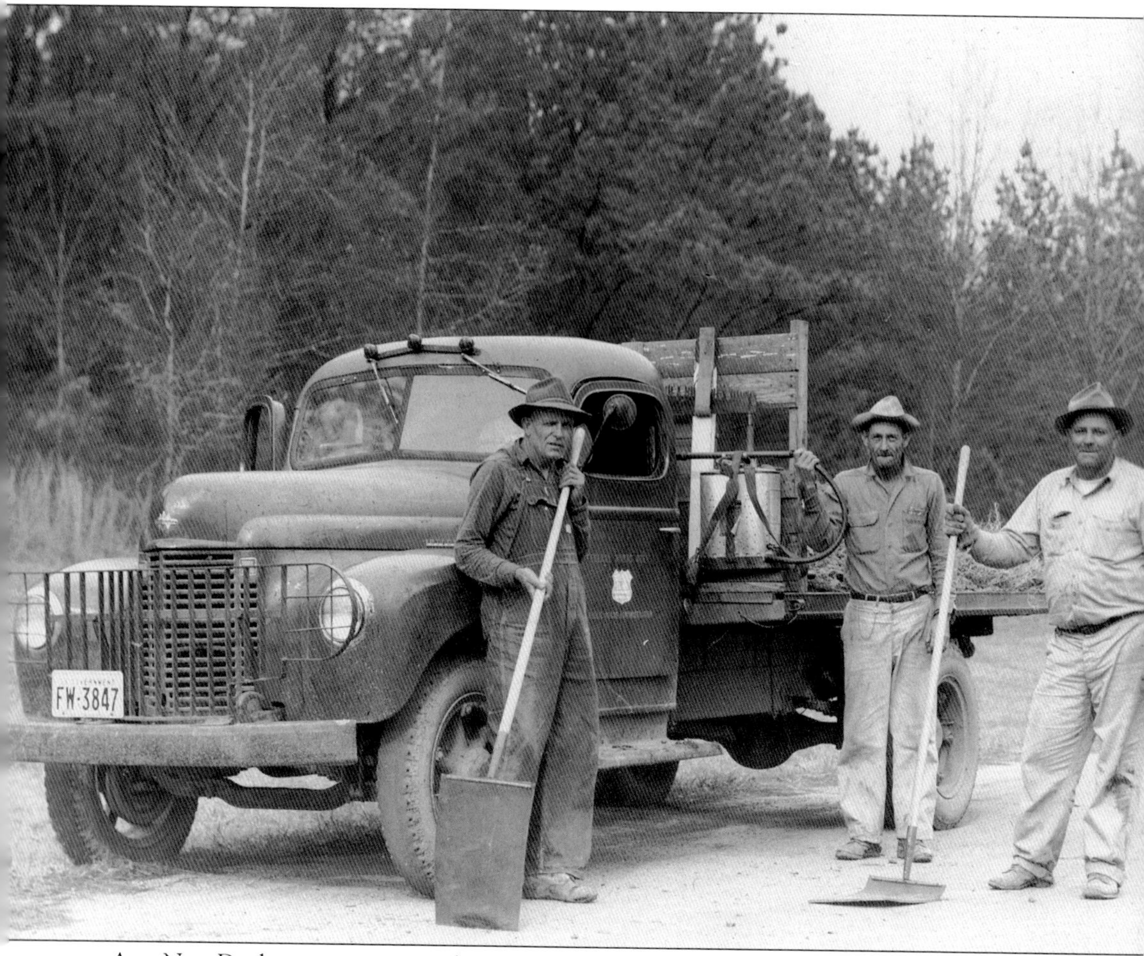

As a New Deal program, one goal was to put large numbers of people to work. Construction in national parks during the Depression was often labor-intensive in order to utilize more workers. Mules and other farm animals were used to clear the forests in construction areas, much as the work had been performed on the old Natchez Trace. (NPS.)

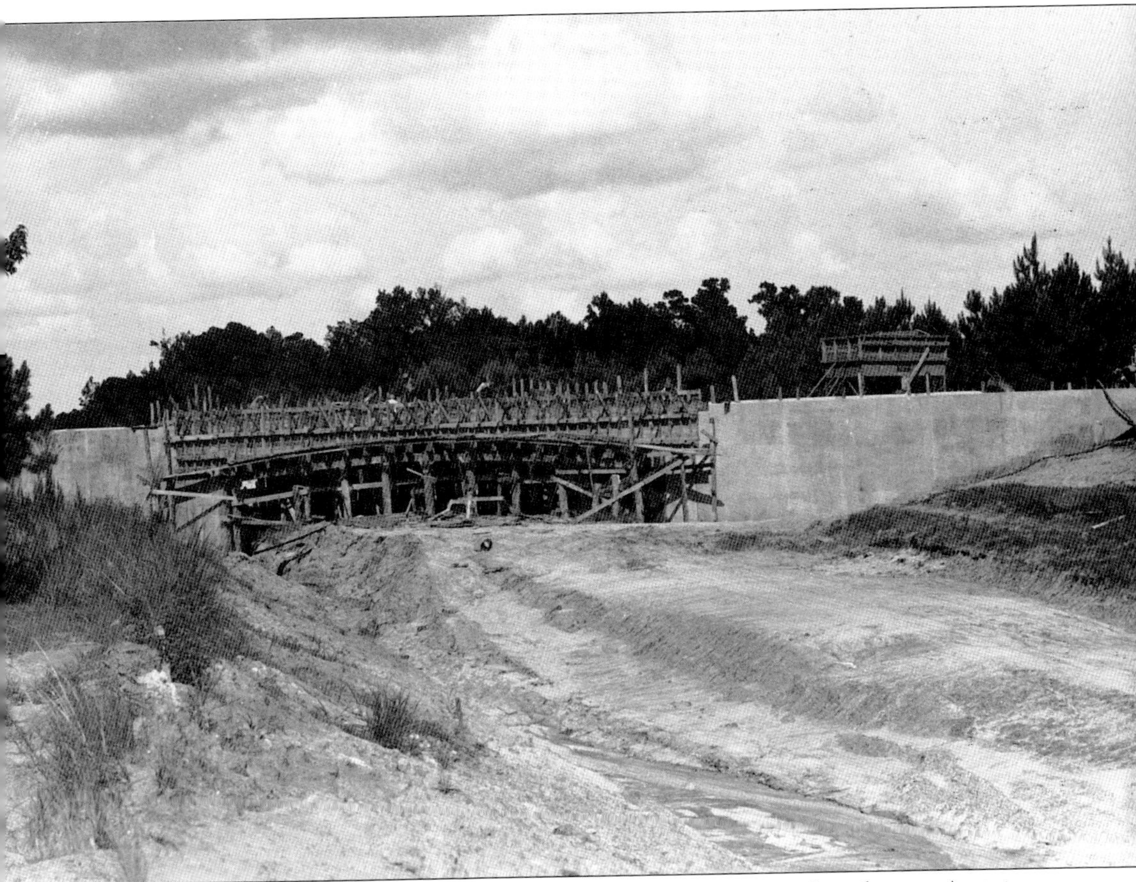

In Depression-era Washington, DC, the novel concept of a parkway combined a new American love of the automobile with scenic sites. Unlike most other parkways, the Natchez Trace was to be a scenic trail of historic sites. Construction methods were modern, but infrastructure would generally be hidden to emphasize the natural aspects of the parkway. This was one of the first overpasses built. (NPS.)

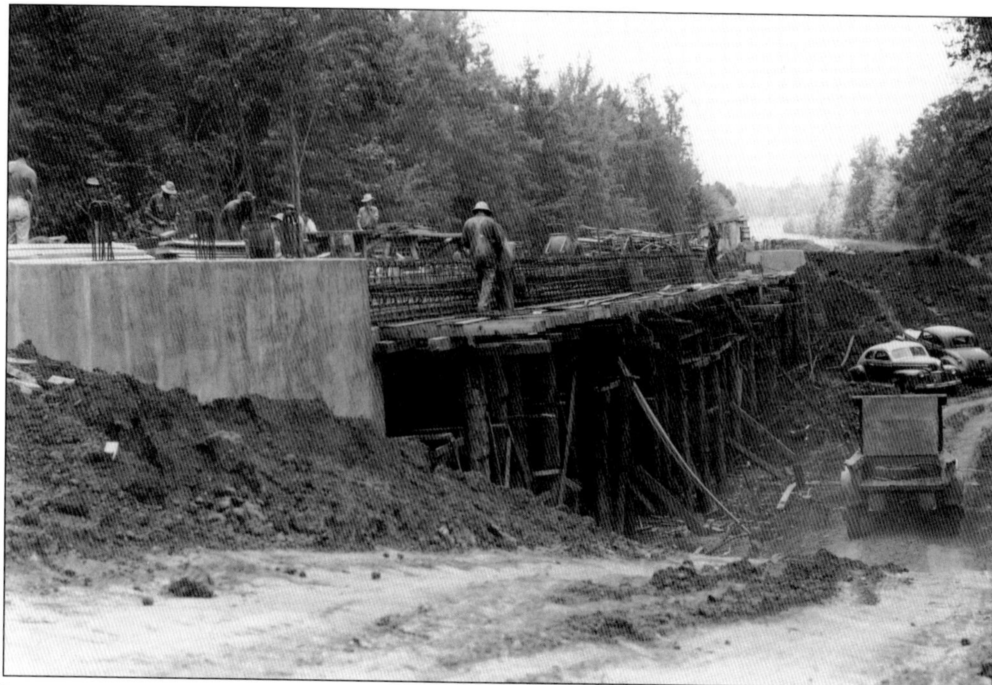

In 1940, a newspaper reported that the parkway was being designed with long sweeping curves for safety and beauty. The curves were intended to slow traffic and to prevent the traveler from seeing too much of the vista at one time. Each new section was to present a different view. The old Natchez Trace, which was built around hills rather than through them, had even more curves. (NPS.)

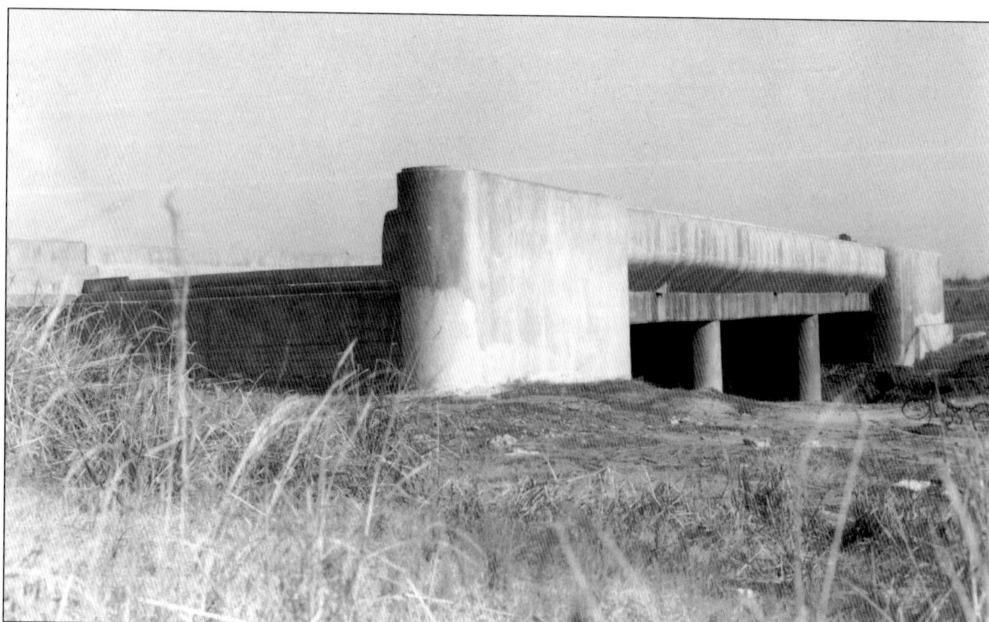

The National Park Service often stained exposed new concrete infrastructure with oil to prevent the stark white of the new materials from detracting from the natural scenery. The oil staining is still apparent on the older structures. This overpass is being constructed at Highway 15. (NPS.)

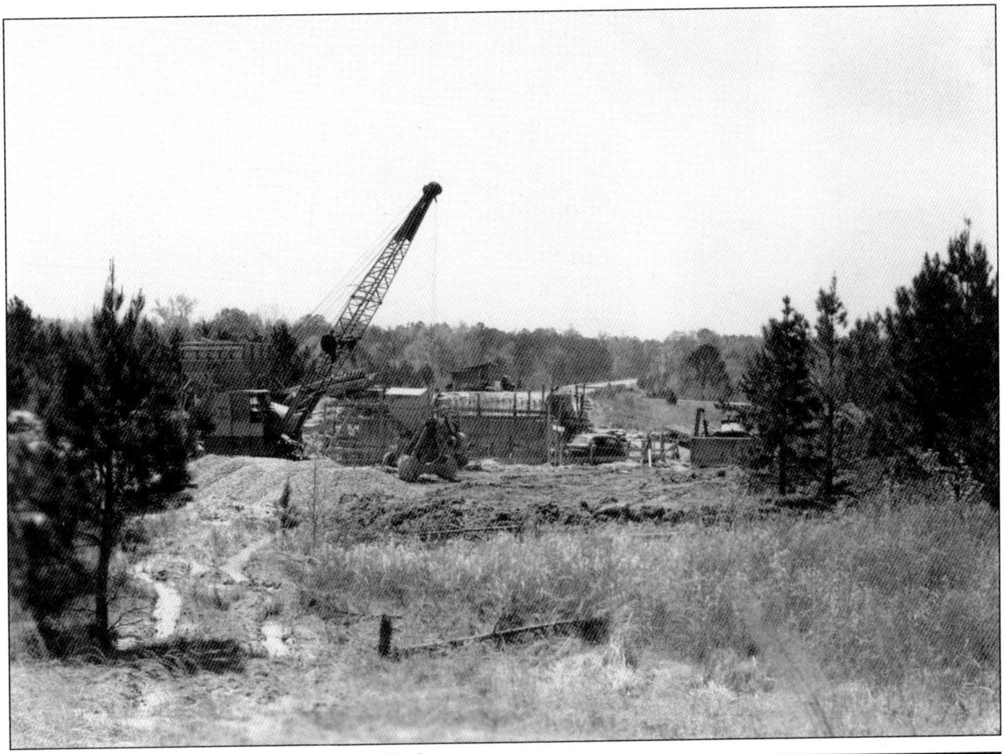

NPS director Newton B. Drury recalled that during the Truman administration the National Park Service often requested little or no money for parkway construction, but powerful House and Senate committee chairs from Mississippi appropriated a few million dollars each year to keep the project moving forward. Roane Fleming Byrnes called on those powerful chairmen each year to report to the parkway association annual meeting, and they complied either by telegram or in person. This bridge is being constructed over Philadelphia Creek at the Highway 16 overpass. (NPS.)

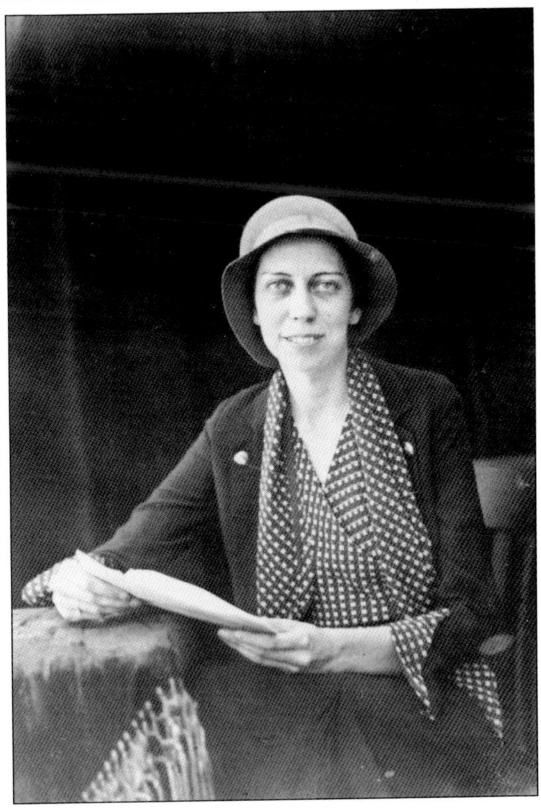

Roane Fleming Byrnes promoted the Natchez Trace and its sometimes mythical lore to writers and artists. Her friend Eudora Welty chose to use the old Natchez Trace as the setting for some of her works, including the classic *The Robber Bridegroom*. The stories brought Natchez Trace history to the attention of a broad readership and increased support for continued construction of the parkway. (MDAH.)

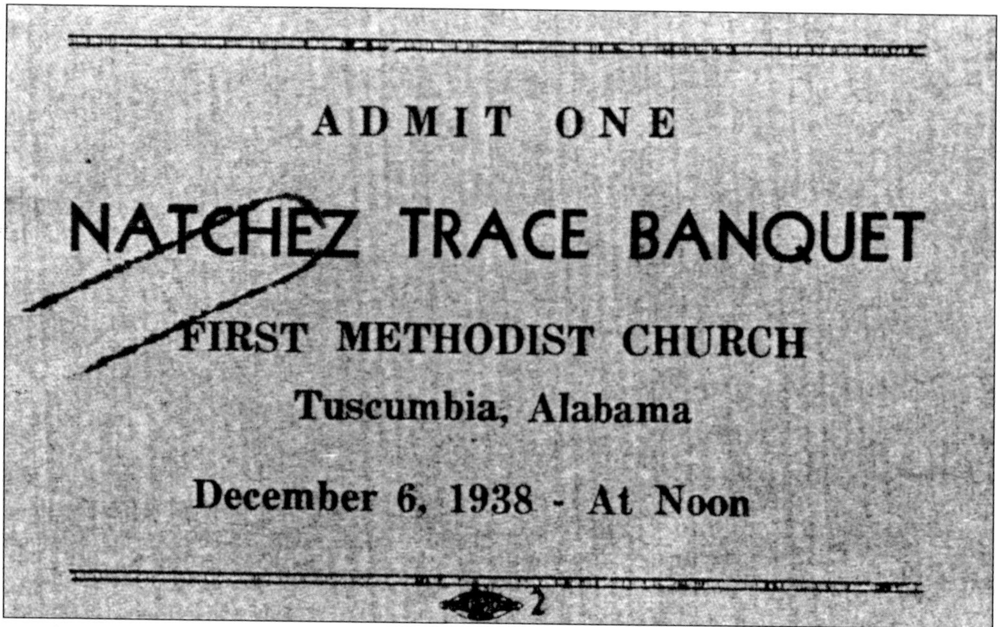

ADMIT ONE

NATCHEZ TRACE BANQUET

FIRST METHODIST CHURCH

Tuscumbia, Alabama

December 6, 1938 - At Noon

2

Natchez Trace associations were also formed in Alabama and Tennessee. Alabama association president Paul Coburn could not obtain support for the purchase of right-of-way in his state until he told a newspaper reporter that Tennessee was making plans to route its portion through Shiloh Military Park to avoid Alabama. Within a week, the Alabama governor announced the beginning of land acquisition. (UMO.)

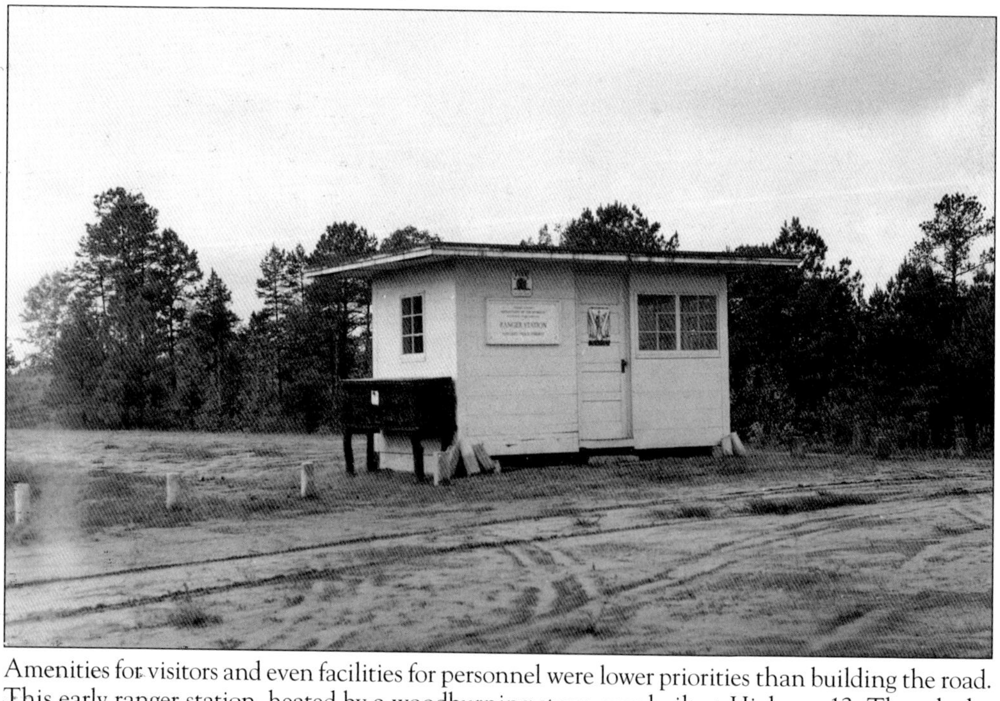

Amenities for visitors and even facilities for personnel were lower priorities than building the road. This early ranger station, heated by a woodburning stove, was built at Highway 12. Though the early buildings were spartan, they gave the National Park Service a visual and physical presence on the future parkway. (NPS.)

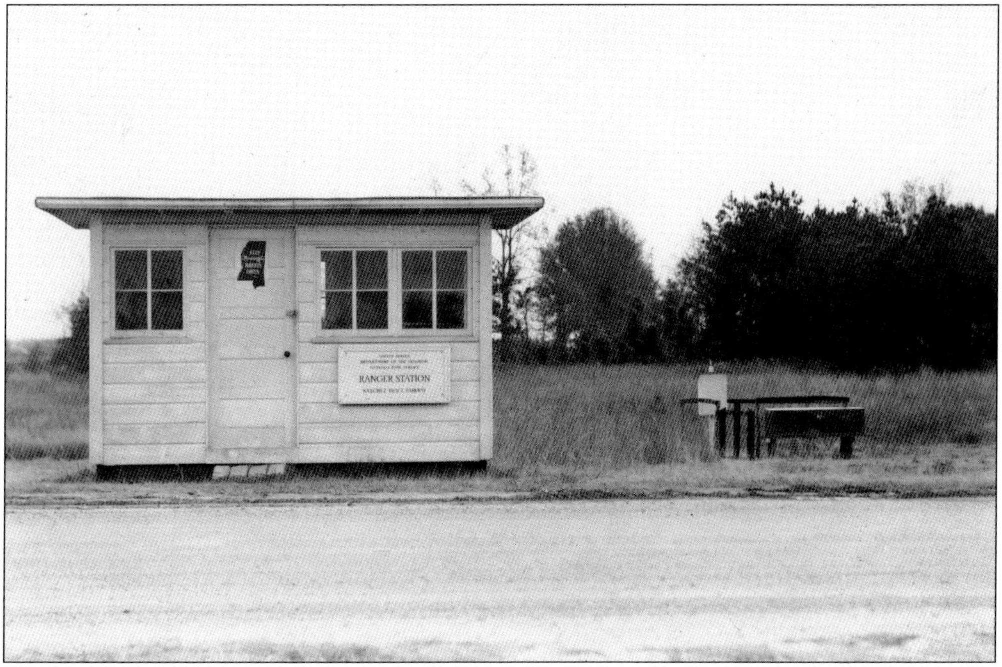

Another early parkway building follows the same functional design. (NPS.)

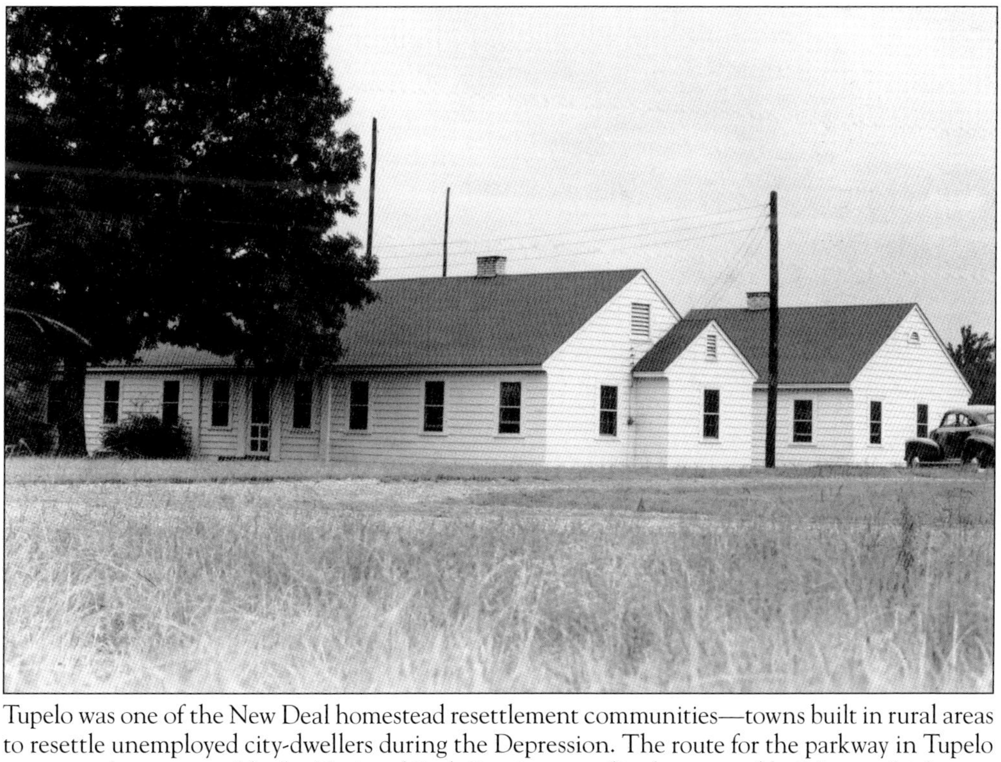

Tupelo was one of the New Deal homestead resettlement communities—towns built in rural areas to resettle unemployed city-dwellers during the Depression. The route for the parkway in Tupelo was moved east to enable the National Park Service to utilize homestead buildings, which were already owned by the government. Workers connected three homestead houses to create the first parkway administration building. (NPS.)

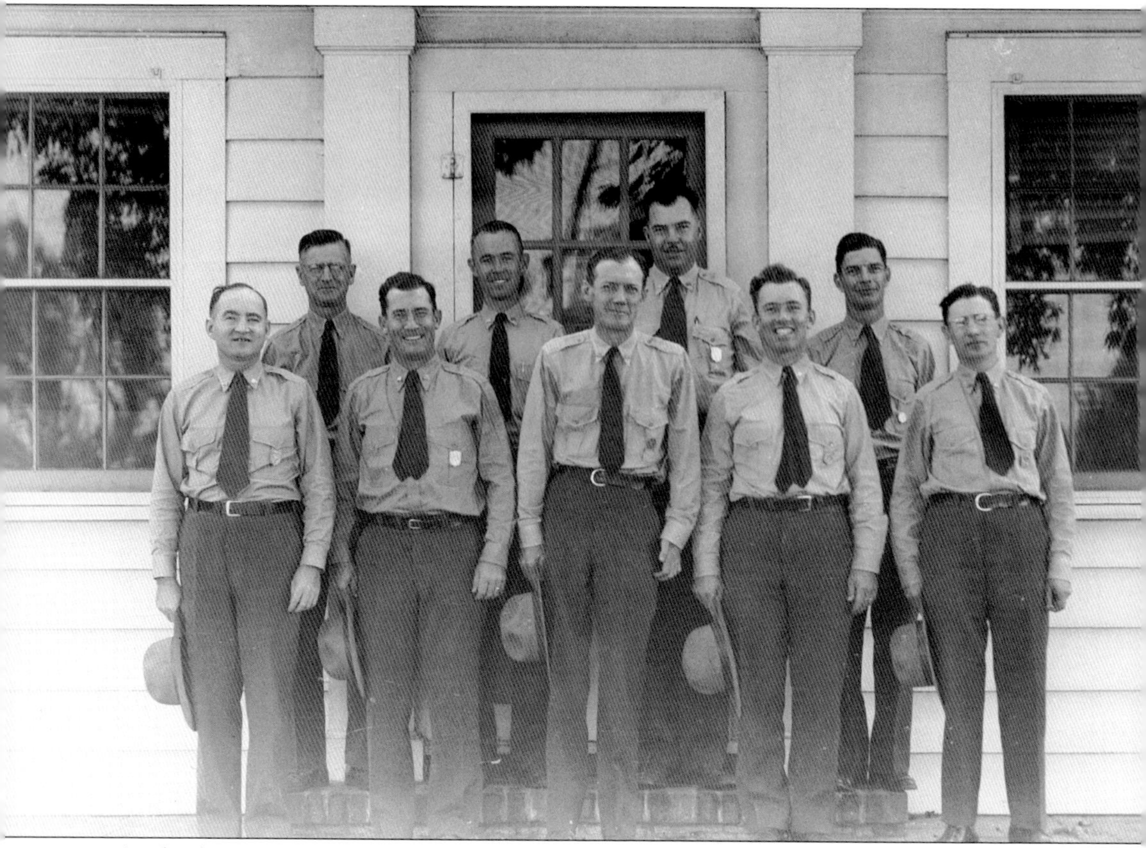

As the first superintendent of the Natchez Trace Parkway, Malcolm Gardner helped shape the National Park Service concept for the parkway. Fred Roush served as custodian of the Meriwether Lewis National Monument. Shown here, from left to right, are (first row) Malcolm Gardner, Ranger Thomas, Ranger Ramstad, Ranger Howe, and custodian Fred Roush; (second row) Assistant Superintendent Hamilton, Chief Ranger Harriman, and District Rangers McCormack and O'Brien. (NPS.)

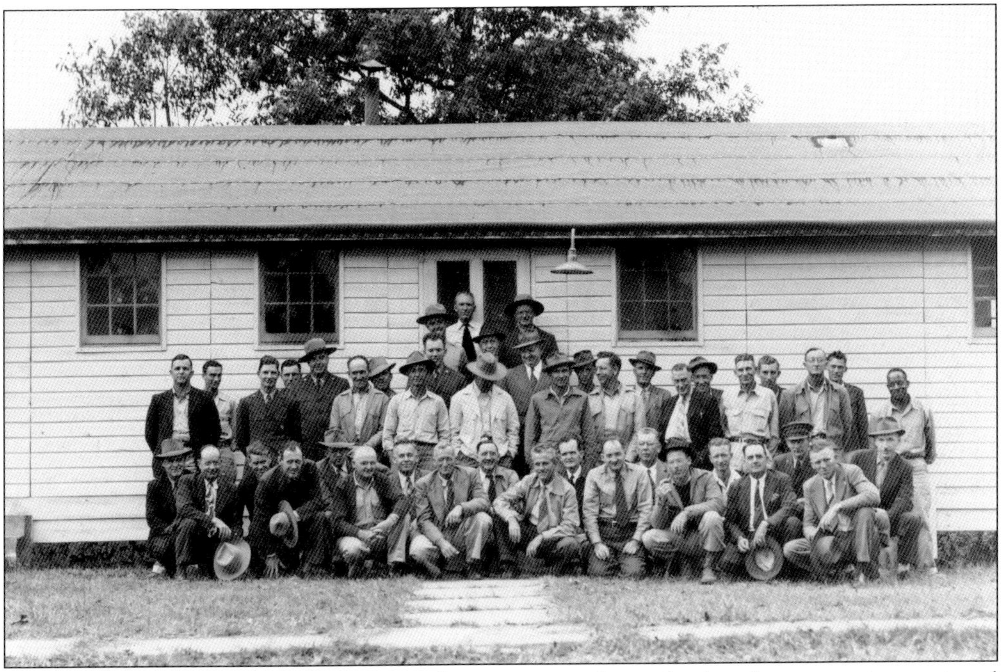

Fire management is critical to preserving the scenic corridor and cultural resources in a national park. An unobserved campfire or lightning can destroy hundreds of acres. This early fire school trained workers in the latest techniques. (NPS.)

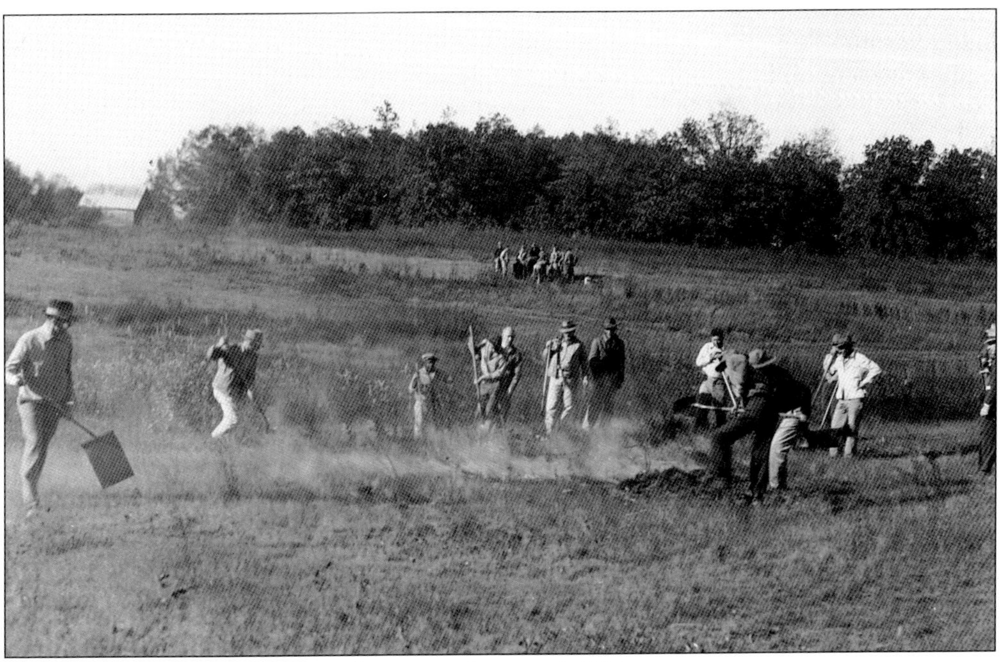

This fire school practices the earth-spray technique. (NPS.)

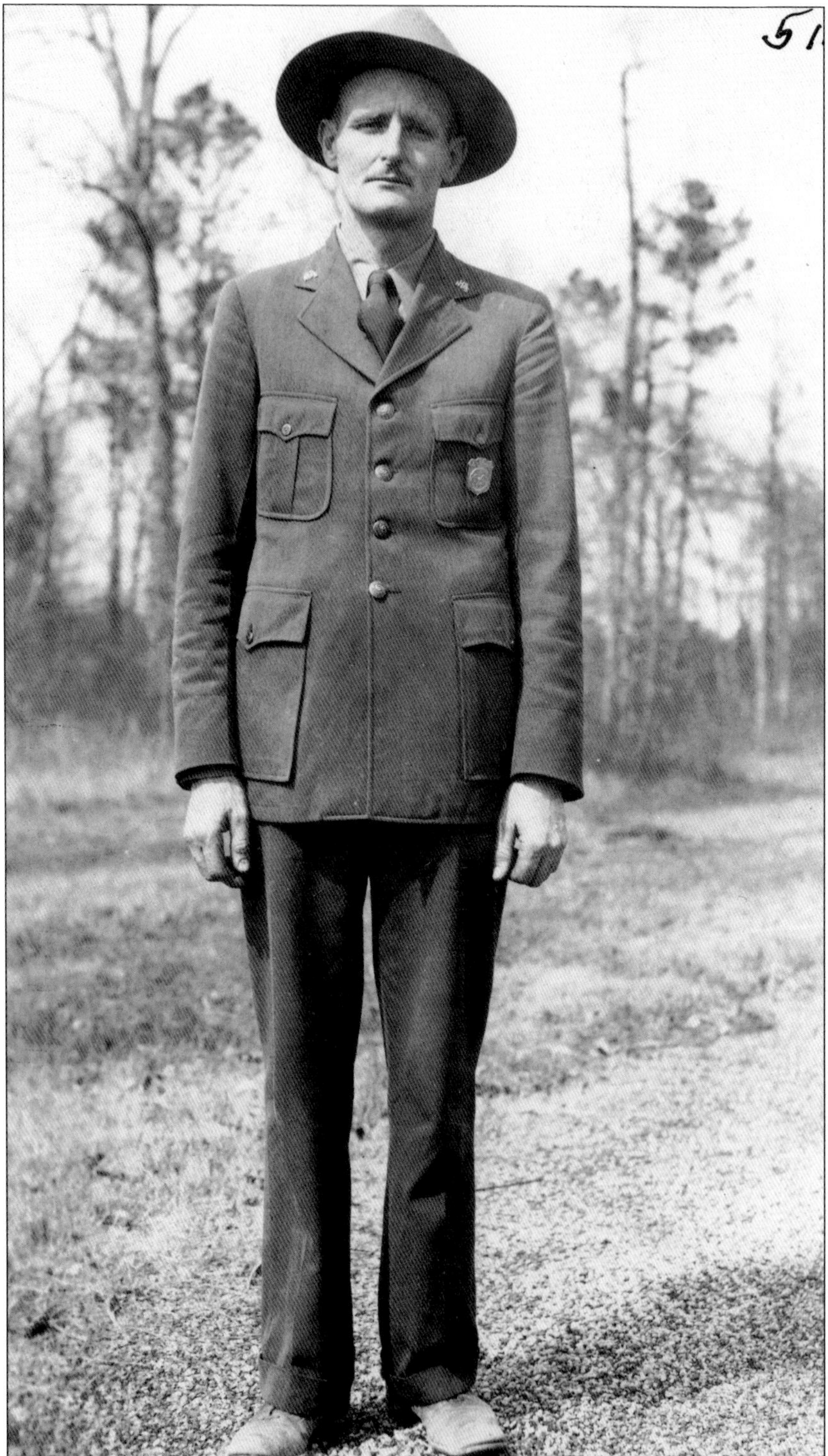

A park ranger's duties can vary daily from law enforcement to emergency medical care, rescue, and interpretation. This ranger is unidentified. (NPS.)

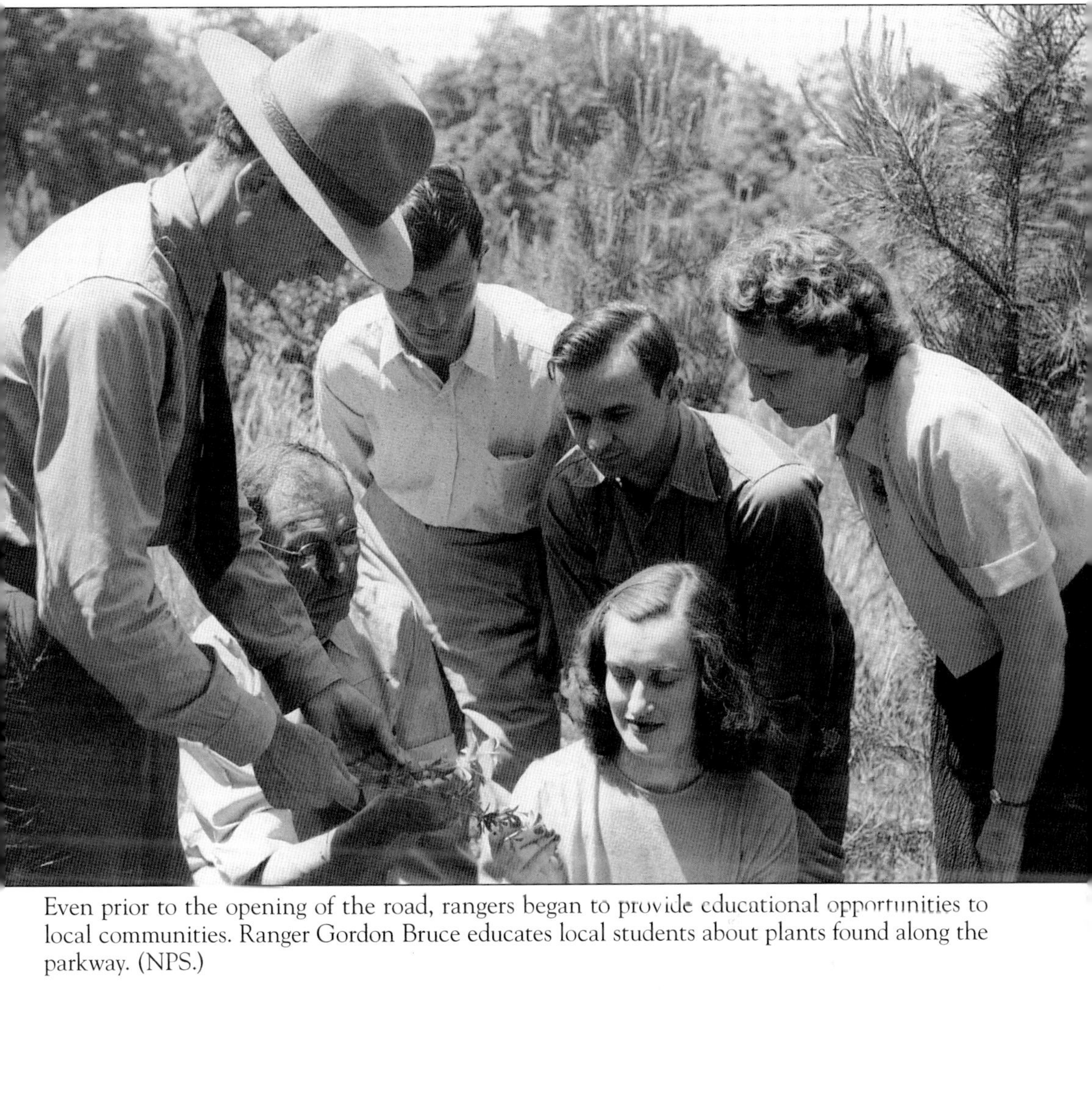

Even prior to the opening of the road, rangers began to provide educational opportunities to local communities. Ranger Gordon Bruce educates local students about plants found along the parkway. (NPS.)

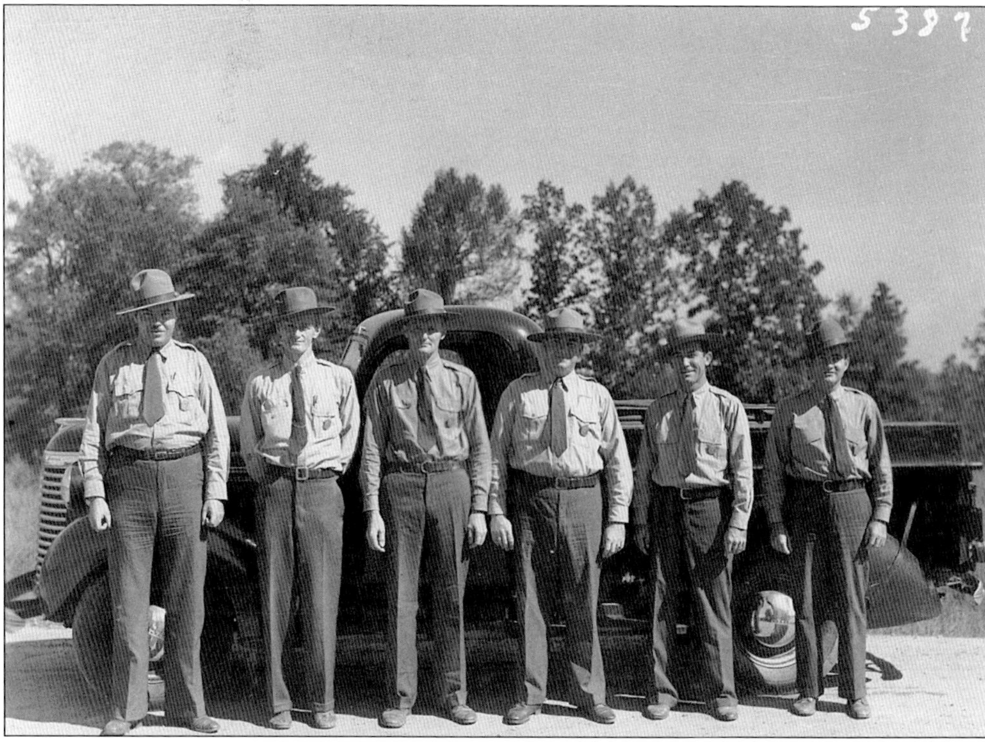

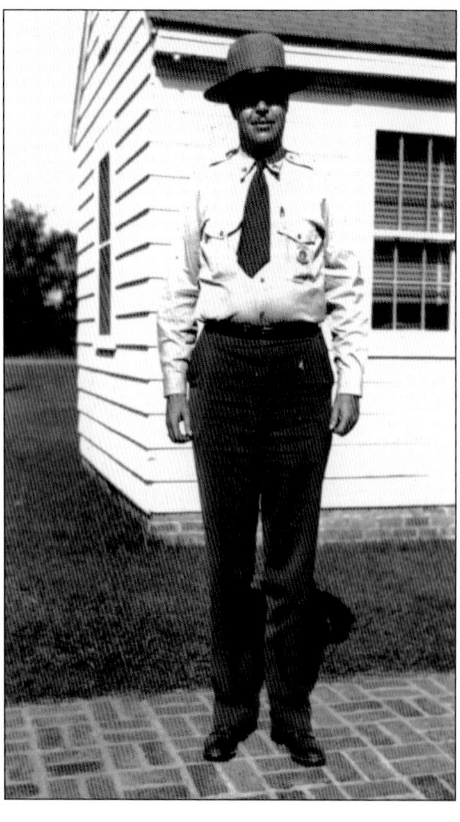

There were more rangers per mile for the opening of the first 22 miles than the parkway administration would ever have again; however, personnel were recruited and trained with the future in mind. In later years, the parkway administration would be responsible for maintaining and controlling much more land with the same numbers of staff members it had when the parkway covered a smaller territory. (NPS.)

Donnell E. O'Brien is shown here outside the former parkway headquarters in Tupelo, Mississippi. (NPS.)

Alvin Timmons makes the routed, lettered, wooden signs that were a trademark feature of national parks. Until the 1950s, when the Mission 66 plan was implemented, the National Park Service designed all improvements to blend with the surrounding environment. The signs were painted a reddish brown to maintain the natural wood look, and engraved letters were painted yellow for visibility. (NPS.)

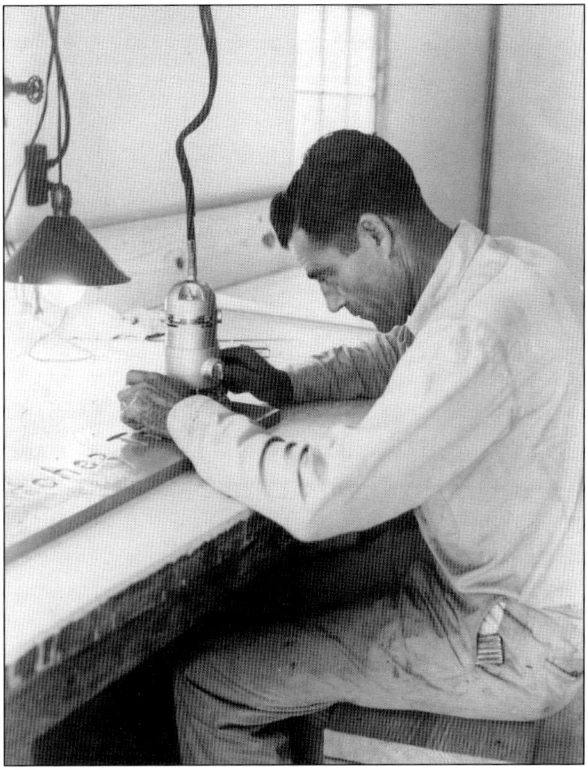

The first parkway logo shown on this early parkway headquarters sign depicts settlers or boatmen walking the old Natchez Trace in the company of a post rider. Later, only the post rider would be used in the logo. (NPS.)

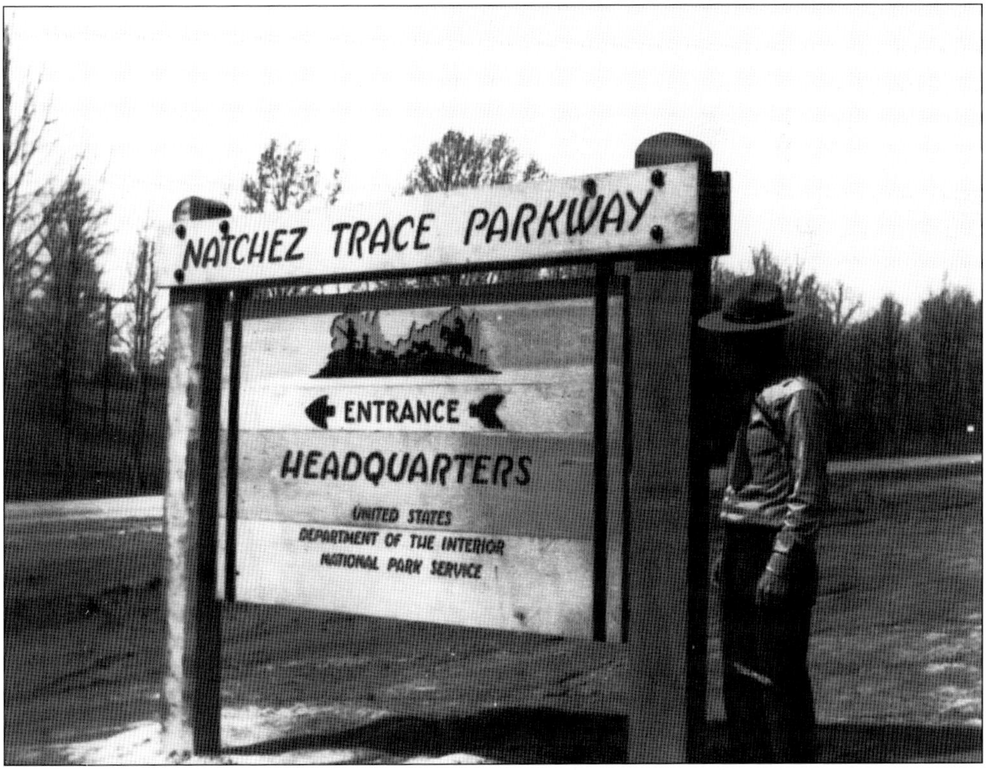

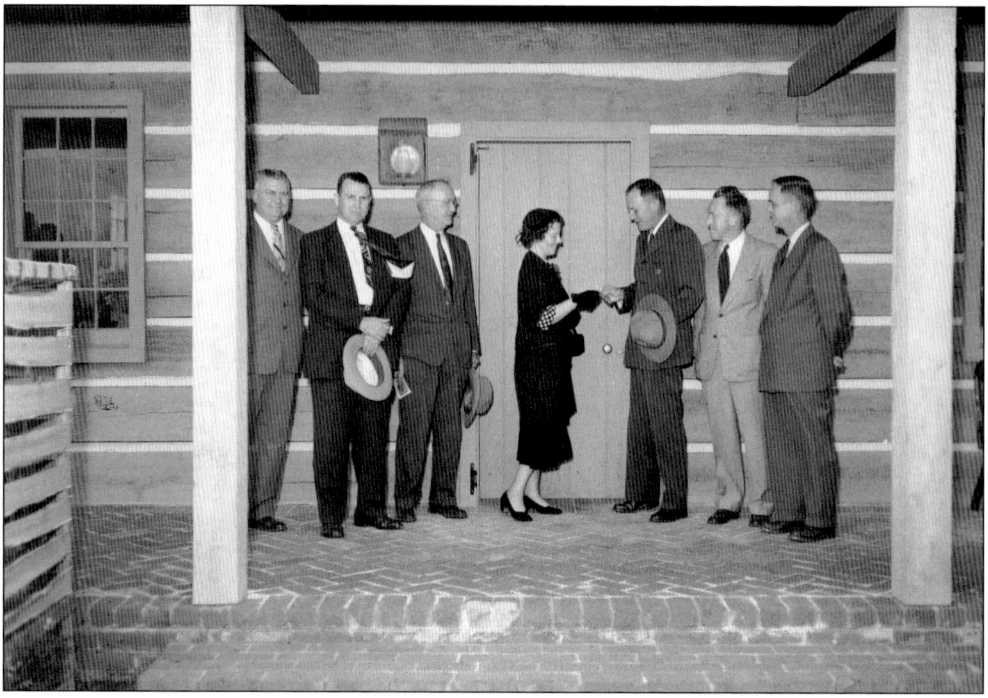

On November 9, 1951, the first 22-mile section was opened. Work on the parkway had been delayed during the World War II years, when all national resources had been devoted to the war effort. This photograph captures Roane Fleming Byrnes's meeting with dignitaries at the cabin where the ceremony would take place. It is clear from their expressions that she is not wasting a moment winning their support for the next phase. (NPS.)

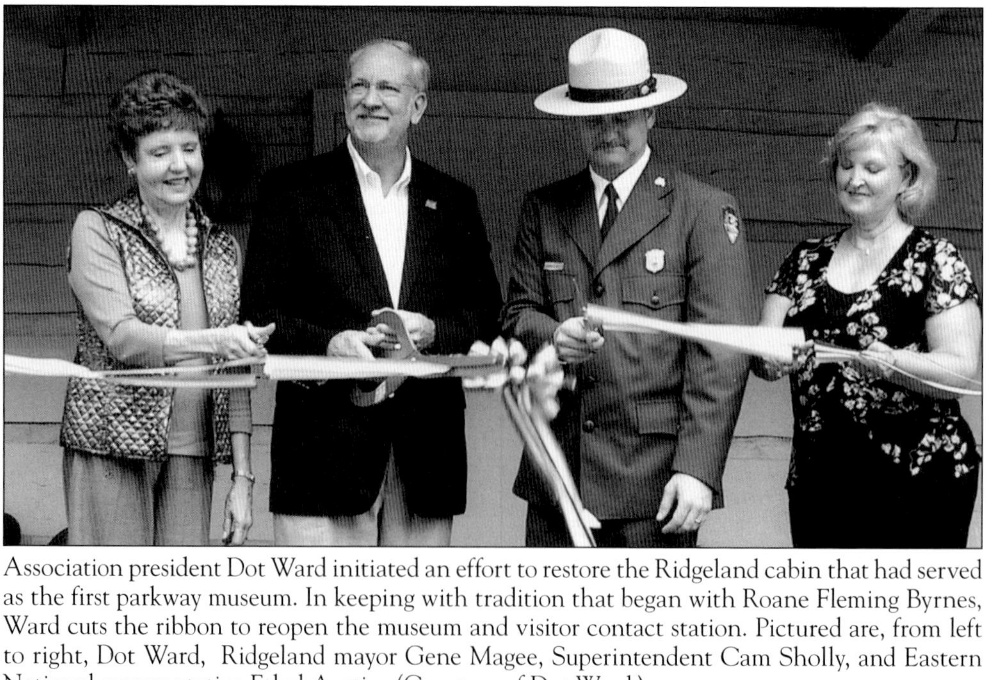

Association president Dot Ward initiated an effort to restore the Ridgeland cabin that had served as the first parkway museum. In keeping with tradition that began with Roane Fleming Byrnes, Ward cuts the ribbon to reopen the museum and visitor contact station. Pictured are, from left to right, Dot Ward, Ridgeland mayor Gene Magee, Superintendent Cam Sholly, and Eastern National representative Ethel Austin. (Courtesy of Dot Ward.)

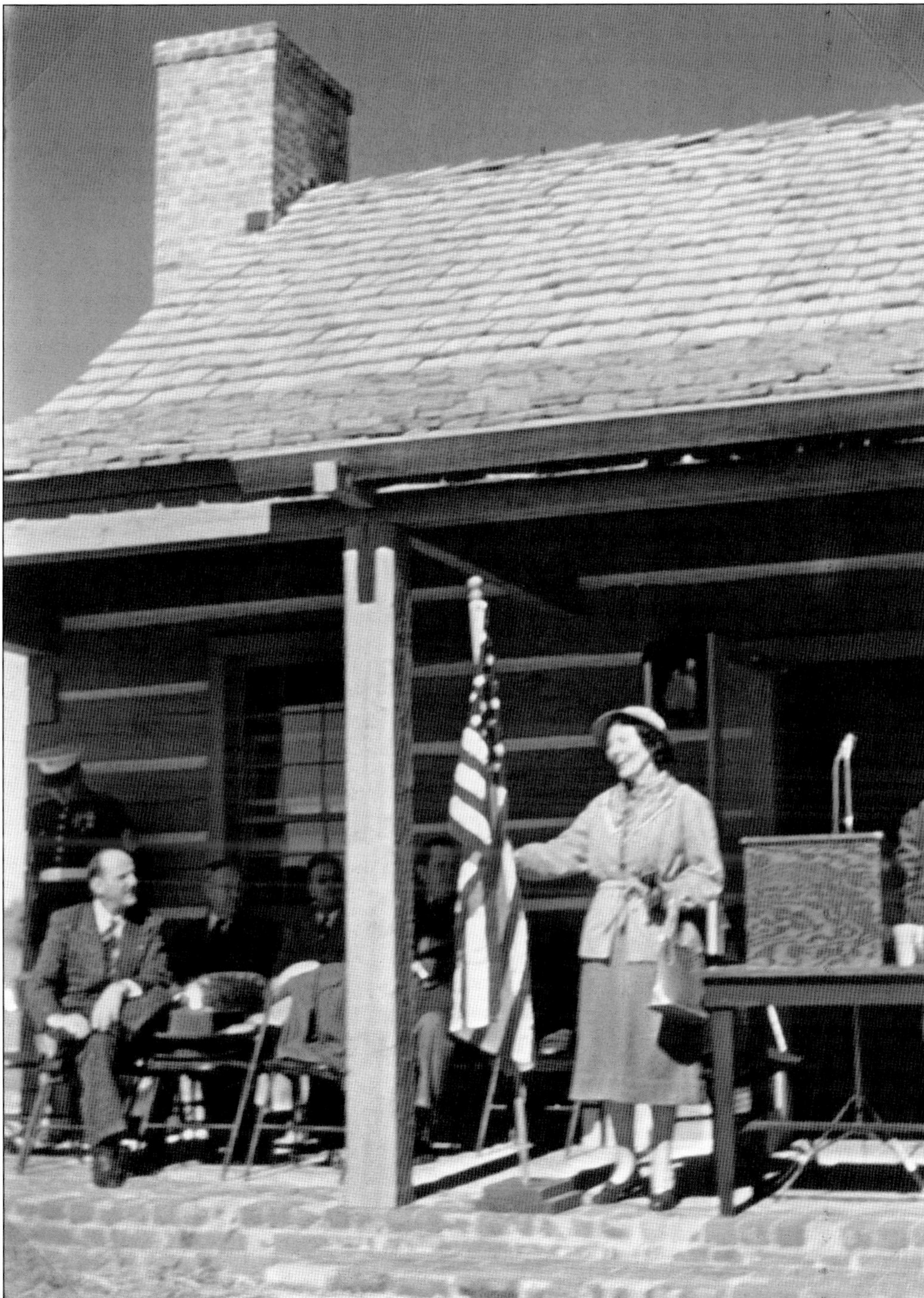

Roane Fleming Byrnes speaks at the opening ceremony at the Ridgeland cabin just prior to cutting the ribbon to open the first segment, beginning a tradition that would continue for the completion of each section of the roadway. (Courtesy of Roane Fleming Byrnes Collection, Special Collections, University of Mississippi Libraries.)

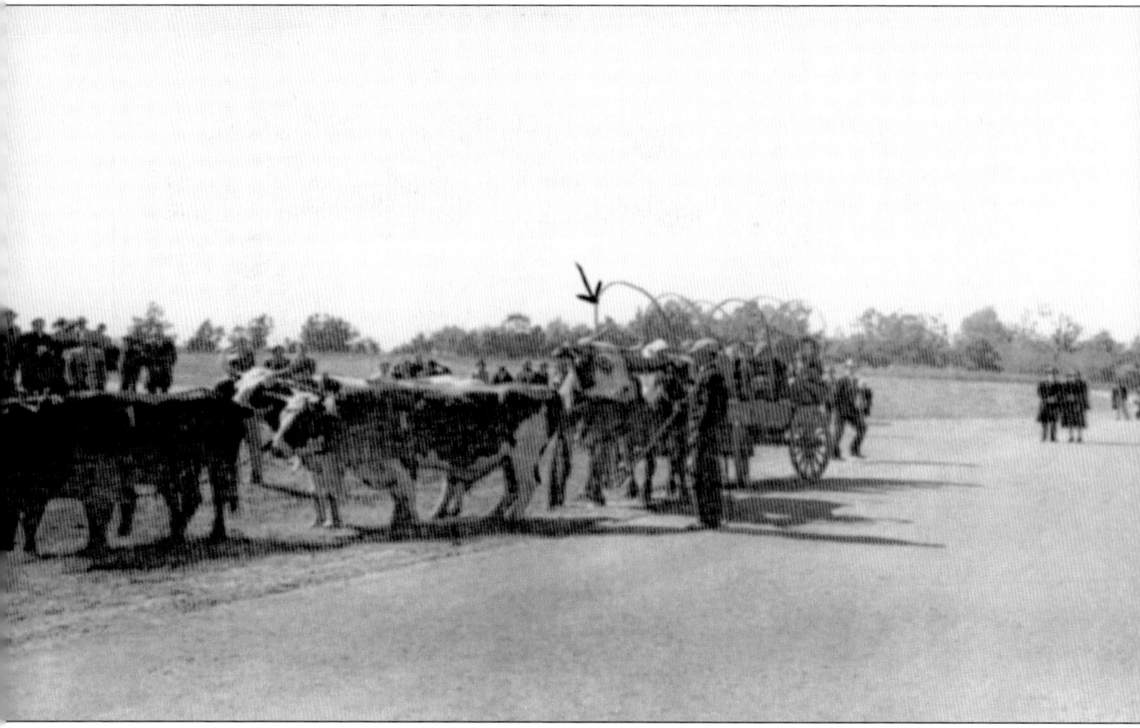

For the opening ceremony, Roane Fleming Byrnes planned to feature a parade depicting the history of the old Natchez Trace from pioneer settlers in ox-drawn wagons to Southern belles in hoopskirts. The characters from the past were to ride first through the ribbon. As shown in this photograph, the lead ox bolted, breaking the tongue on the wagon and leaving the characters from the past stranded. Undaunted, Byrnes made historical pageants part of association annual meetings. (NPS.)

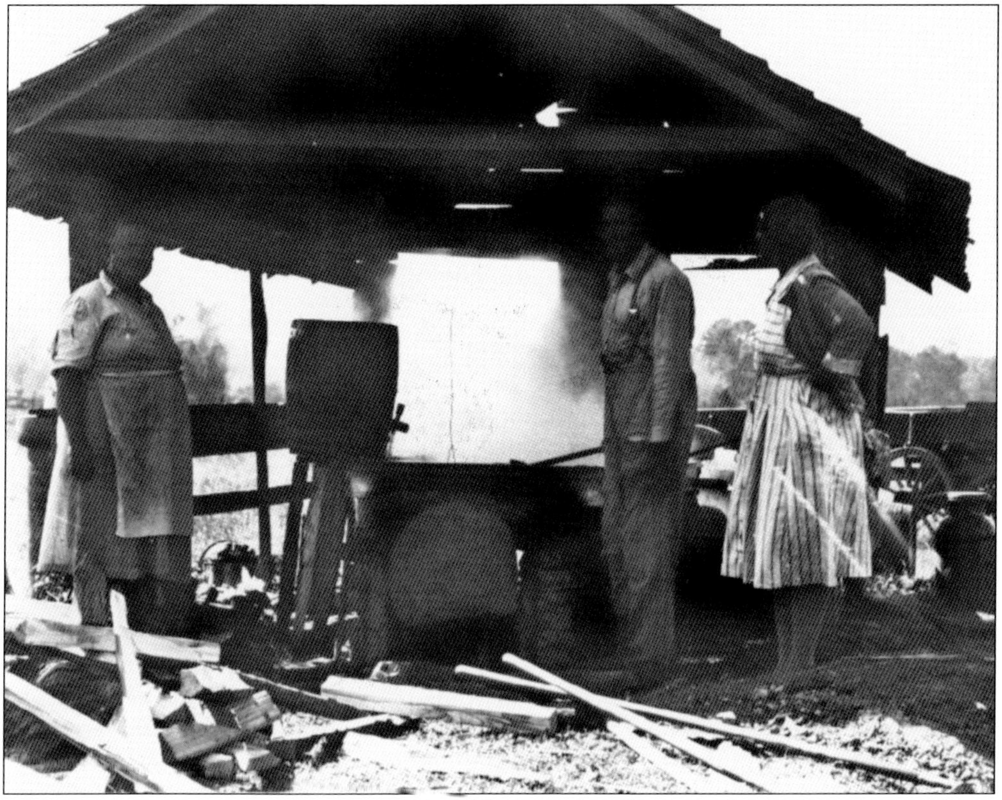

At first, it was unnecessary to recreate the old Southern culture on the parkway to provide an educational experience for visitors. Travelers only had to look out the windows of their automobiles to see people carrying on the same traditions as those practiced by early settlers. Here, Henry Howard and his unidentified assistants are making molasses. (Both, NPS.)

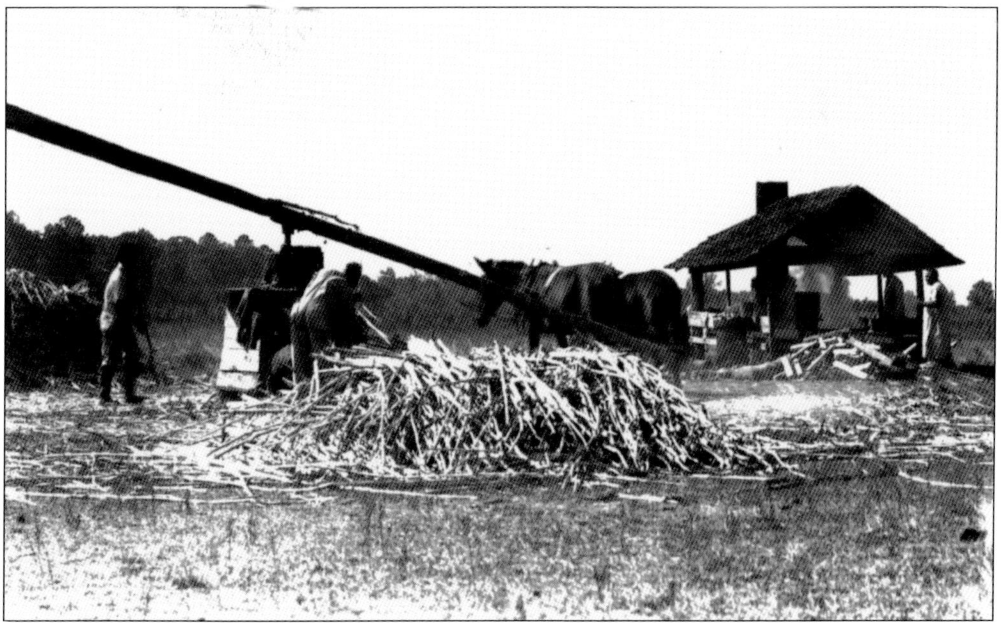

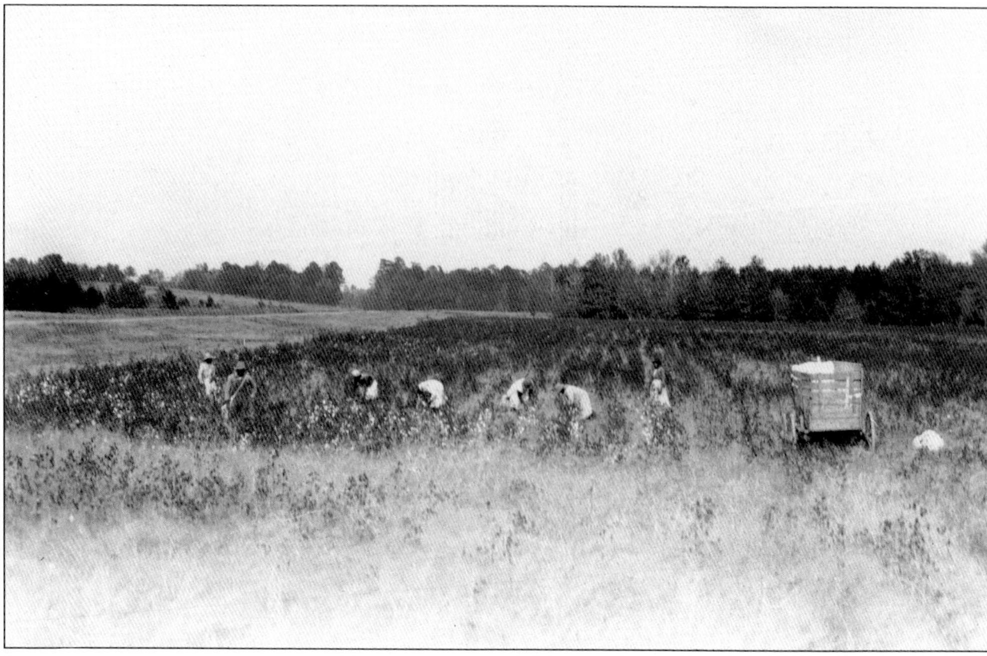

In Mississippi, miles of fields were still planted with cotton when the parkway first opened, reminding visitors of the important role the cotton industry had played in the Southern economy. The National Park Service interpretation later expanded to include a discussion of enslaved African Americans. (NPS.)

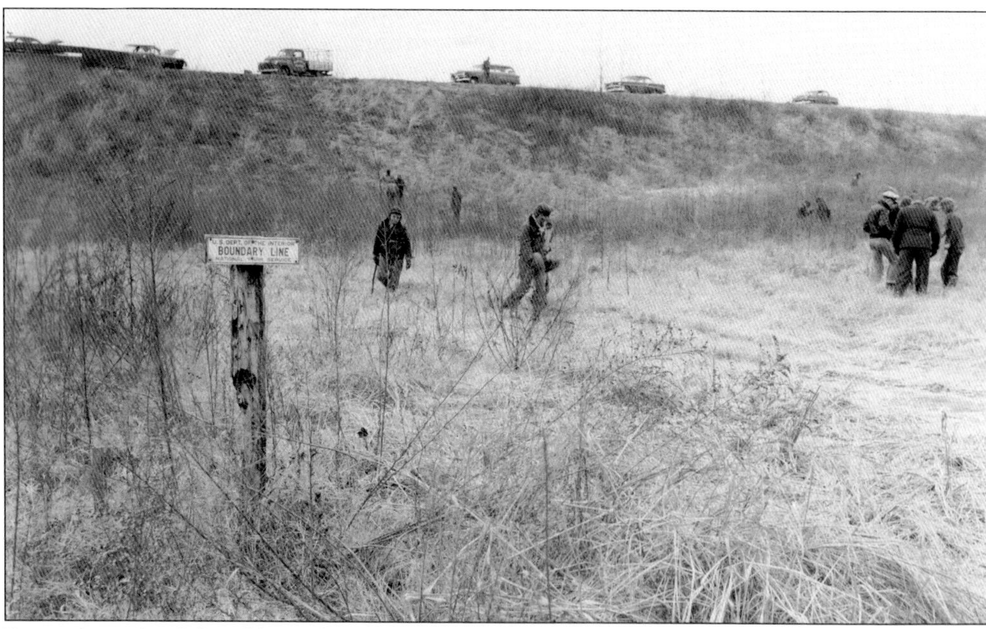

Because much of the old Natchez Trace continued to be used for local roads, old-growth trees had already been cleared in several areas. Some landowners also cut their trees for additional income when they learned the government would be buying their land. New trees had to be planted to recreate the historic experience of traveling the Natchez Trace and to protect the scenic views. (NPS.)

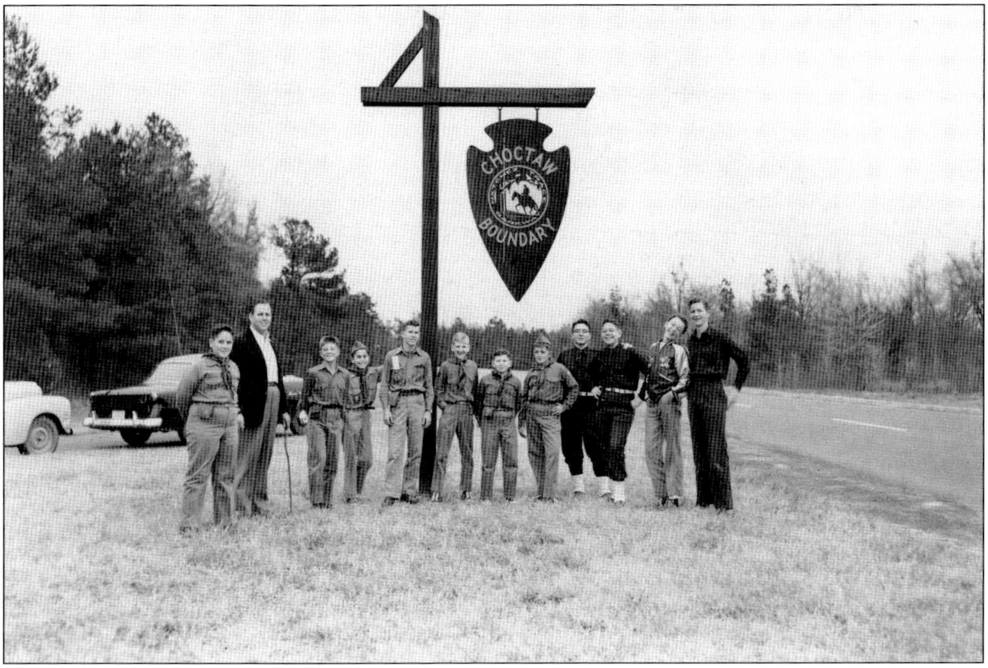

Building the parkway coincided with the development of Scouting programs in the three states. Numerous Scouts earned merit badges for service to their country by planting trees, clearing trails, and building bridges. (NPS.)

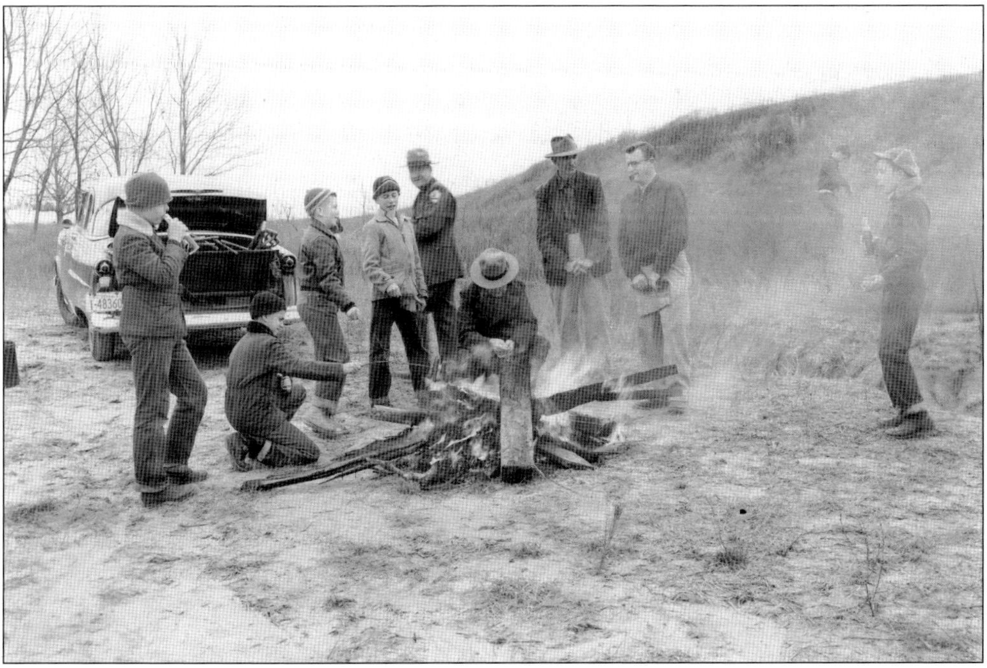

Standard practice encouraged contractors to clear all trees in construction zones, change the grades of the land as needed, and then plant small trees on the new grades. The National Park Service often marked mature trees it wanted to remain; however, saving trees required full-time supervision. Here, a Boy Scout group is gathered around a fire. (NPS.)

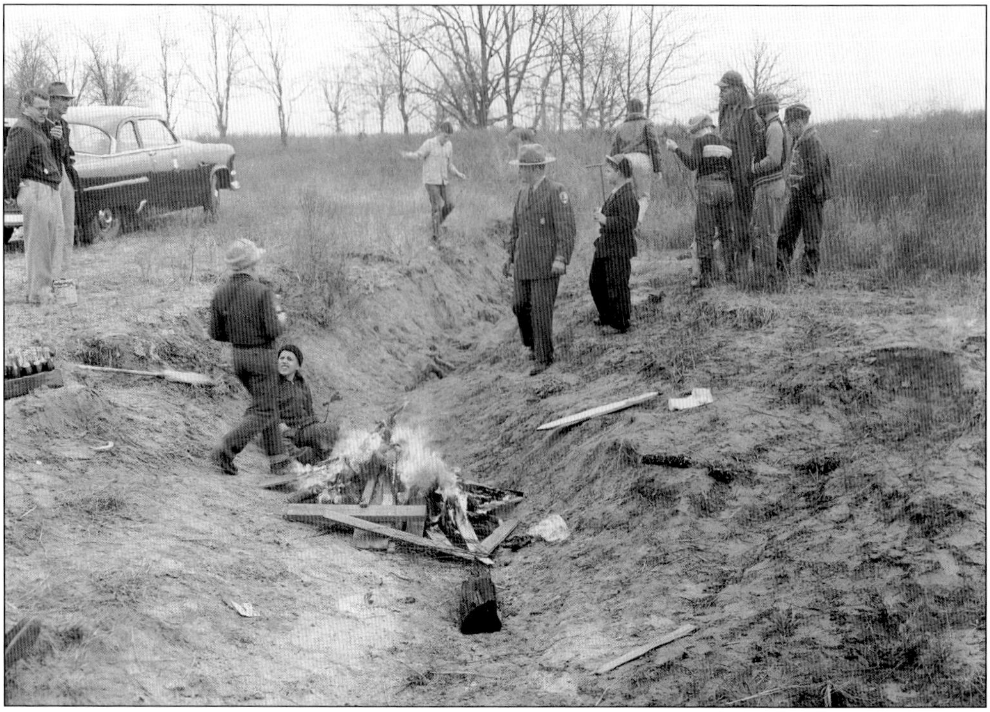

To earn a special patch, Scouts had to walk 20 miles of the old Natchez Trace, camp near it, and talk to a park ranger for two hours. (NPS.)

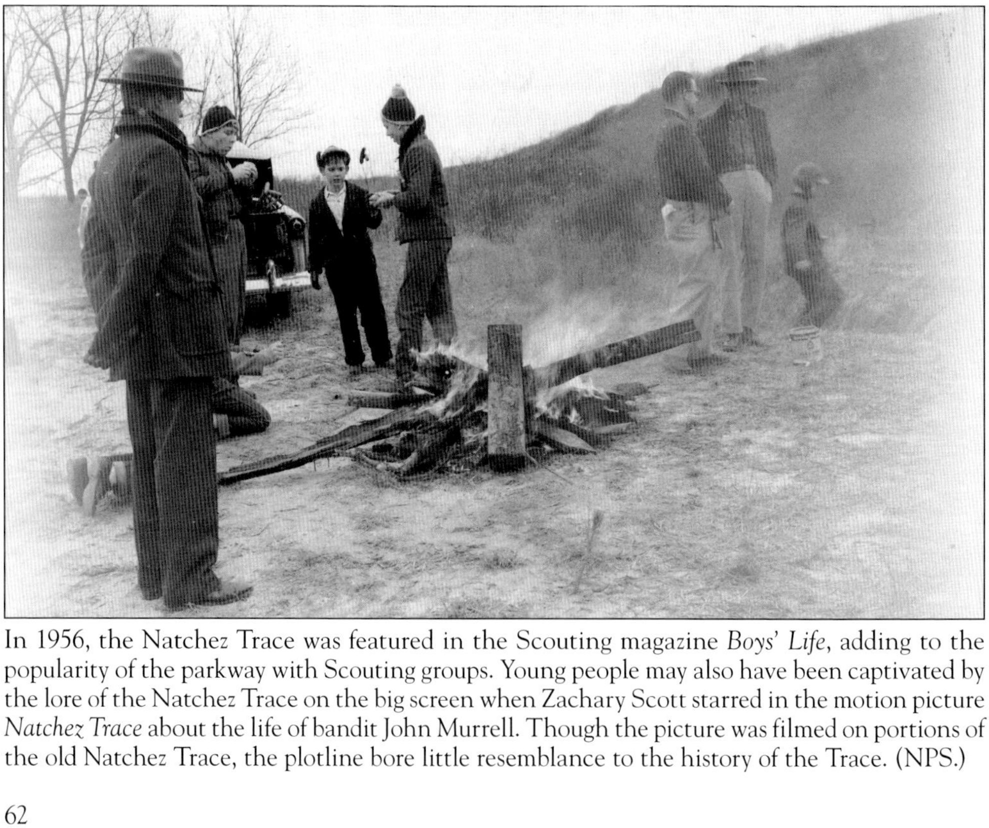

In 1956, the Natchez Trace was featured in the Scouting magazine *Boys' Life*, adding to the popularity of the parkway with Scouting groups. Young people may also have been captivated by the lore of the Natchez Trace on the big screen when Zachary Scott starred in the motion picture *Natchez Trace* about the life of bandit John Murrell. Though the picture was filmed on portions of the old Natchez Trace, the plotline bore little resemblance to the history of the Trace. (NPS.)

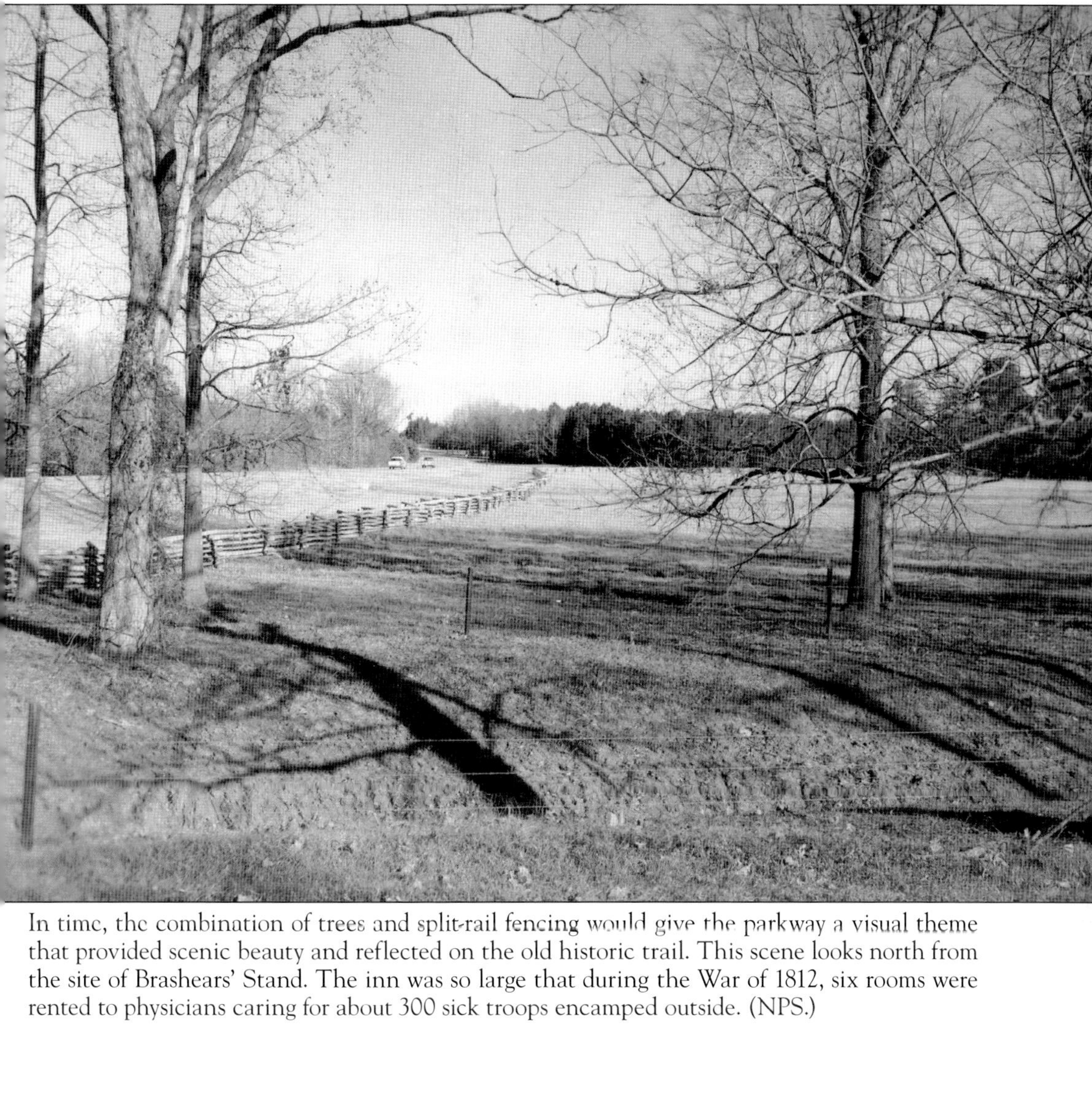

In time, the combination of trees and split-rail fencing would give the parkway a visual theme that provided scenic beauty and reflected on the old historic trail. This scene looks north from the site of Brashears' Stand. The inn was so large that during the War of 1812, six rooms were rented to physicians caring for about 300 sick troops encamped outside. (NPS.)

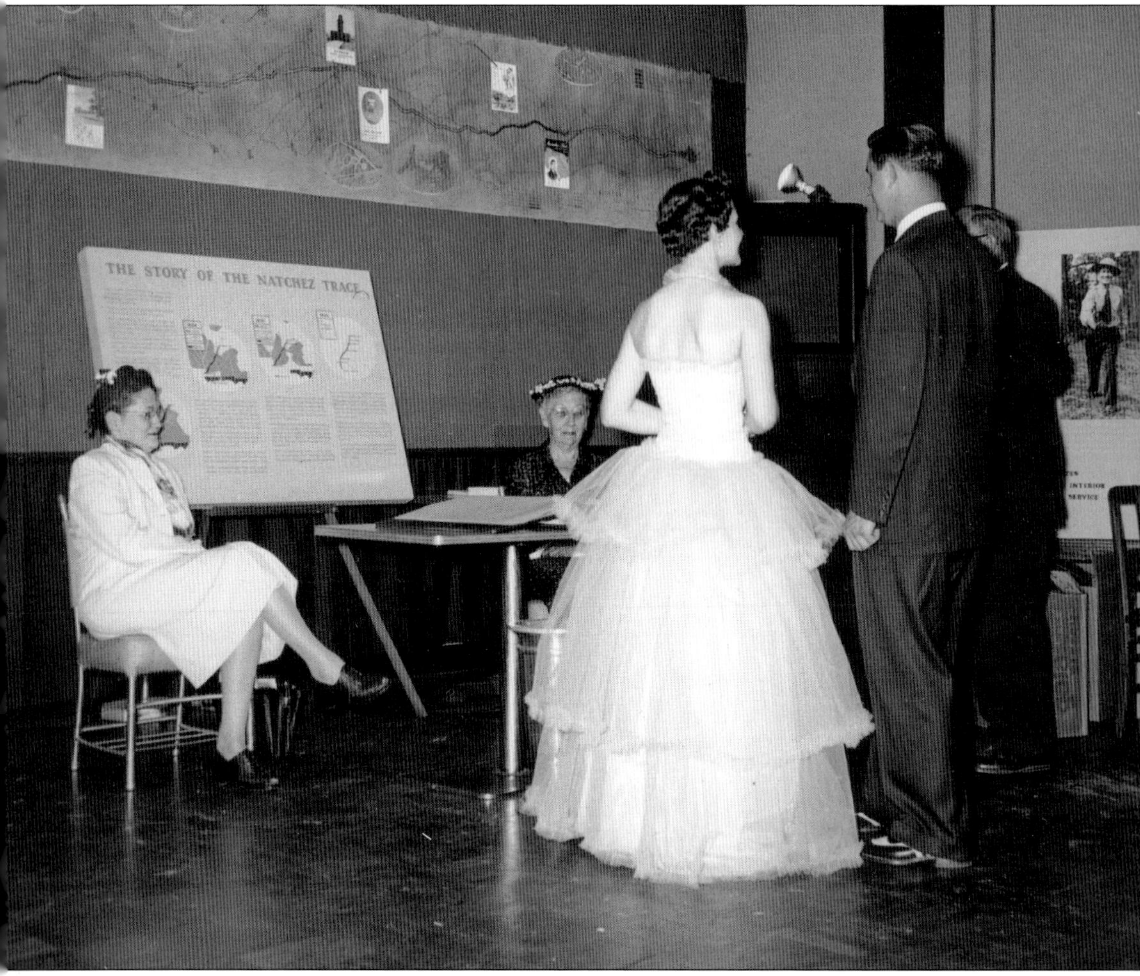

The parkway association added a new dimension to its 1934 promotional drawing when it created an exhibit for travel shows to educate the public about the history of the Trace and to give them an idea of the experiences a completed Natchez Trace Parkway would provide. This exhibit was shown at the Heidelberg Hotel in Jackson, Mississippi. (NPS.)

Three

Mission 66
Building a Modern Park
1955–1969

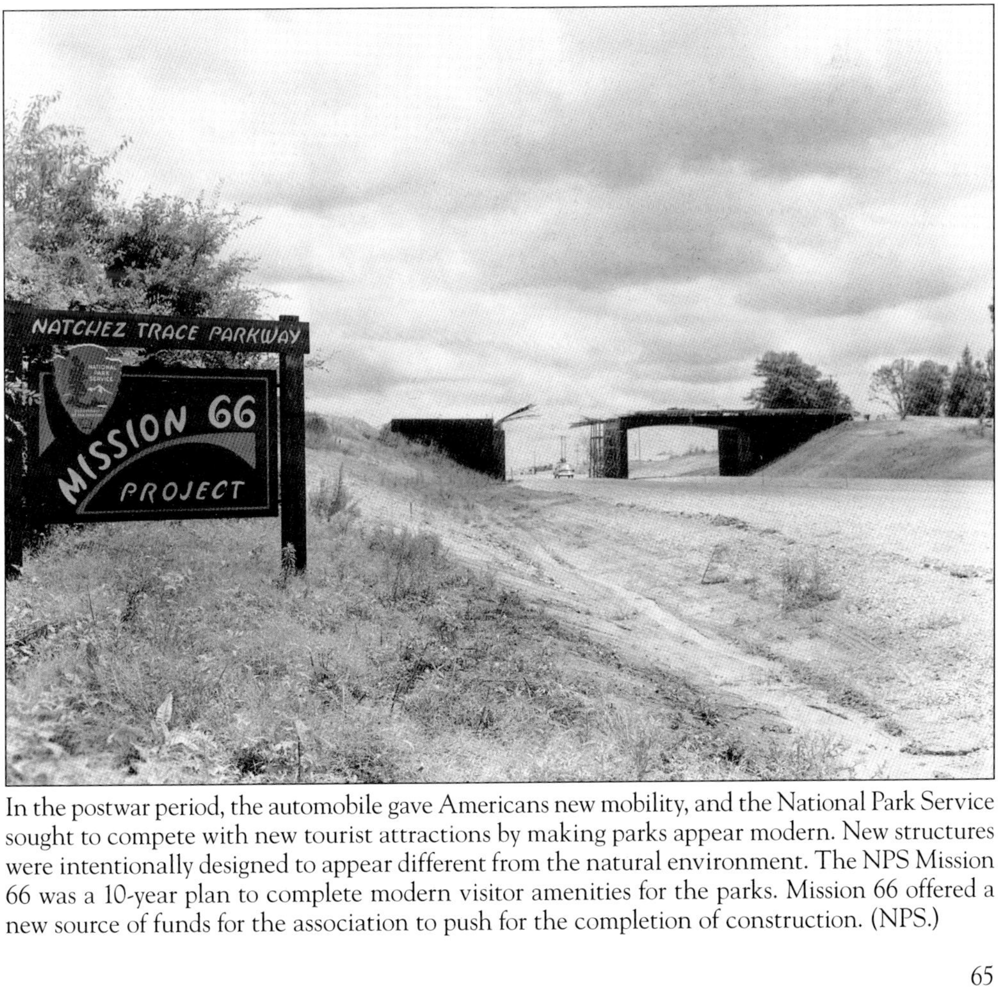

In the postwar period, the automobile gave Americans new mobility, and the National Park Service sought to compete with new tourist attractions by making parks appear modern. New structures were intentionally designed to appear different from the natural environment. The NPS Mission 66 was a 10-year plan to complete modern visitor amenities for the parks. Mission 66 offered a new source of funds for the association to push for the completion of construction. (NPS.)

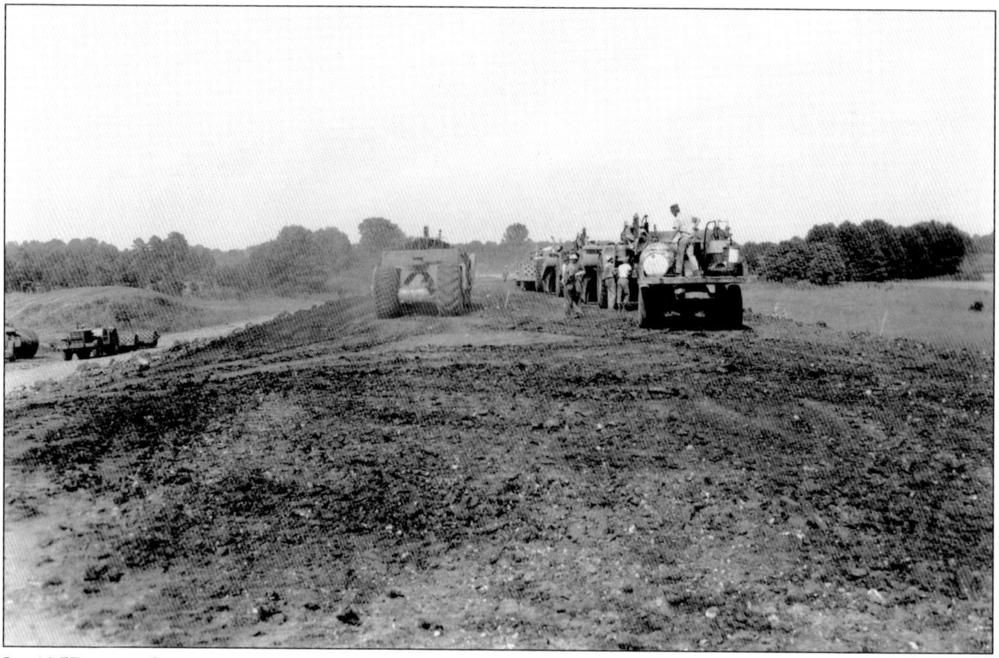

In 1957, just when postwar cost-cutting measures in Washington, DC, threatened the future of the parkway, Mission 66 provided more than $6 million for new parkway construction. Work was slated to begin on 107 miles. Superintendent Gardner told an encouraged parkway association that the project would be completed by 1966. (NPS.)

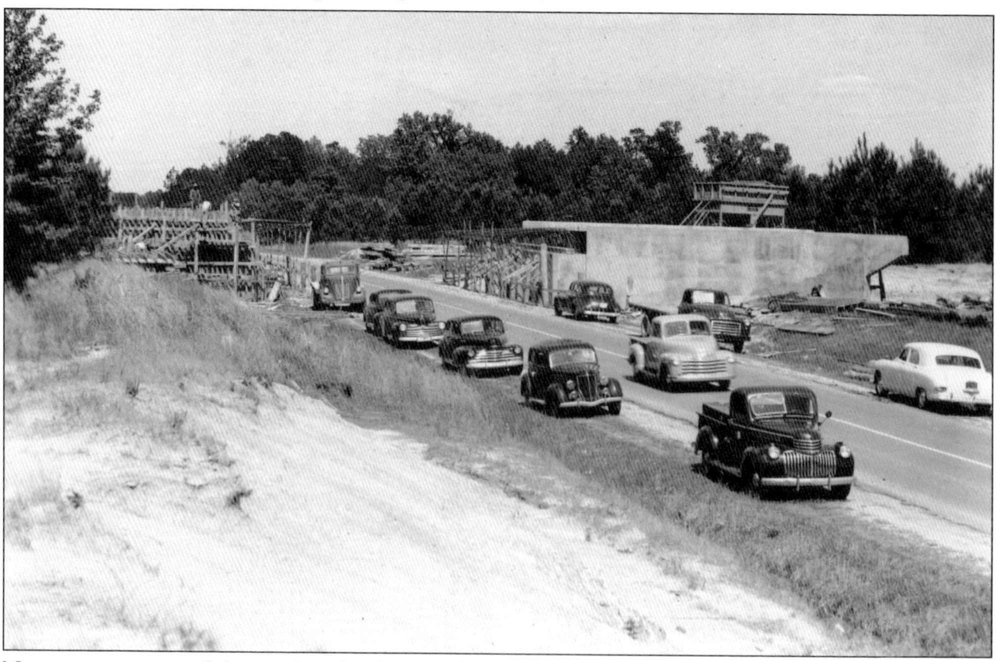

New construction of about a fourth of the parkway generated excitement. Survey crews, engineers, heavy-machine operators, and other workers took up residence in several towns along the Trace. Skeptics who had argued that the parkway was a dream that would never be realized faced the reality of massive construction. (NPS.)

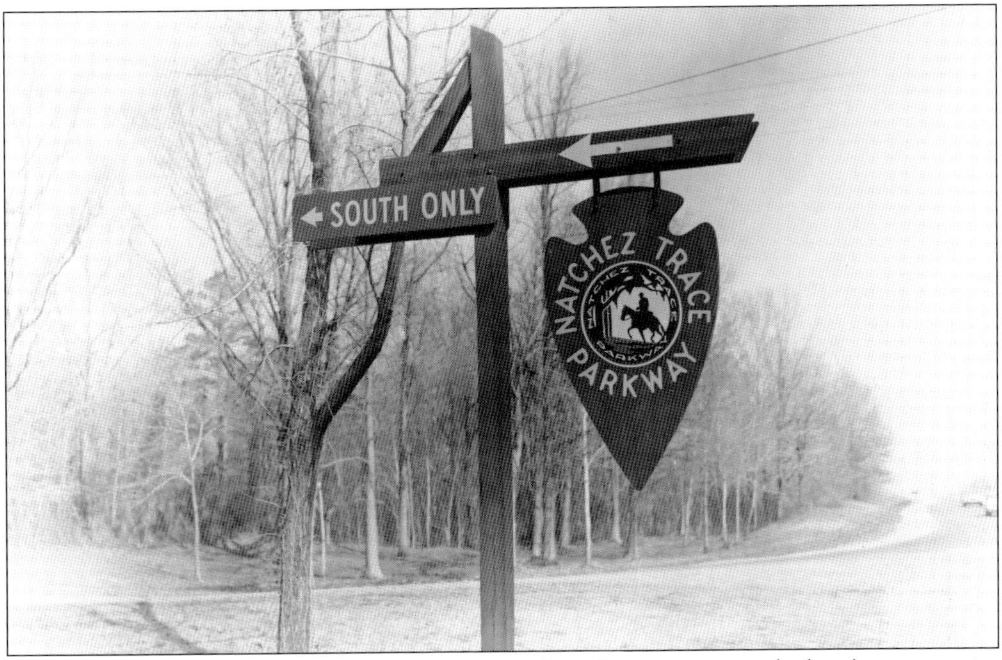

One-way signs were commonplace for decades. Stretches of construction took place between major highways so that visitors never faced a dead end. Pull-off exhibits or trails were usually built for each section to provide travelers an interpretive or recreational experience even on small sections of the parkway. (Both, NPS.)

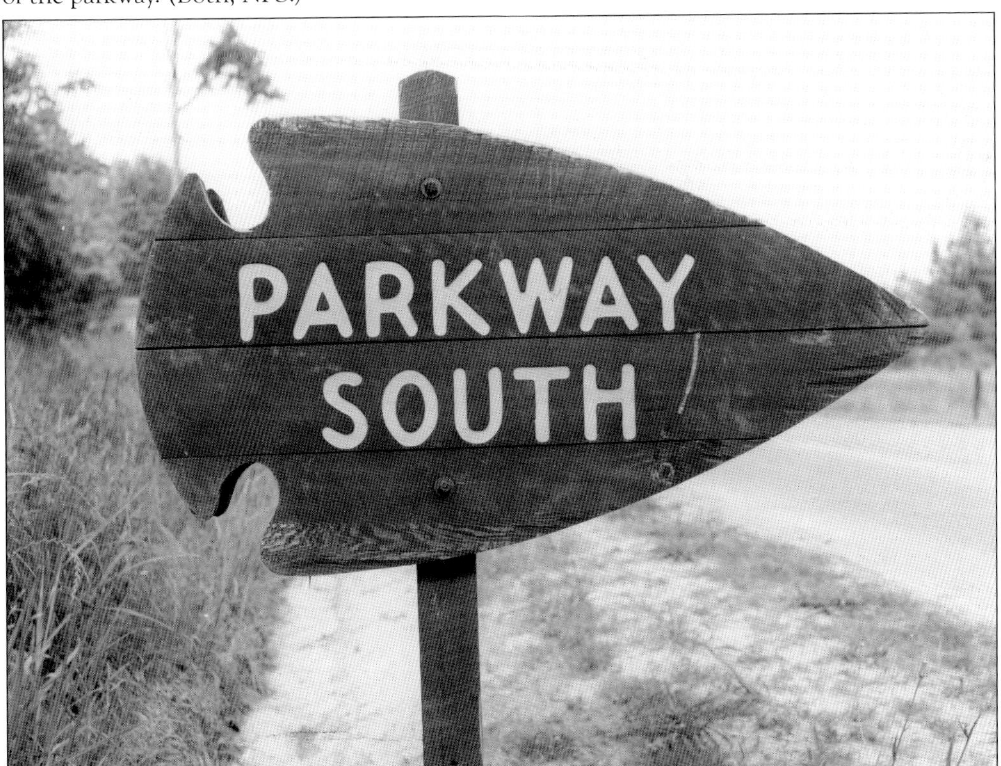

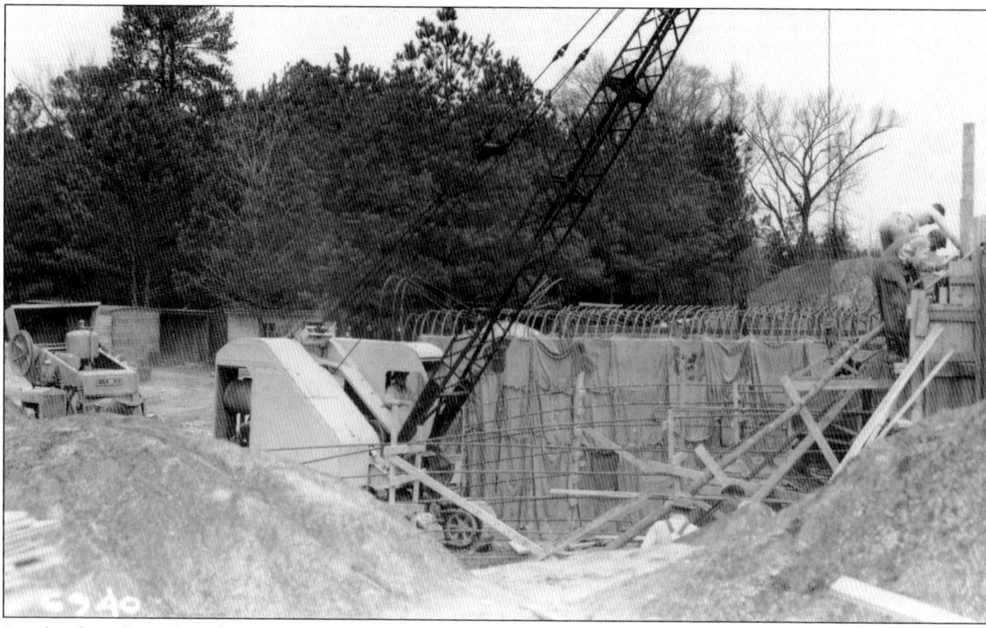

In the height of enthusiasm generated by new construction in national parks, the Kennedy administration briefly considered extending the Natchez Trace Parkway north to Kentucky's Mammoth Cave and then east to the Smoky Mountains. Someone even suggested that connecting it to Oak Ridge would make it the "Atomic Road." In 1961, (on a lesser scale) Congress incorporated the Meriwether Lewis National Monument and the Ackia Battlefield into the parkway. (NPS.)

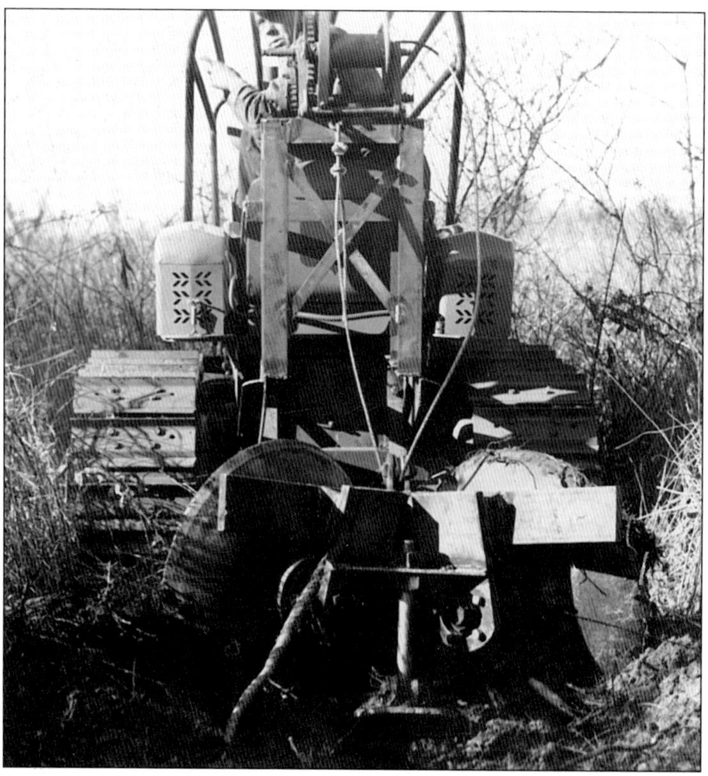

Unlike the Depression-era public works projects, Mission 66 favored private contractors and equipment that could perform a job with the least expense possible. This machine allowed the removal of tree stumps up to five feet in diameter in construction areas, speeding up the process over the handsaws and mules used during earlier periods. (NPS.)

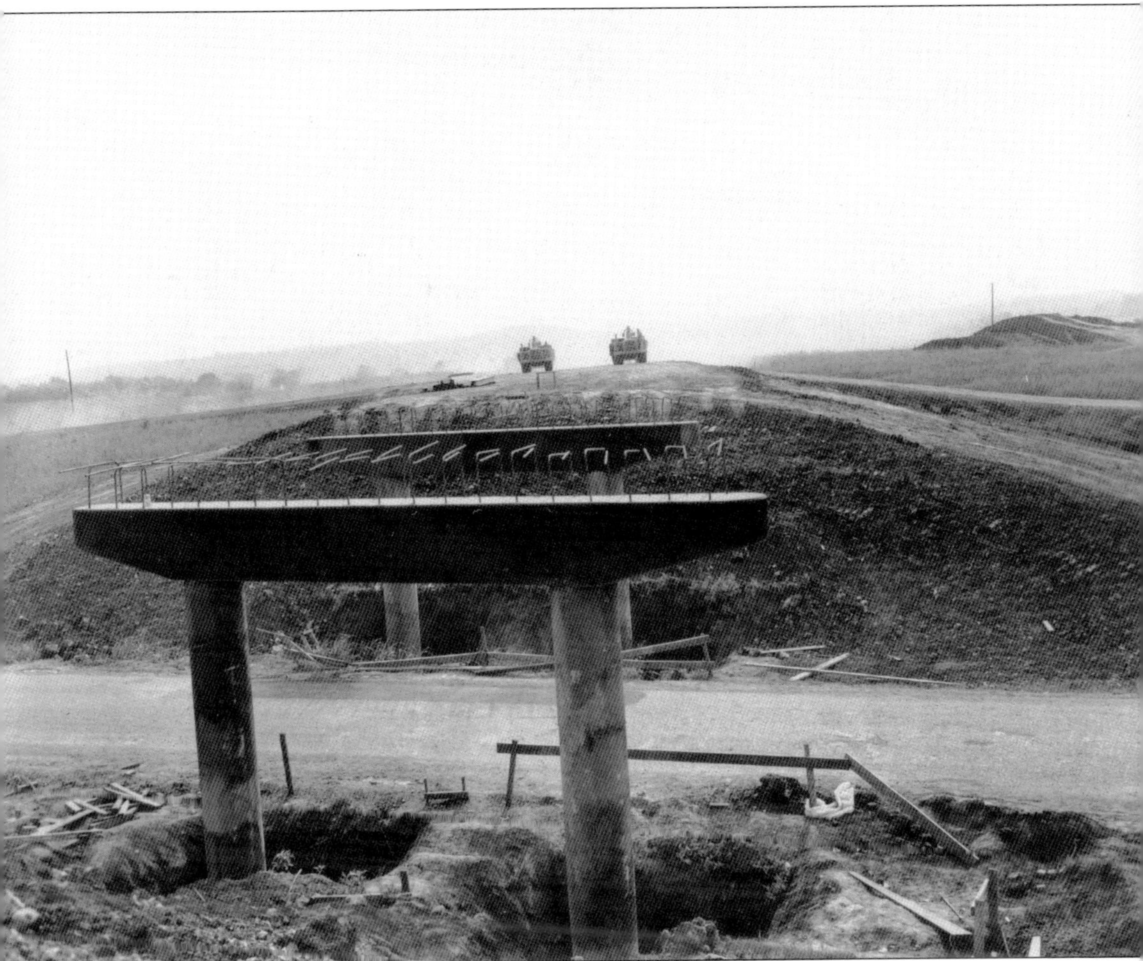

Construction projects funded by Mission 66 were divided among Mississippi, Alabama, and Tennessee to garner political support from each state. Completion of the bridge shown here over Highway 15 north of Cherokee, Alabama, edged traffic closer to the Tennessee River. (NPS.)

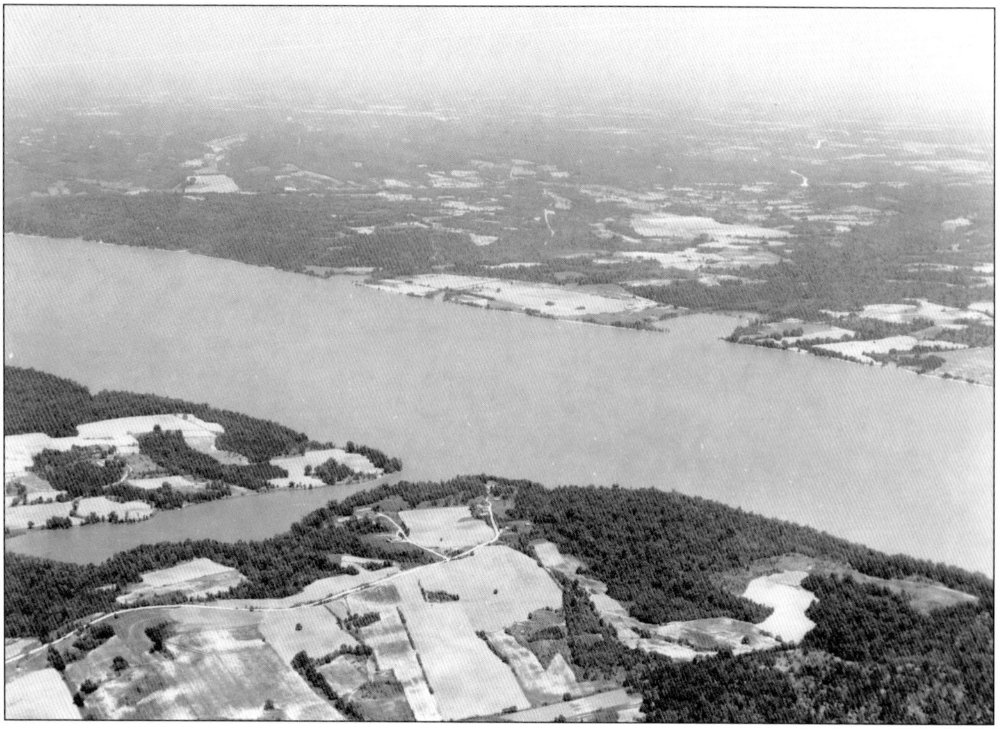

One of the greatest construction challenges was building a bridge to cross the mile-wide expanse of the Tennessee River. On the old Natchez Trace, travelers waited for a ferry for a crossing on water at Colbert's Shoals, but Americans on the move in the 1960s were not so patient. (NPS.)

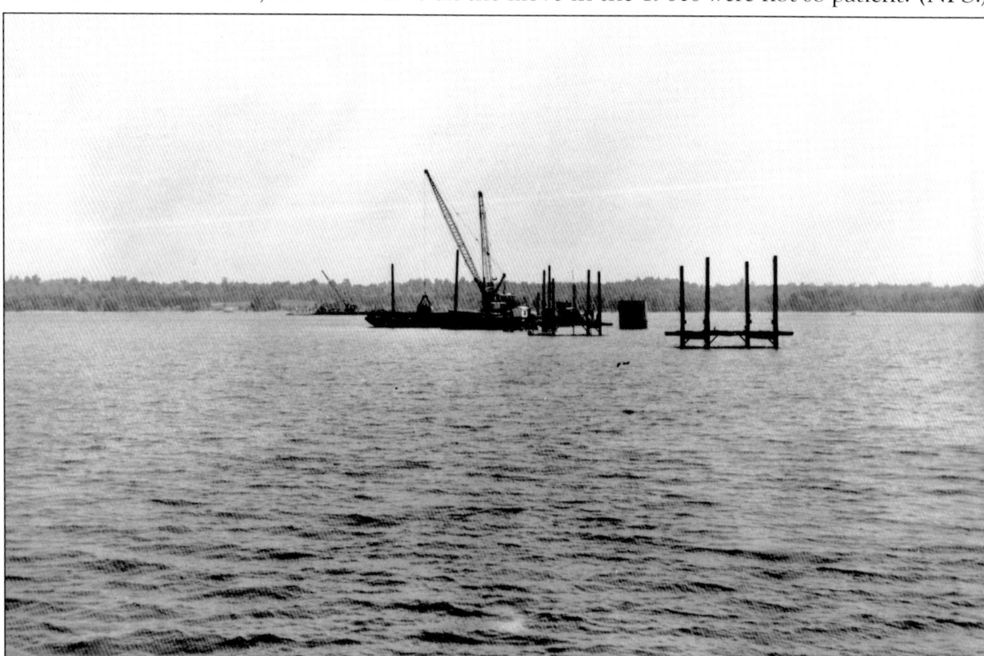

Piers for the bridge across the Tennessee River were set in 1962. Construction began in 1963. Large cranes placed on barges on the Tennessee River hoisted steel beams into place. (NPS.)

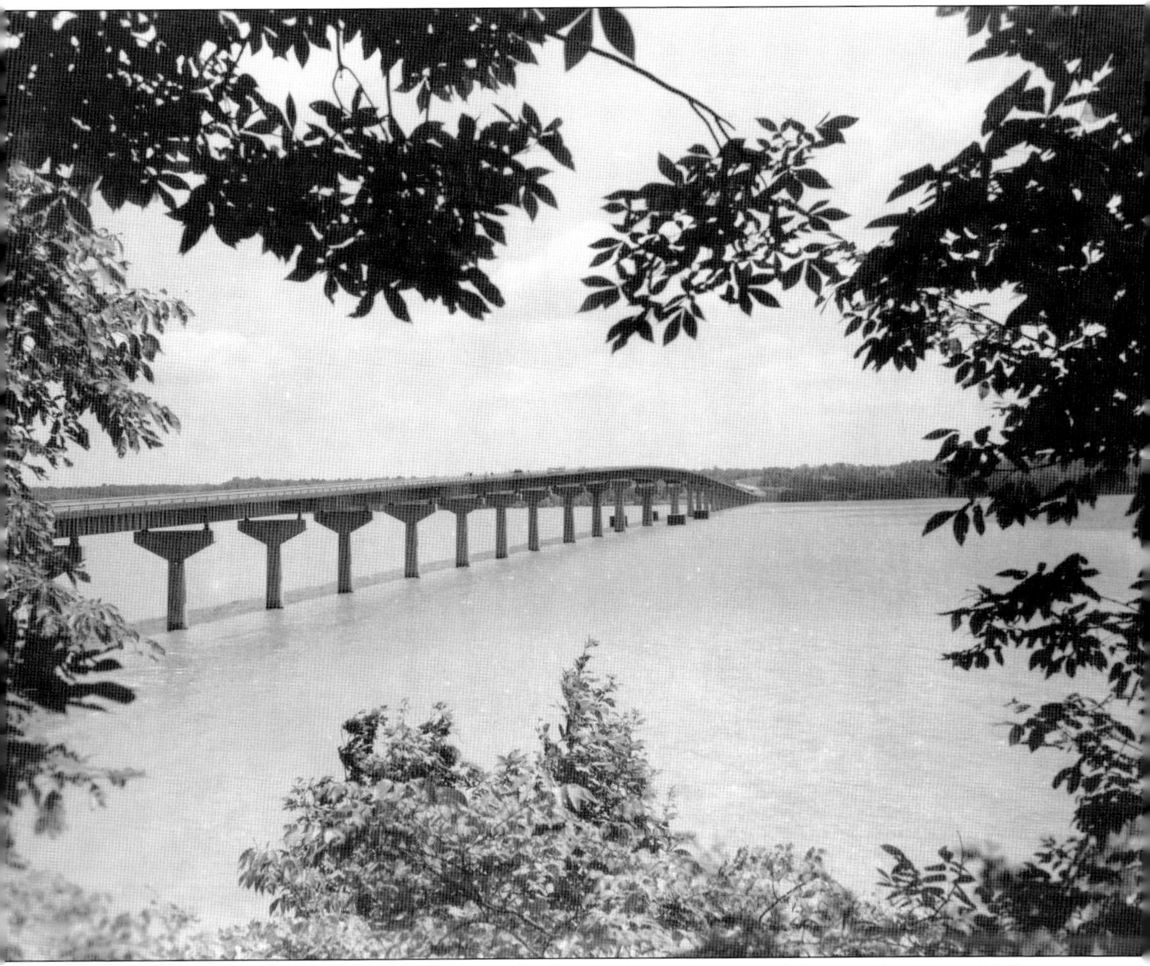

The completed bridge was named in honor of John Coffee, who served during the War of 1812 as Andrew Jackson's adjutant general. After the war, Coffee became an important political and business leader in the northern Alabama area. (NPS.)

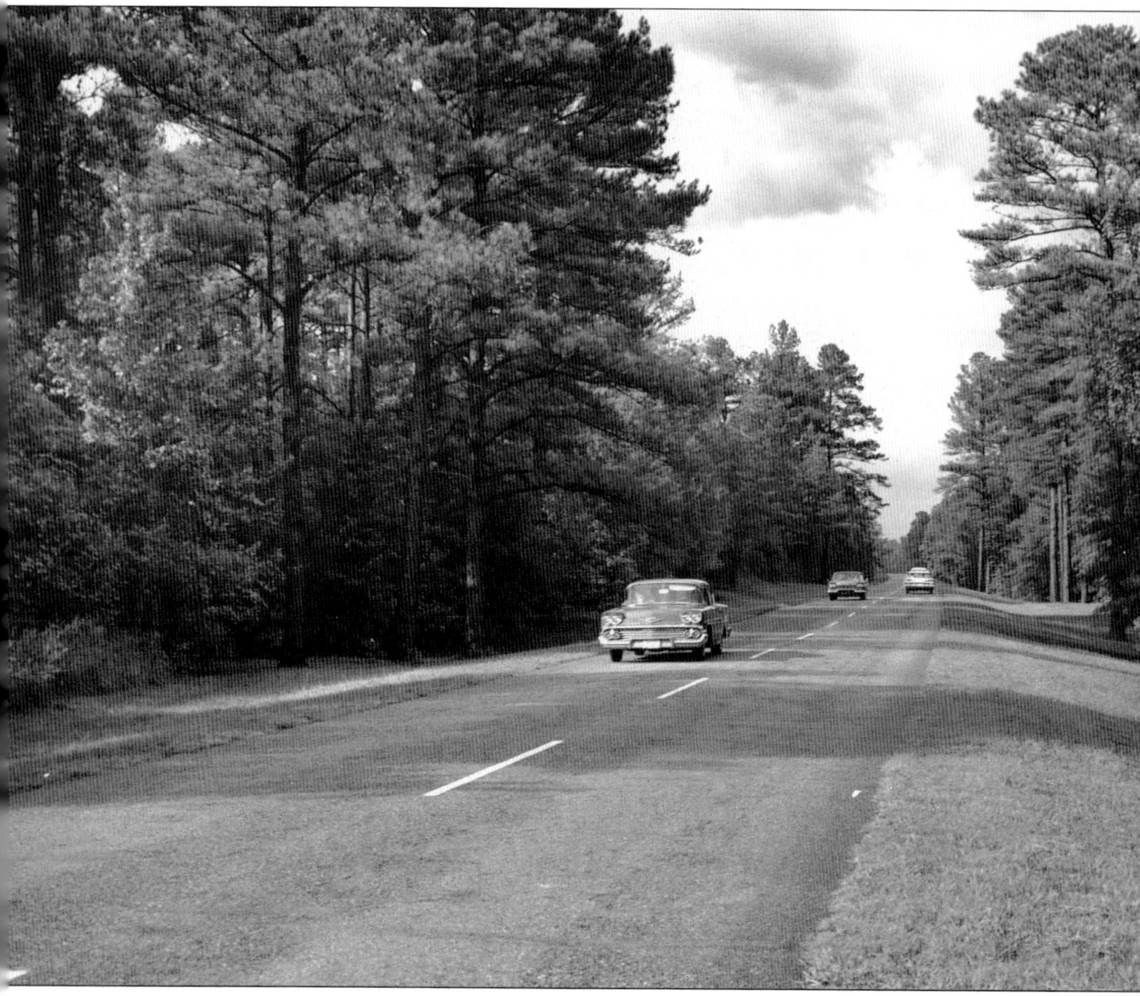

Visitation exceeded five million people by 1962. By December 1963, half the parkway road had been completed. Travelers could drive on long sections through southern Tennessee and parts of Alabama and Mississippi. (NPS.)

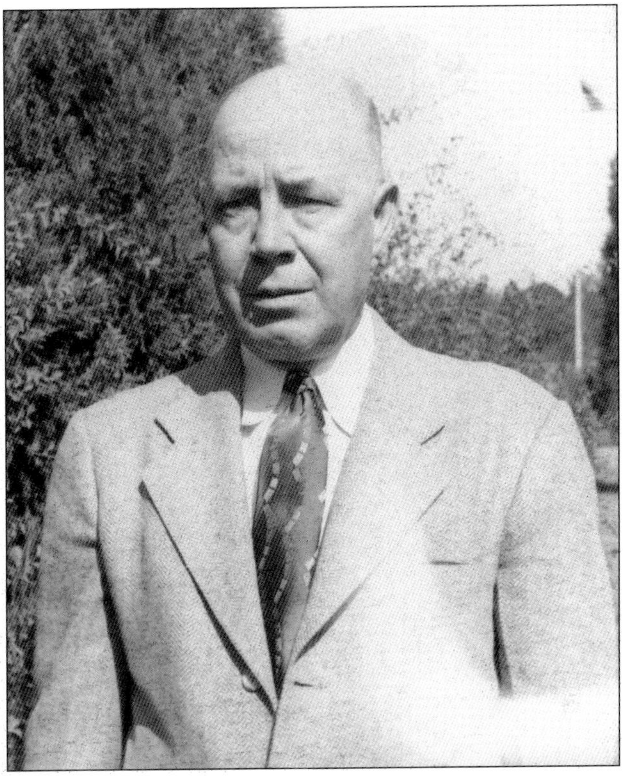

Historian Dawson Phelps's writings shaped the interpretation of Natchez Trace history for decades. When Phelps began working on the parkway, he discovered that few historians had researched the Trace. Young National Park Service employees instructed to complete a survey of historic sites in 1937 had rummaged through courthouses and interviewed older residents to obtain information. Phelps took the research one step further by placing interpretation in a scholarly context. (NPS.)

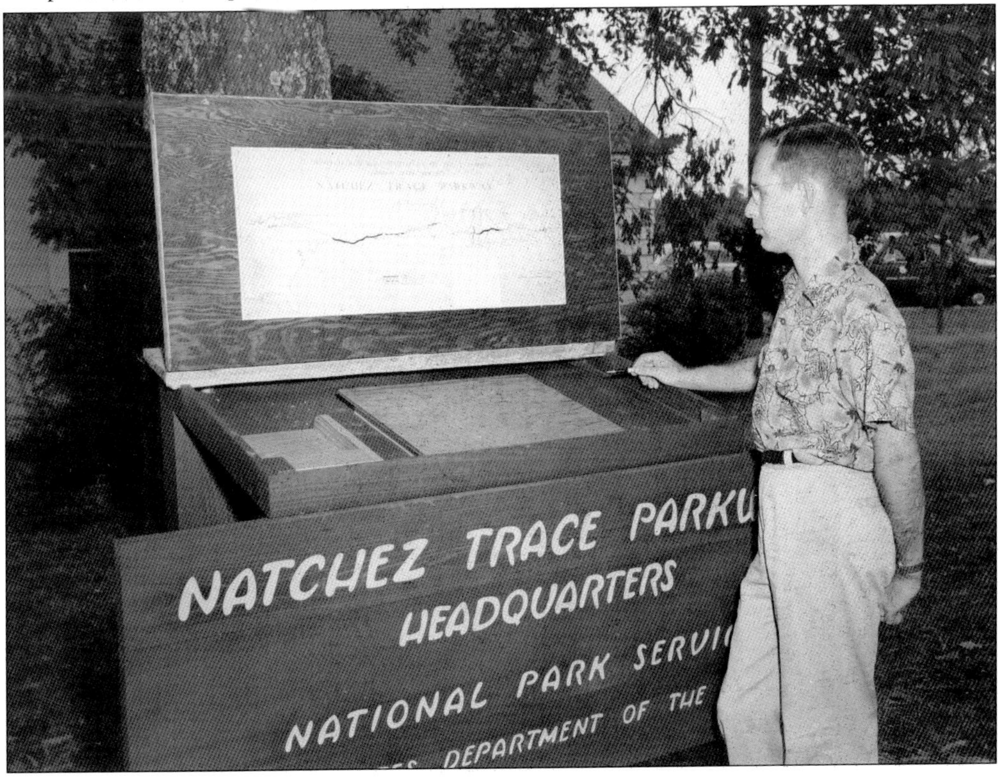

The novelty of the project generated excitement. Visitors followed progress of completion and imagined a distant day when they could make the complete 444-mile trip. (NPS.)

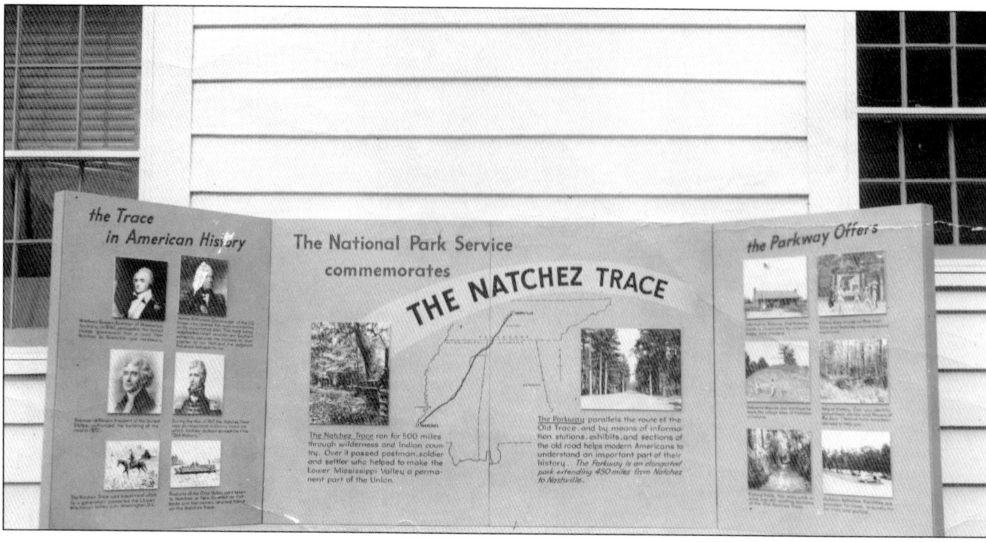

A parkway was a relatively new concept even to the National Park Service. It would take time to help people understand how it would differ from other public roads. NPS created a portable exhibit as an outreach to communities along the parkway to fulfill the mission of making the public aware of the parkway and to give more information about its historic and natural resources. NPS took advantage of county fairs as opportunities to make contact with many people at the same time. (Both, NPS.)

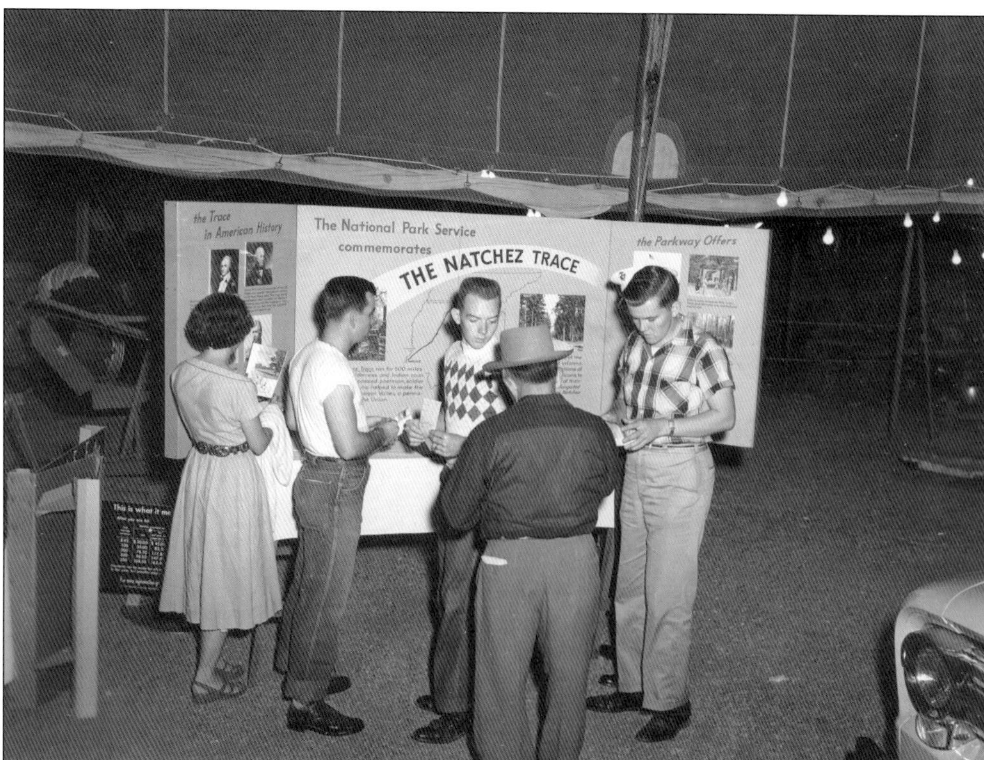

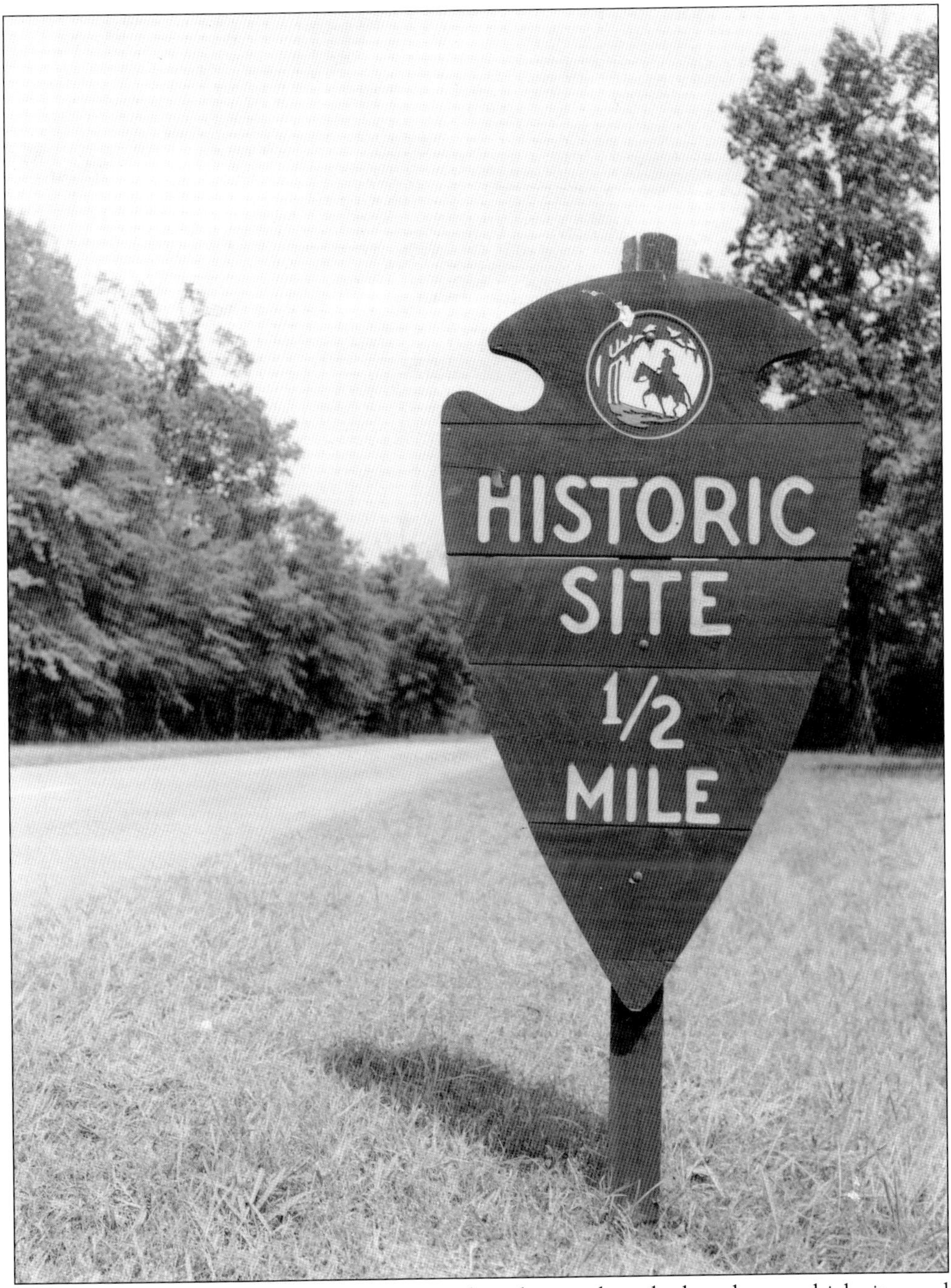

The parkway contains so many historic sites that planners have had to choose which sites and themes to interpret. At first, sites of lesser national significance were interpreted to provide visitors something to see even in sections completed over a short distance. Later, as the parkway neared completion, some smaller sites were closed so that they would not detract from the larger storylines. (NPS.)

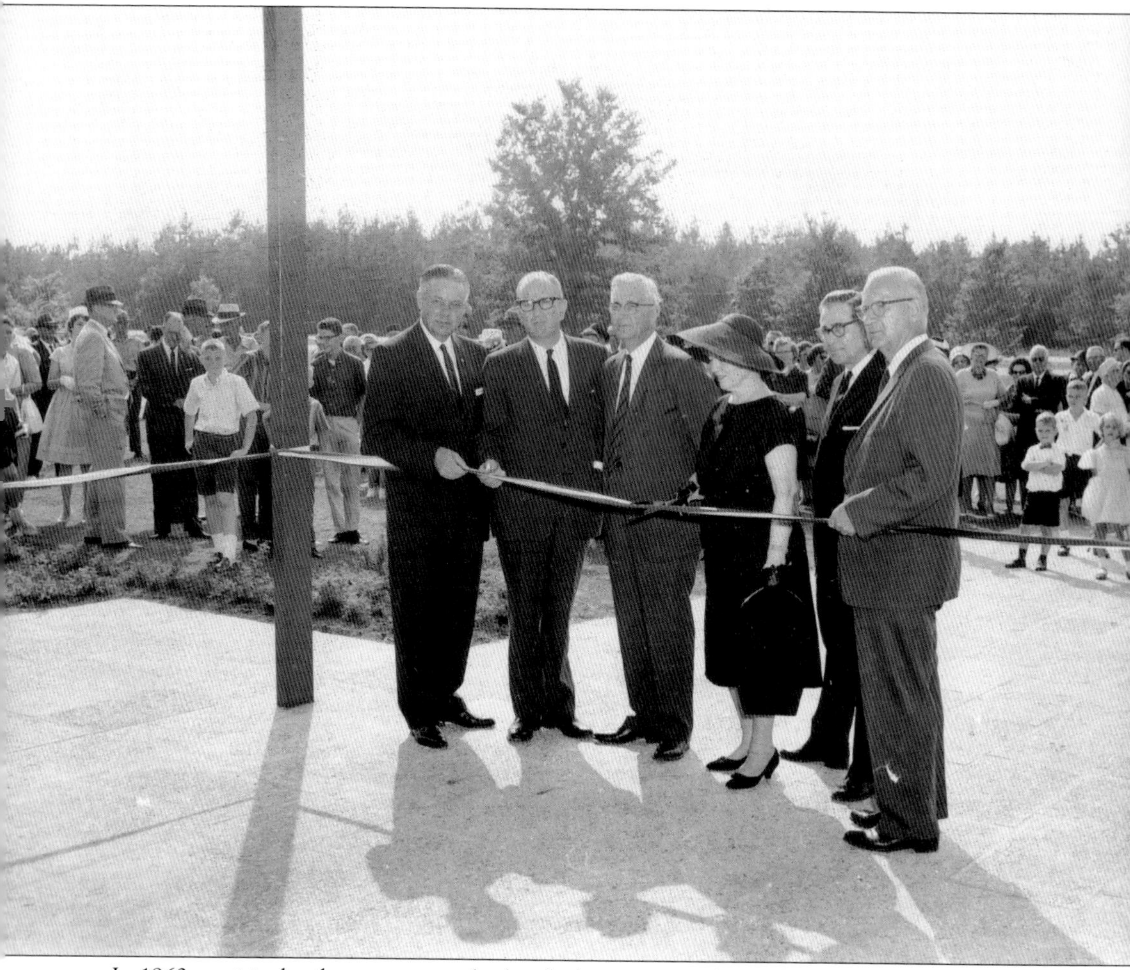

In 1963, a critical milepost was reached with the opening of a modern visitor center and facilities for parkway administration in Tupelo, Mississippi. Pictured at the ribbon-cutting are, from left to right, Tupelo mayor James Ballard, Elbert Cox, former congressman Jeff Busby, Roane Fleming Byrnes, Congressman Tom Abernethy, and National Park Service director Conrad Wirth, who developed the Mission 66 plan for national parks and the new concept of visitor centers. For Byrnes and Congressman Busby, the opening was the climax of the numerous meetings they had held since 1934. (NPS.)

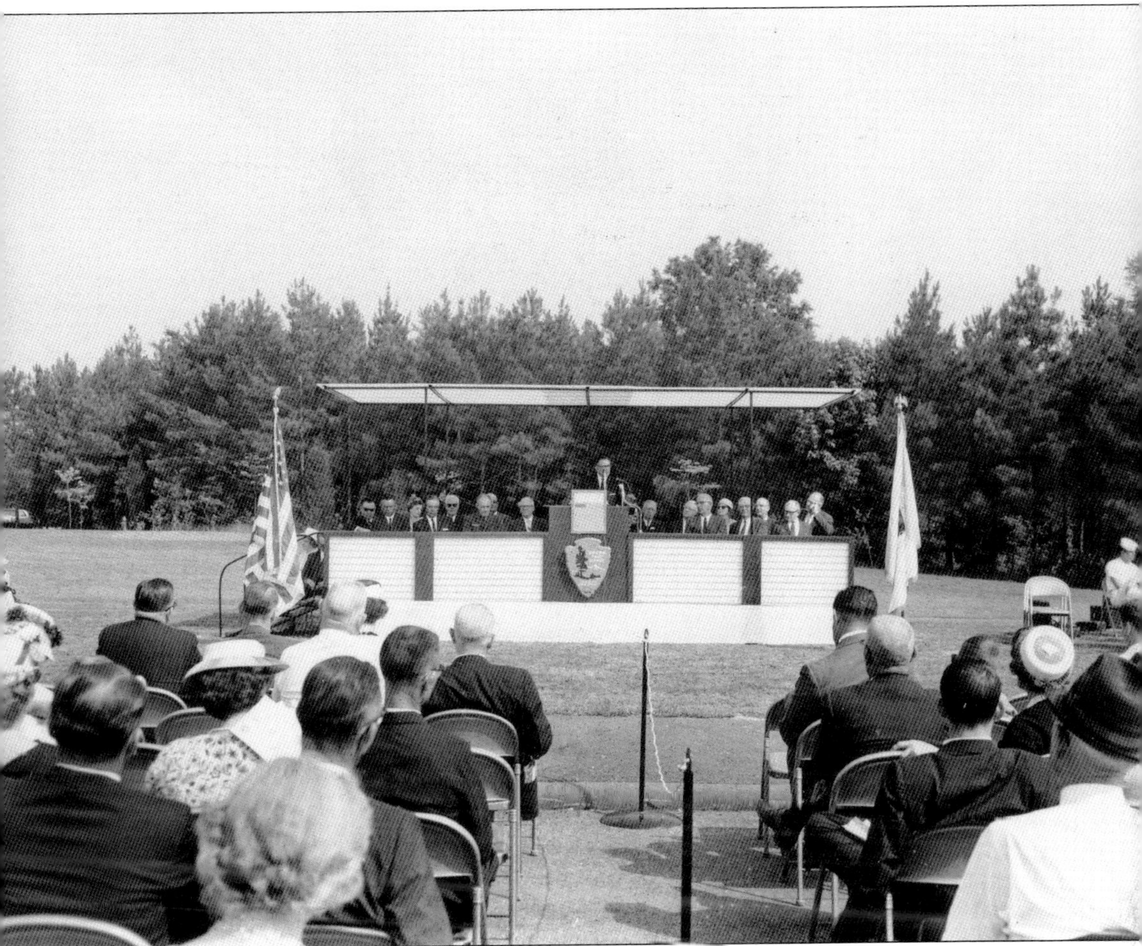

The visitor center opening ceremony was cosponsored by the Community Development Foundation of Tupelo (CDF). CDF director Harry Martin would step forward to lead the push to complete the road. (NPS.)

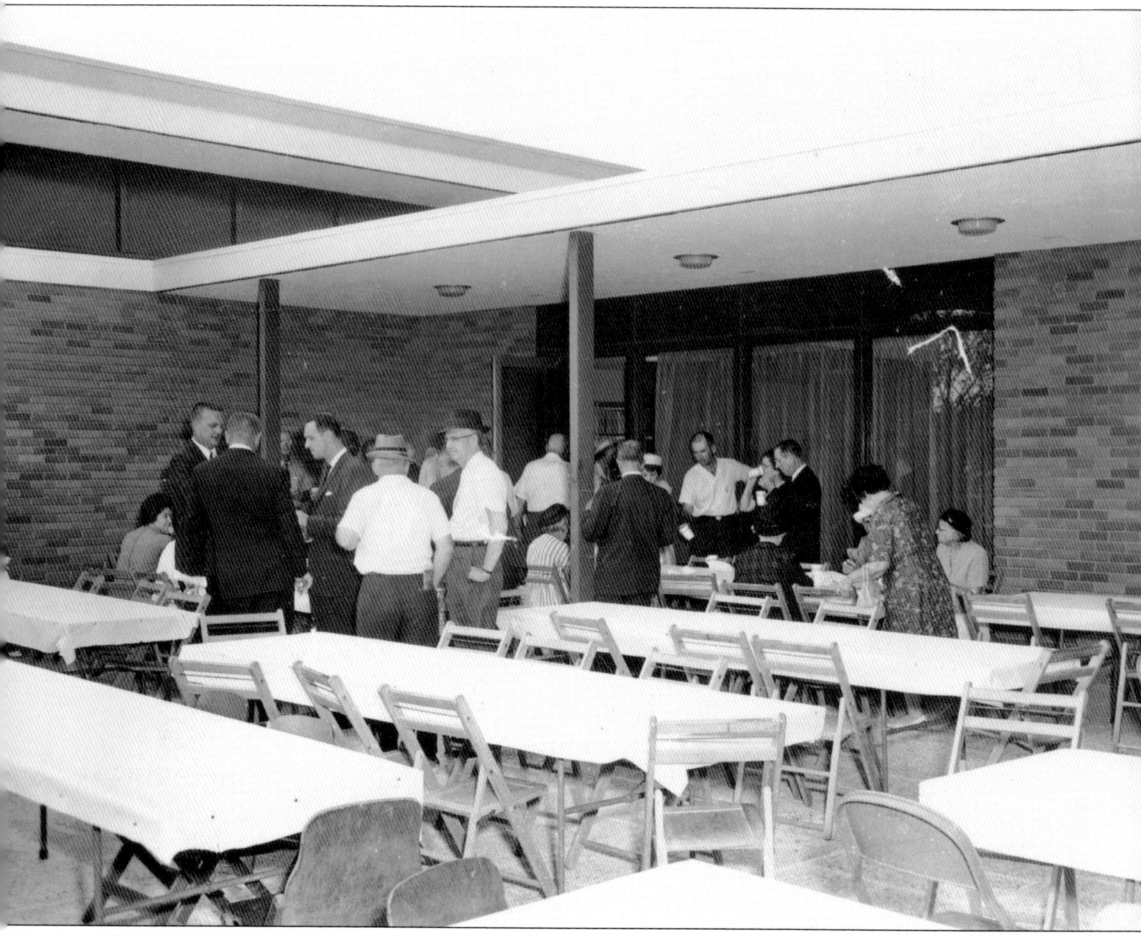

The brick visitor center was designed to reflect Mid-Century Modern architecture, a stark change from the heavy stone and wooden beam designs used by the National Park Service in the 1930s and the simple frame construction the parkway had utilized from its inception. (NPS.)

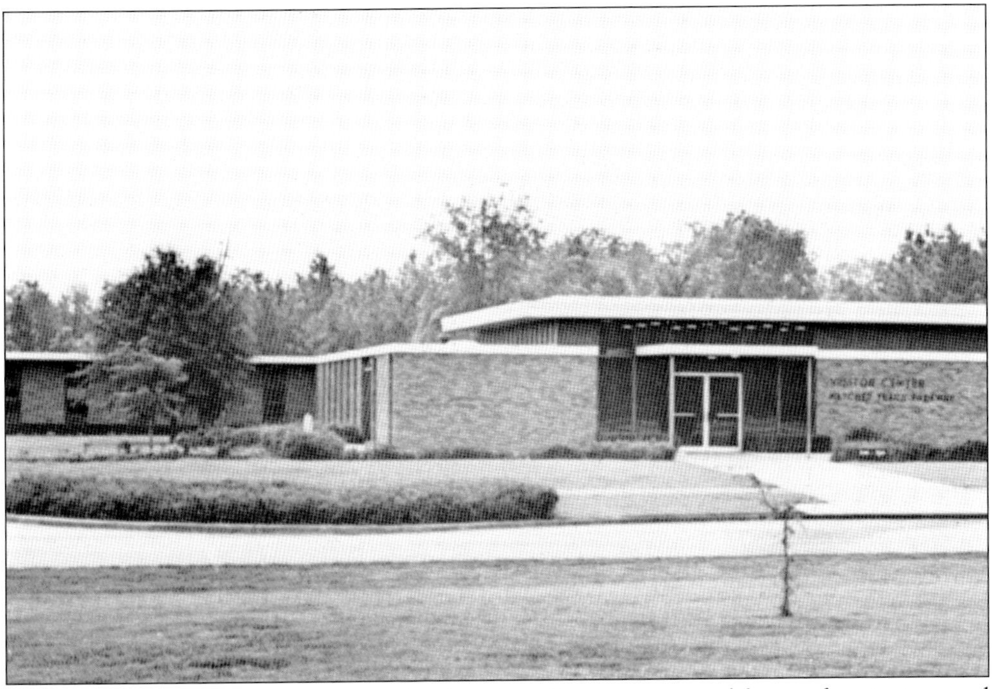

Similar modern designs incorporating brick and steel beams were used for comfort stations and significant wayside stops along the parkway. Elements of the style are strikingly similar to the design Frank Lloyd Wright selected for the Rosenbaum house in Florence, Alabama. (NPS.)

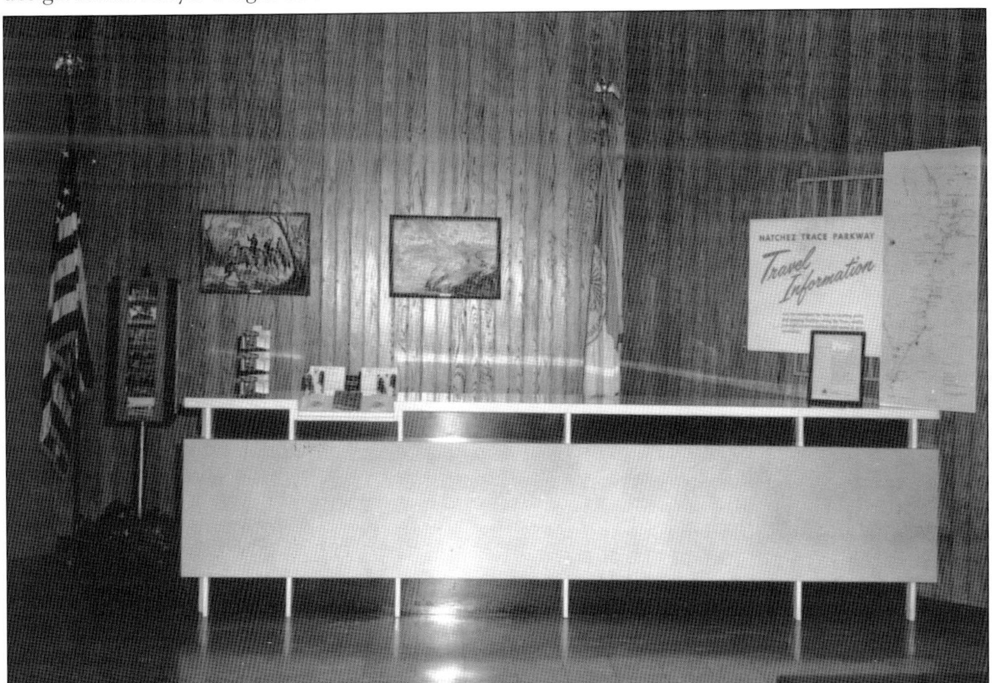

In keeping with Mission 66, the visitor center interior was designed to give visitors an experience similar to any other cutting-edge tourist attraction. (NPS.)

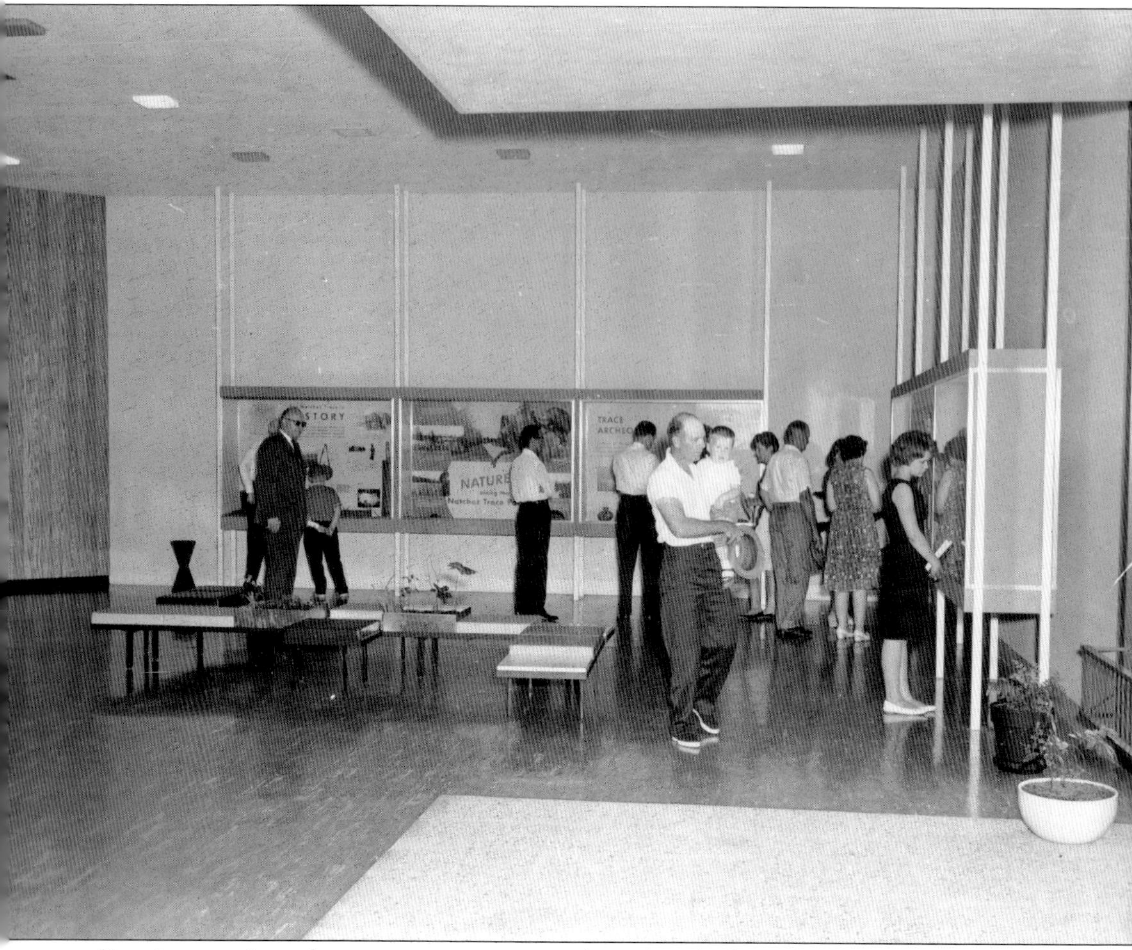

People attending the opening ceremony take a first look at the new visitor center and exhibits. (NPS.)

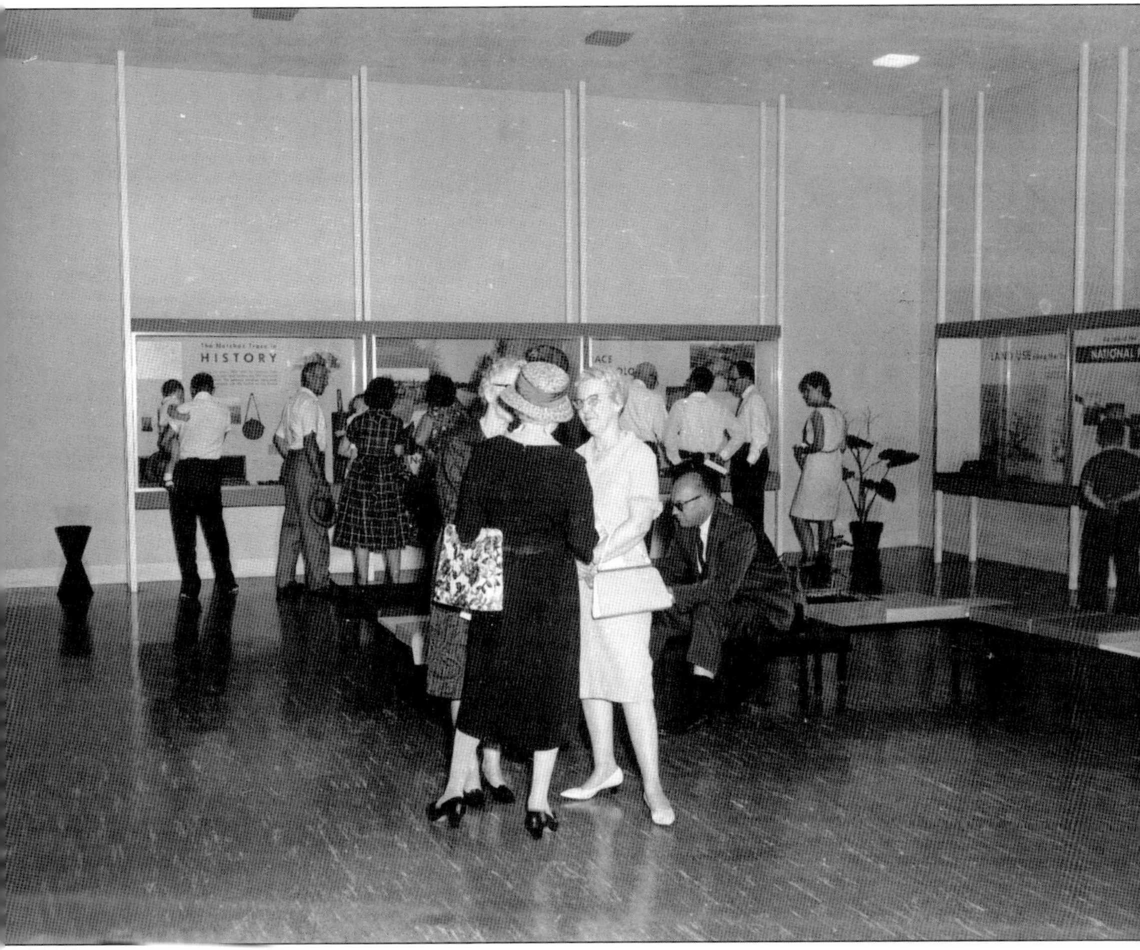

Exhibits in the new visitor center emphasized both history and nature along the parkway. The designs at first were simple introductions to themes that visitors would find along the road. (NPS.)

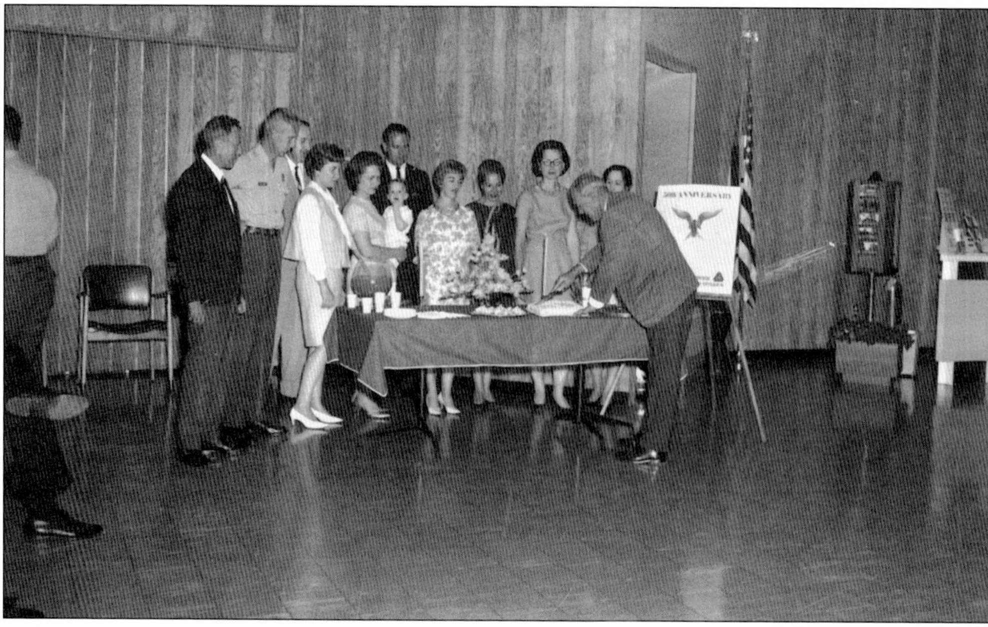

An open house was held at the visitor center to reflect on Mission 66 and to obtain public comment. All Mission 66 programs encouraged parks to choose a primary focus as historic, scenic, or recreational. The parkway administration determined that the parkway should become primarily a recreational park and provide a place for people living along the route to unwind on weekends. (NPS.)

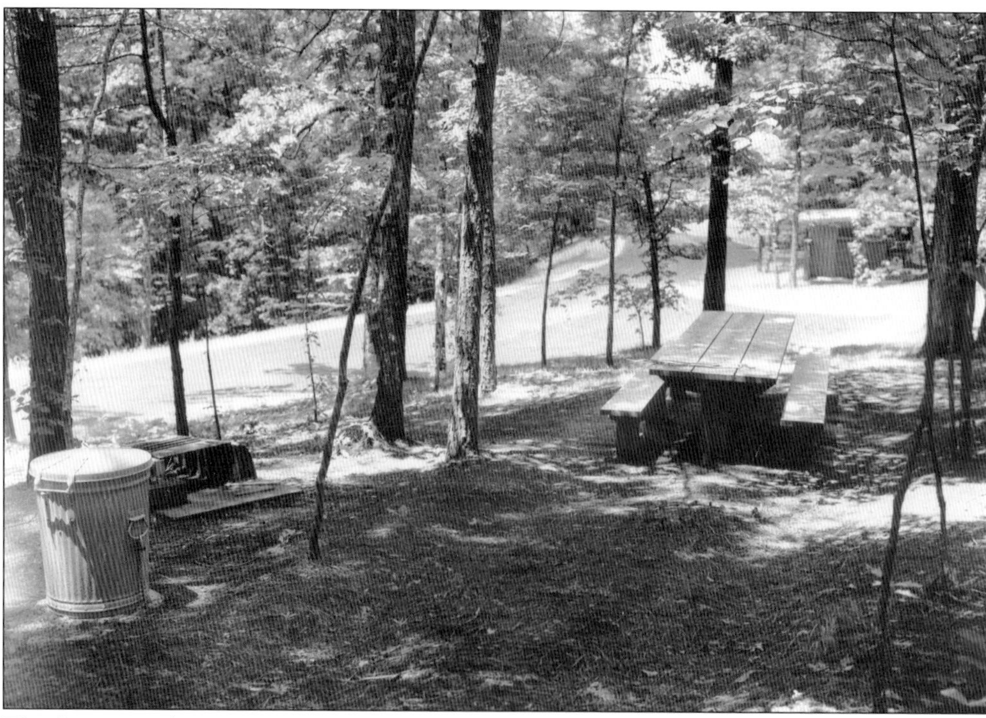

The decision to become primarily a recreational park directed funds toward development of new campgrounds and picnic areas and away from historic preservation and interpretation. (NPS.)

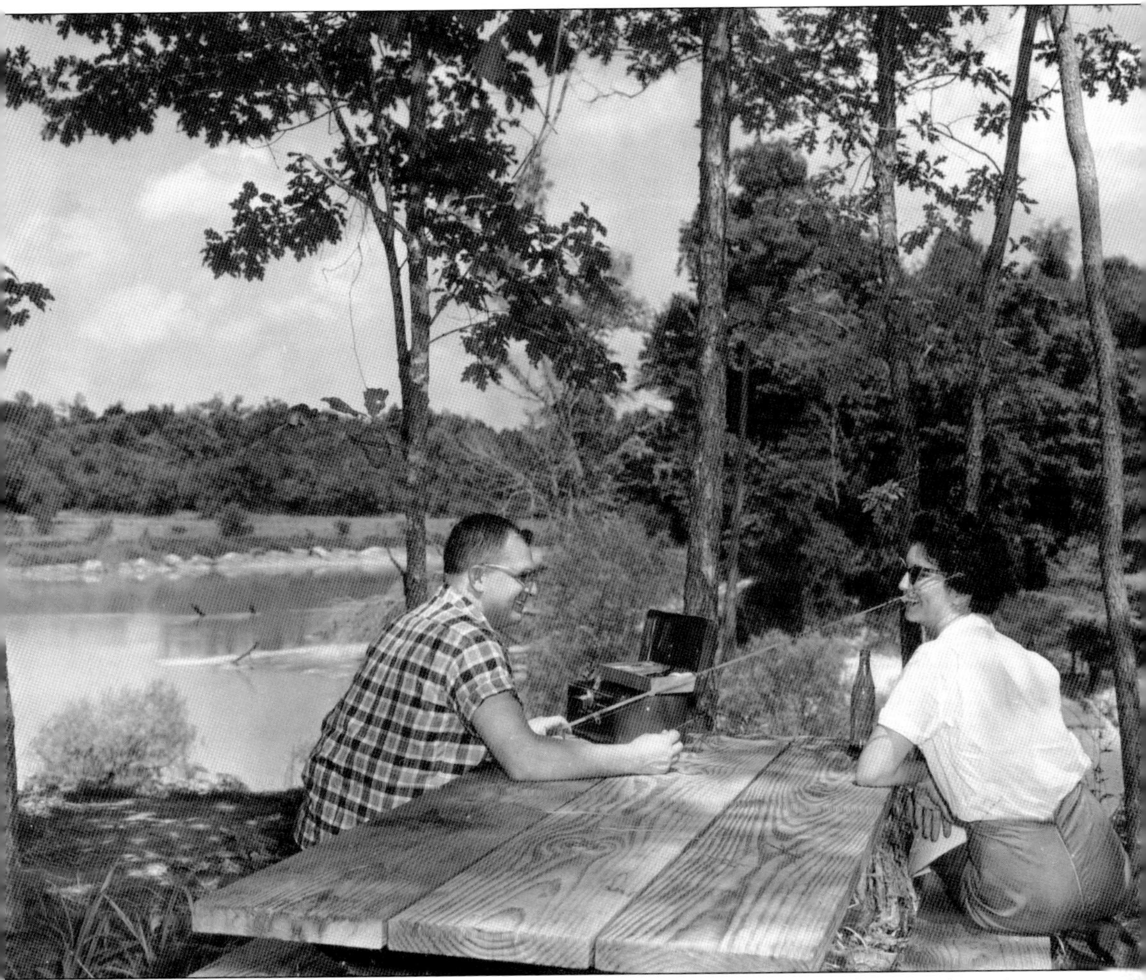

The development of the recreational aspects of the park encouraged local residents, such as this unidentified couple seen here in 1959, to visit the parkway to enjoy the outdoor experience. Picnic tables, grills, shade, and access to a lake for fishing added a parklike experience to Natchez Trace. (NPS.)

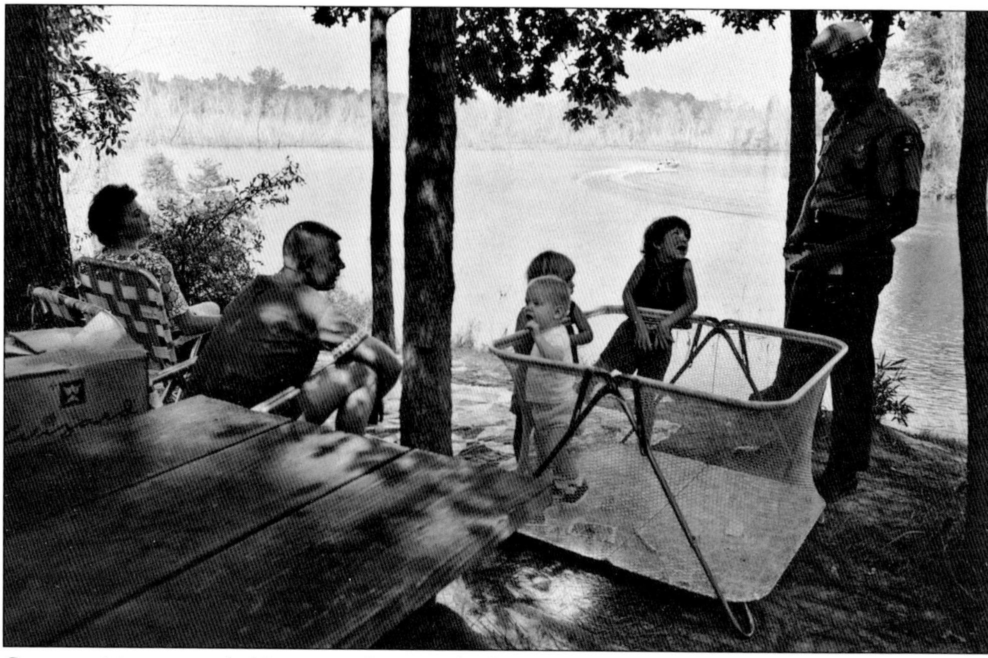

Communities responded by using the new facilities for community and family gatherings. The association mission of focusing on the preservation of the history of the old Natchez Trace was compromised during the Mission 66 years to obtain the funds needed for continued construction of the road. (NPS.)

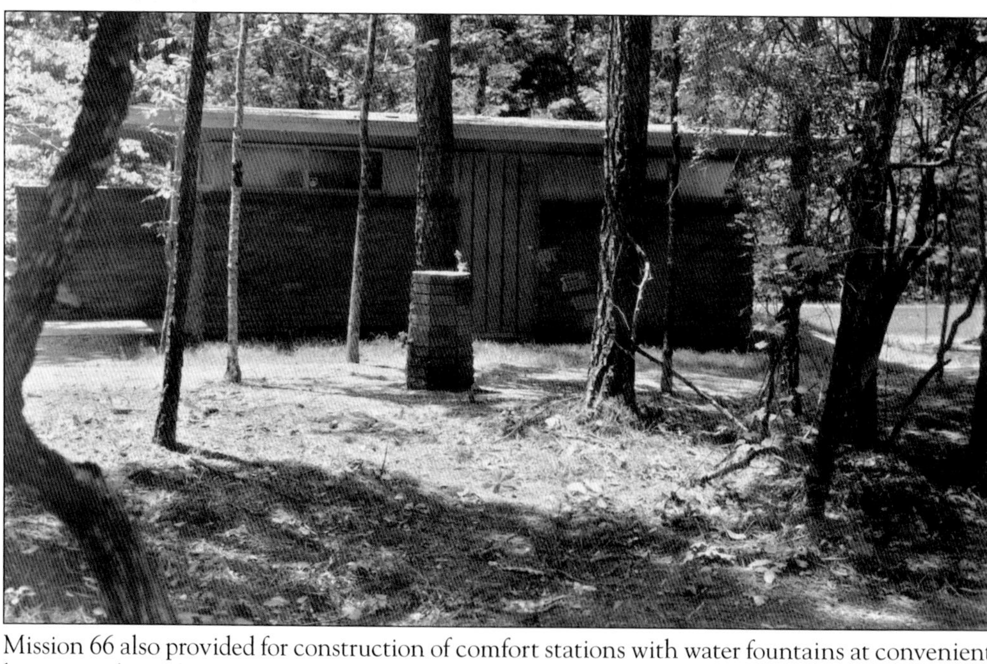

Mission 66 also provided for construction of comfort stations with water fountains at convenient locations along the parkway. Motorists would no longer have to search for springs for drinking water. Comfort stations were often located at sites that also had a history or nature feature. Travelers were encouraged to spend time at the stops to learn but also to become more alert when they resumed driving. (NPS.)

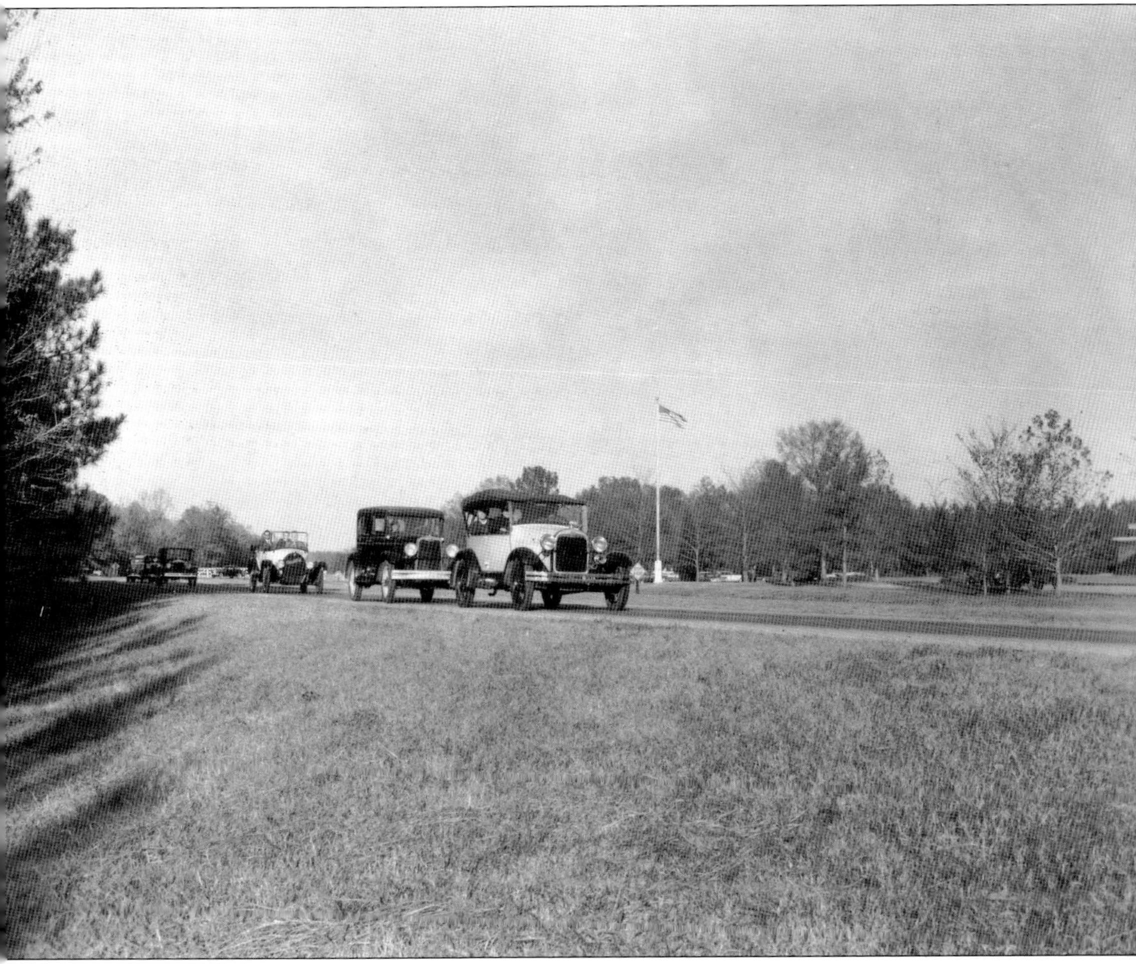

The parkway has long appealed to antique car enthusiasts, who enjoy drives at a leisurely pace without competition from commercial traffic. National car clubs regularly choose to hold annual drives on the parkway. (NPS.)

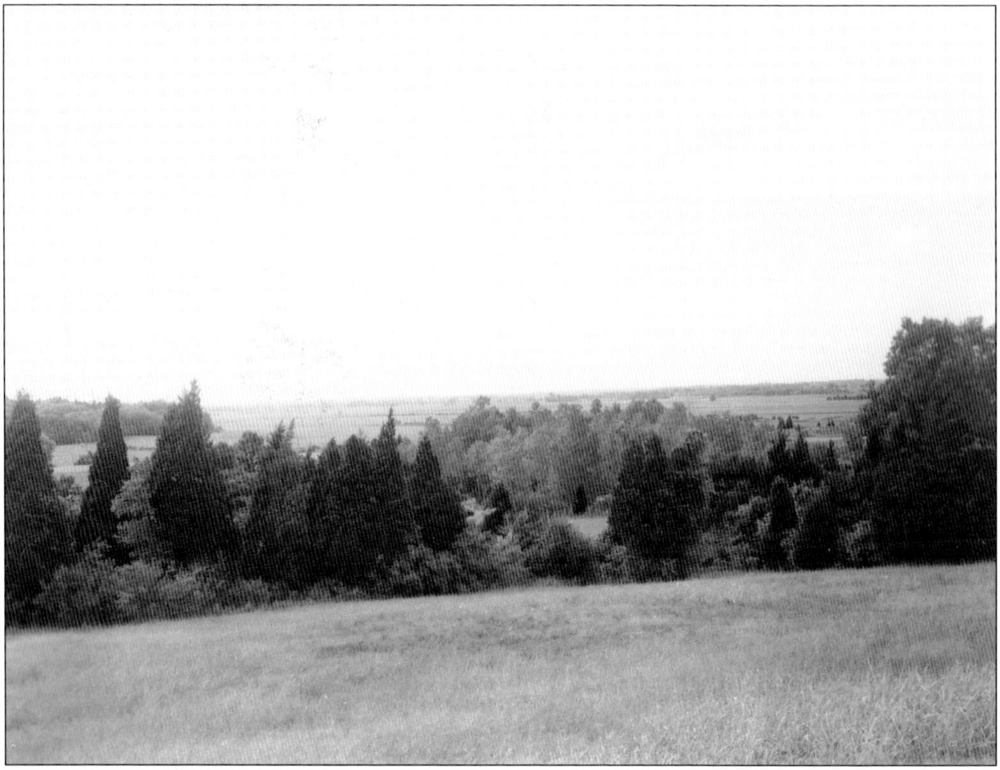

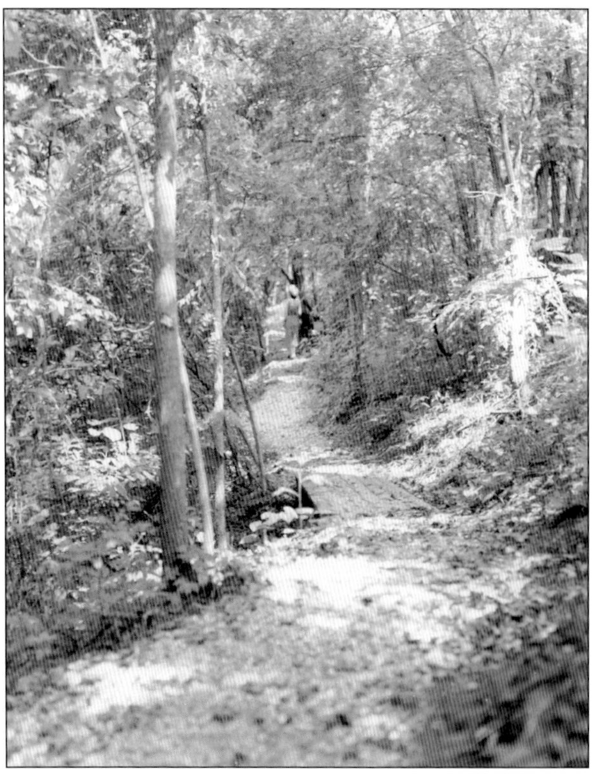

Though the parkway would not be selected as a national scenic trail until 1983, designers understood the importance of highlighting scenic vistas along the road. Little Mountain, Colbert Ferry, and Baker Bluff Overlook are just three spectacular views from pull-off areas. (NPS.)

Trails to historic, natural, or scenic areas were designed to allow travelers to get out of their automobiles and take brief walks in the natural environment. At certain points along the parkway, visitors can also walk along segments of the old Natchez Trace military road just as thousands of soldiers and other travelers 200 years earlier. (NPS.)

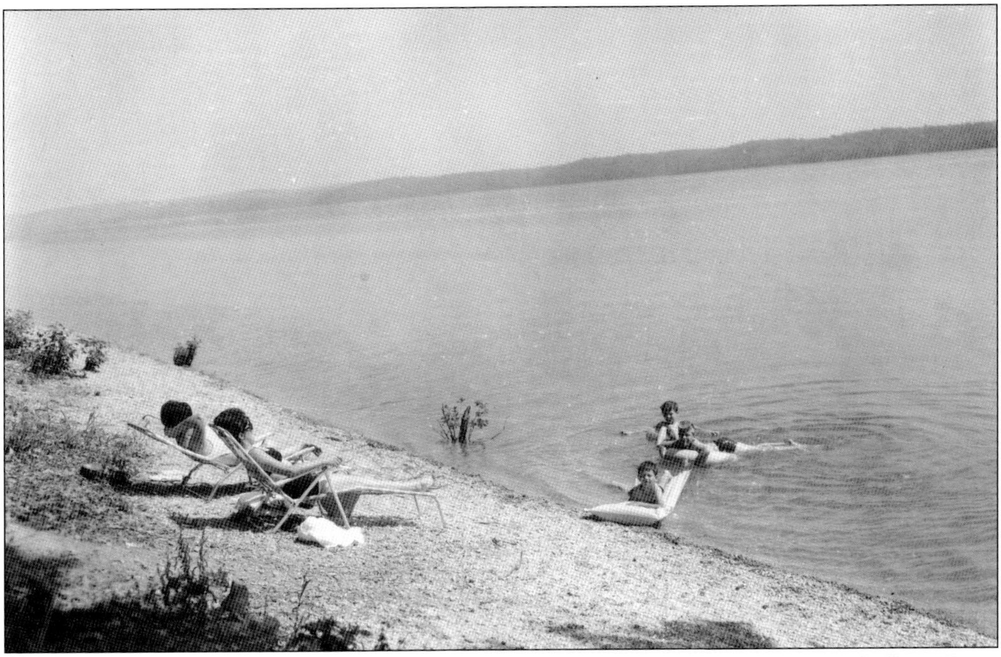

Recreational parks within the parkway land were planned at Little Mountain, Colbert Ferry (above and below), and Meriwether Lewis. Campgrounds with outdoor grills, picnic tables, and comfort stations would provide the services residents would need for a weekend getaway. Early plans also included building gas stations and sandwich shops at the parks. Hiking, fishing, and boating would be encouraged. Park rangers planned weekend educational programs for campers and showed outdoor educational films. (Both, NPS.)

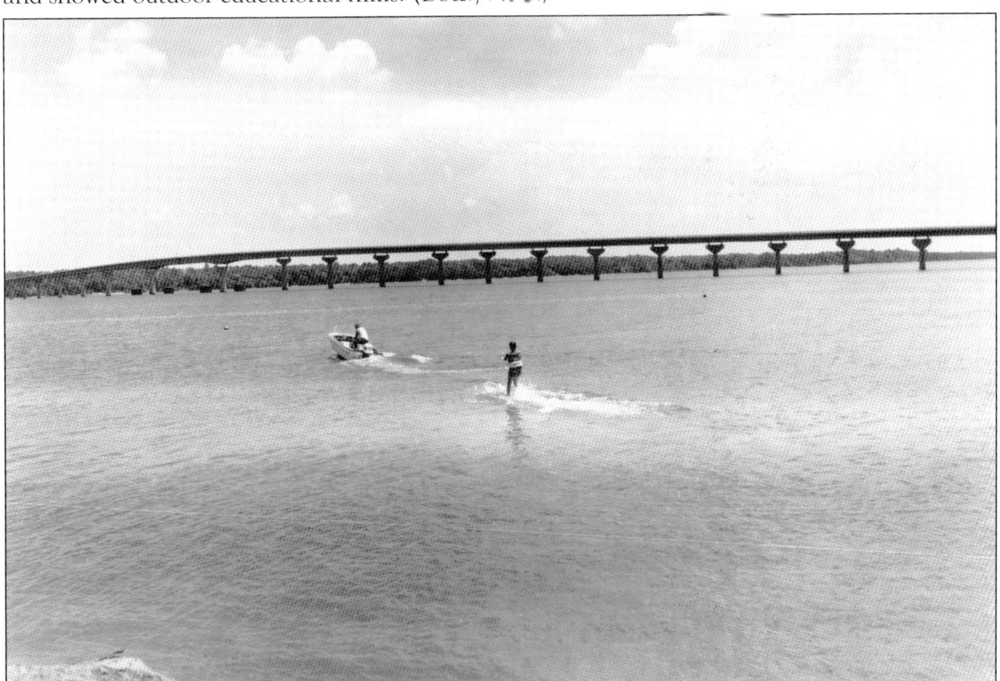

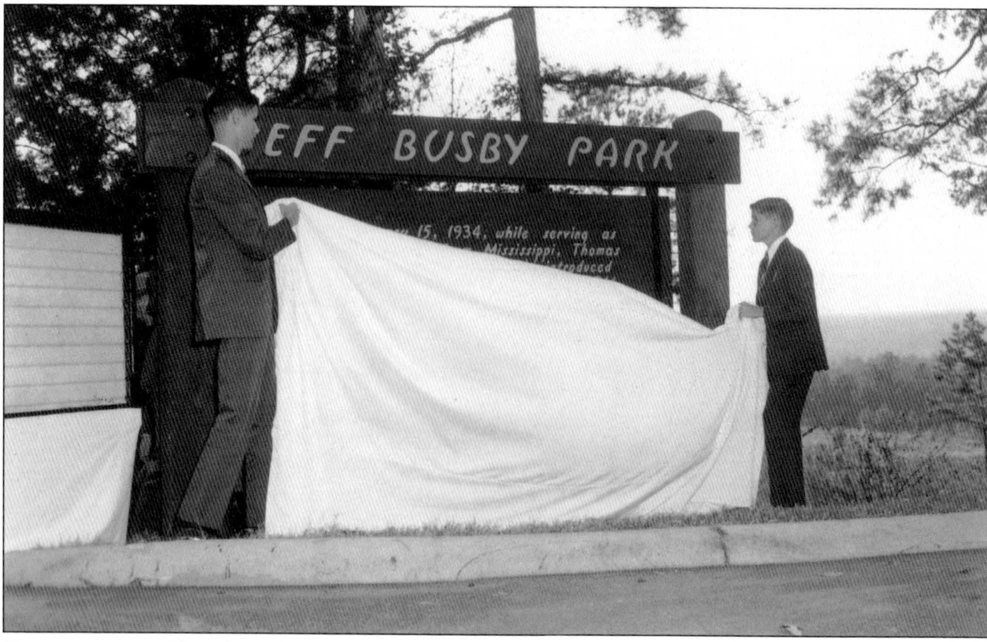

Congressman Jeff Busby, who introduced the bill in the House of Representatives to appropriate funds for the parkway, died in 1964. Though Busby lost his congressional seat in the 1930s, he returned to his law practice in Mississippi and continued to support the parkway, viewing the project as one of his legacies. Congressman Abernethy suggested that Little Mountain Park be renamed in honor of Busby to remind travelers of his efforts in introducing the first appropriation bill for the parkway. Congressman Busby's family participated in the ceremony, and his grandsons unveiled the new marker at the top of Little Mountain, the highest point of the parkway in Mississippi. (Both, NPS.)

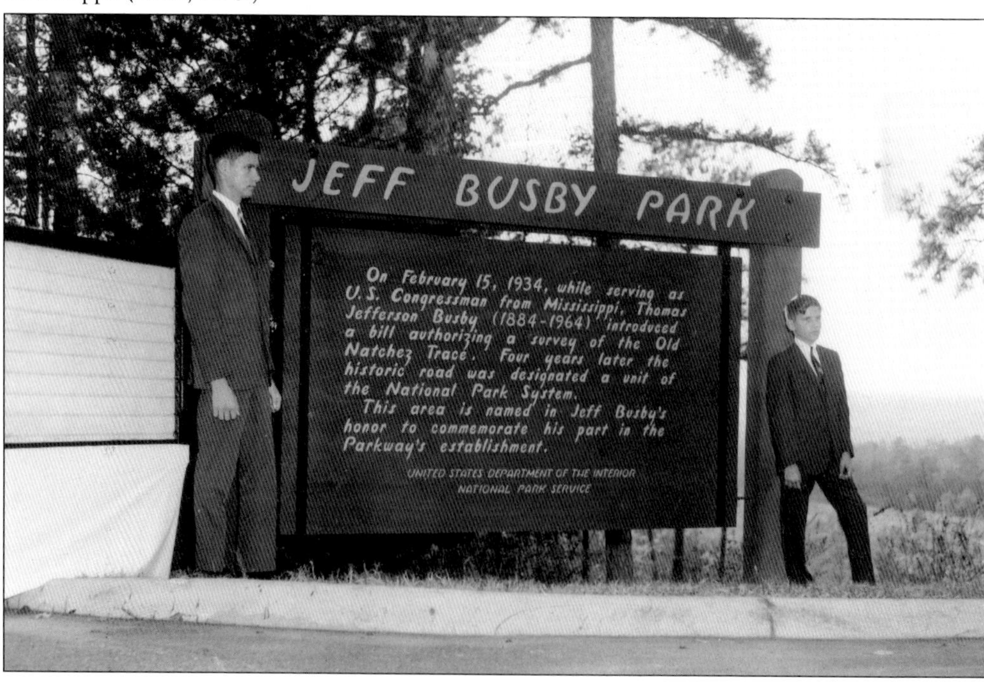

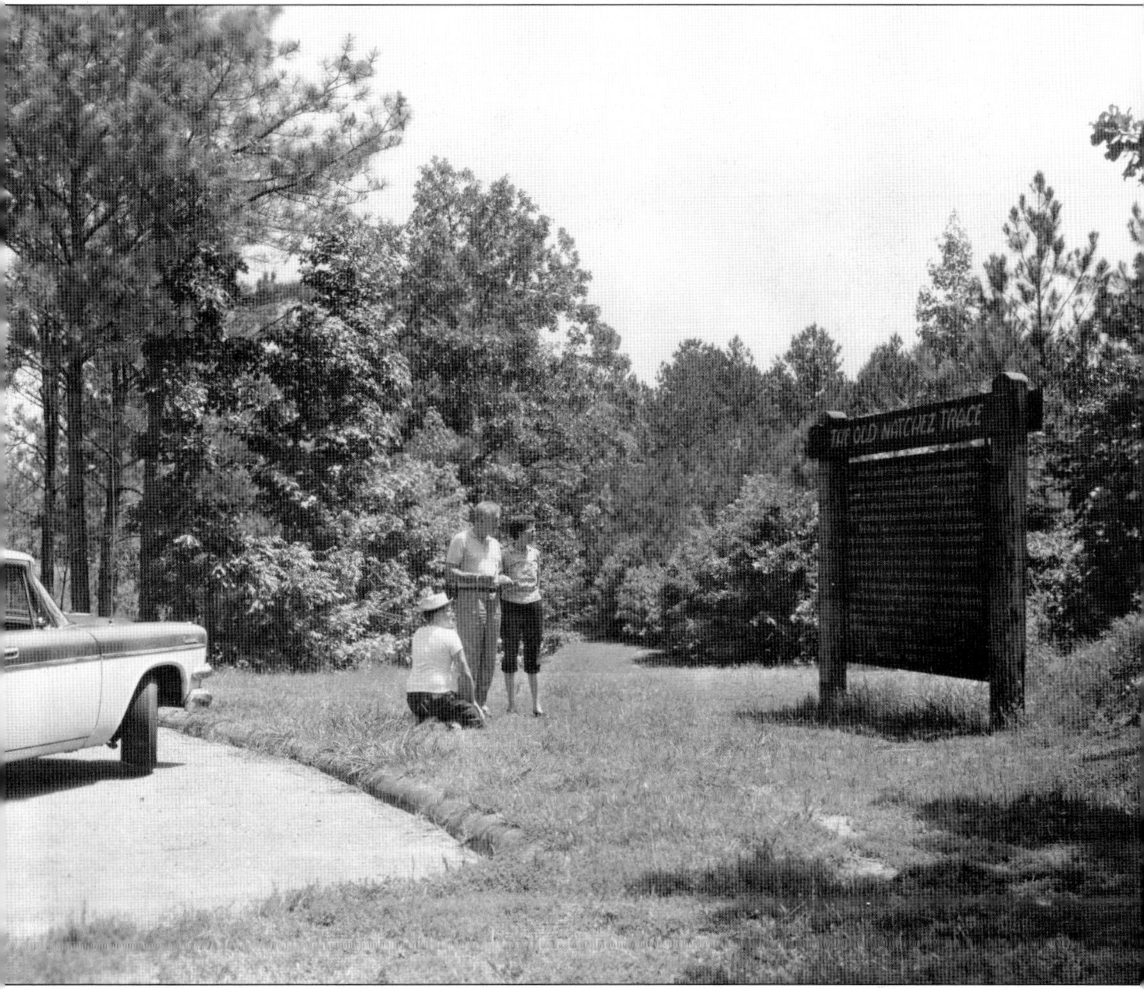

Sites along the parkway at pull-off areas were interpreted on wooden signs. (NPS.)

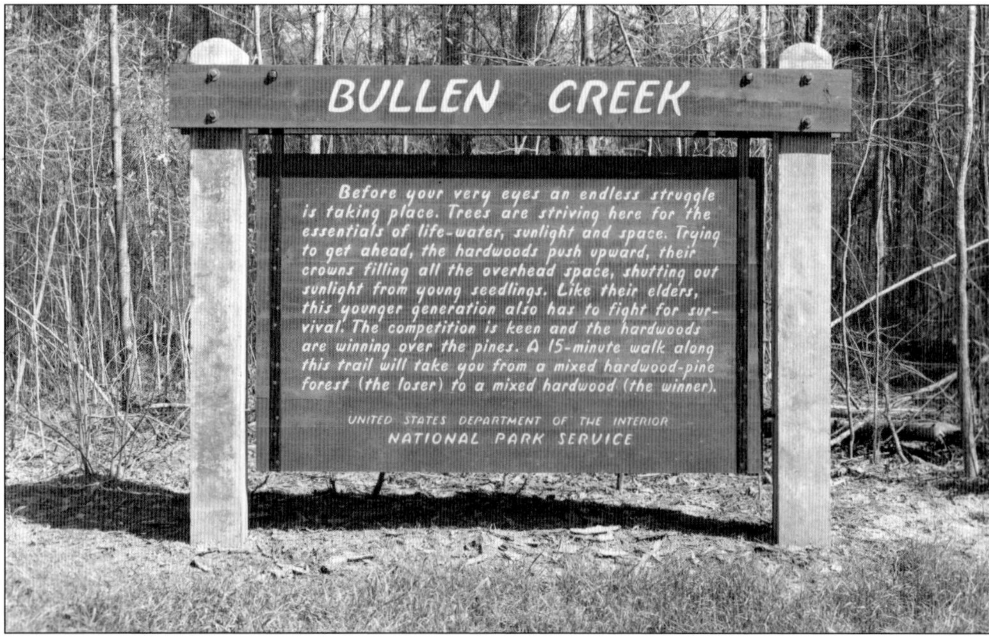

Some interpretation related to the forest areas along the length of the parkway. (NPS.)

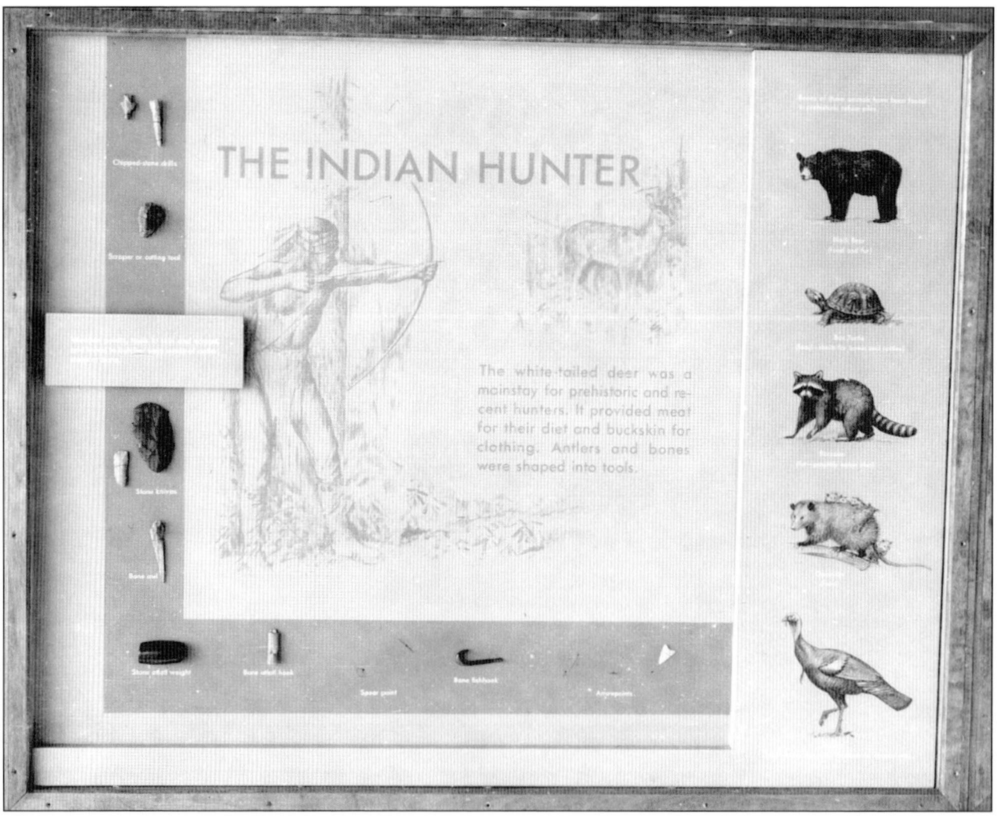

At Jeff Busby Campground, a Mission 66 outdoor shelter also contained exhibits on nature and history. (NPS.)

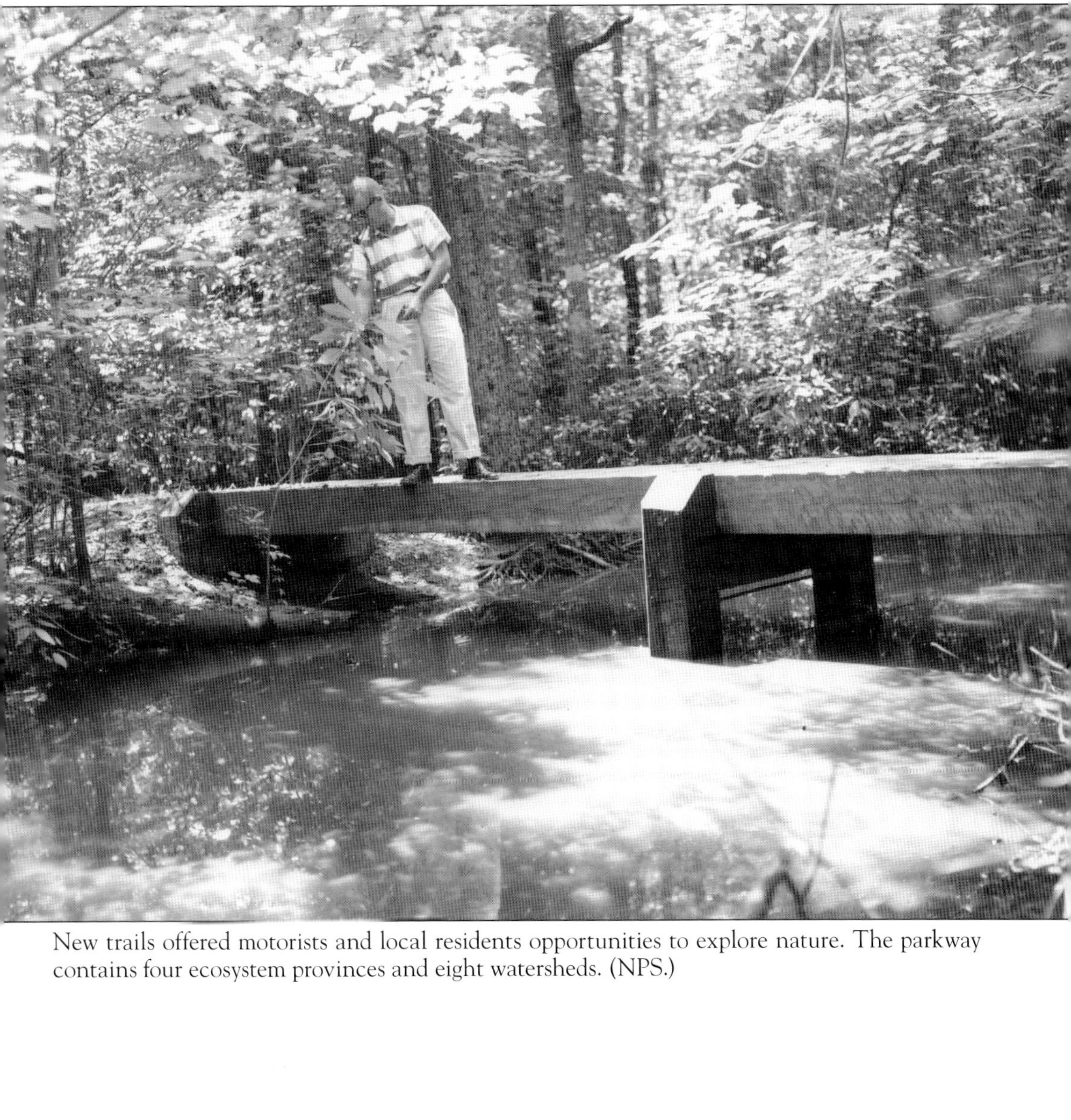

New trails offered motorists and local residents opportunities to explore nature. The parkway contains four ecosystem provinces and eight watersheds. (NPS.)

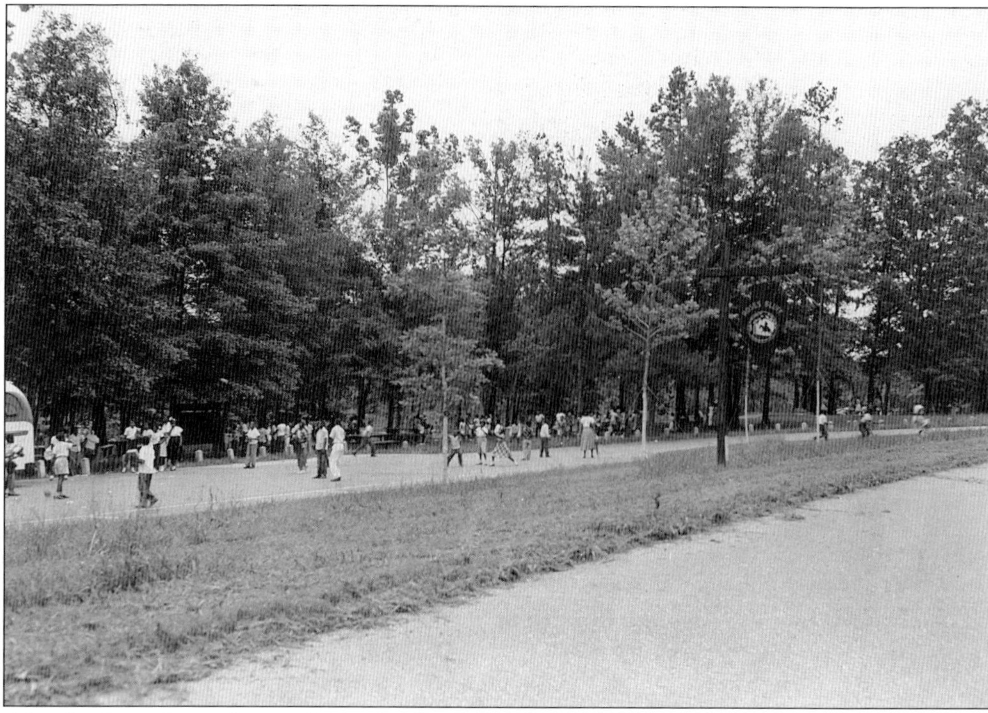

Schools along the parkway also took advantage of the educational opportunities the parkway offered. (NPS.)

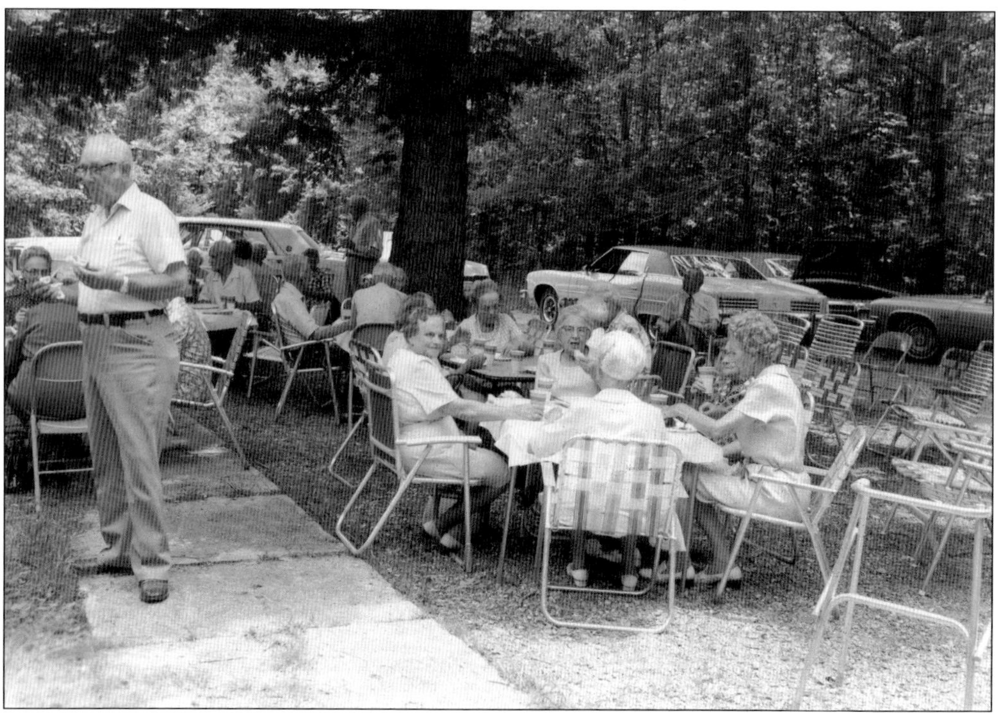

The park areas quickly became popular meeting and picnic areas for civic groups. This group of senior citizens is from Saltillo, Mississippi. (NPS.)

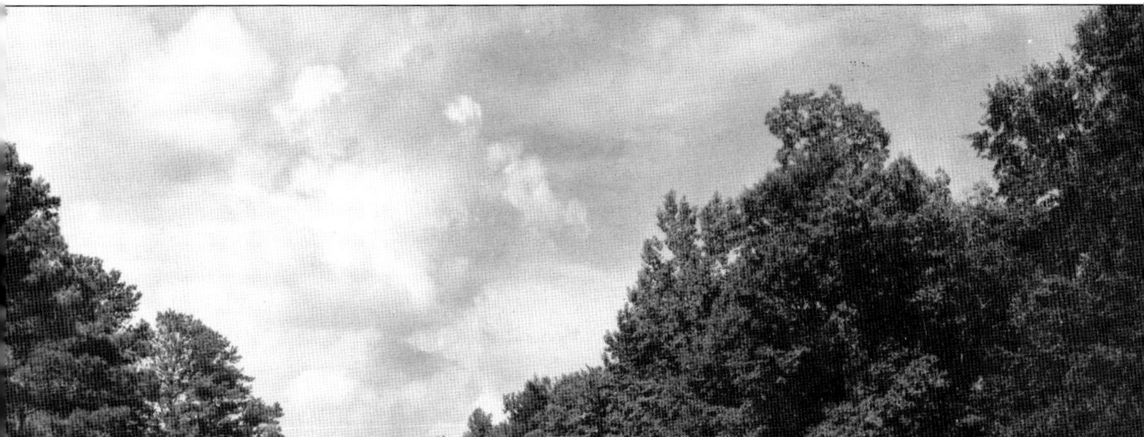

By the time the Mission 66 projects were completed, the parkway experience had changed. The focus was on providing motorists a great driving experience along the scenic route and local residents a place to camp and enjoy recreation on the weekends. (NPS.)

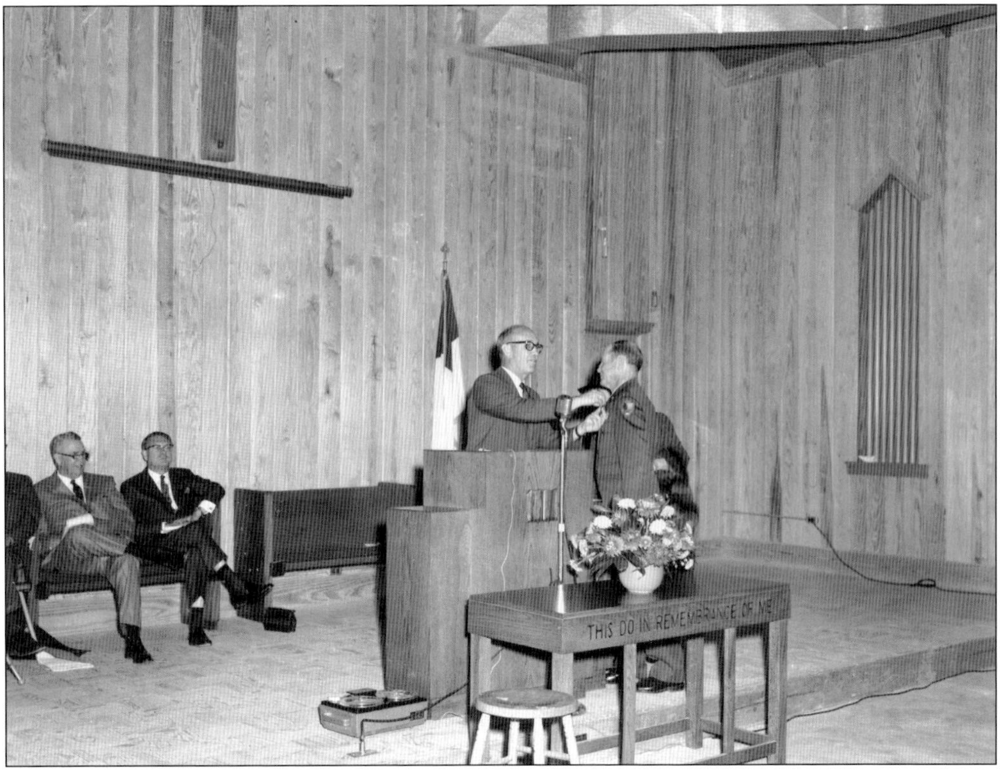

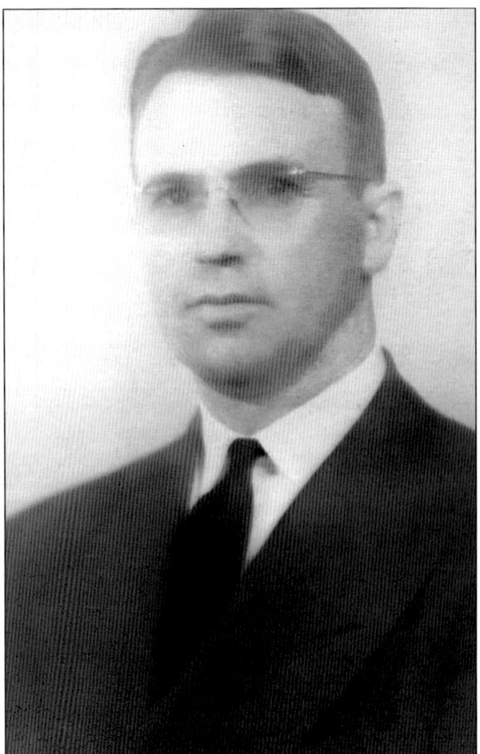

On October 30, 1969, the annual meeting at French Camp, Mississippi, would be transitional. Superintendent Robert Haraden awarded Roane Fleming Byrnes the first Post Rider Award for her 36 years of service. It was the last annual meeting Byrnes was able to attend. She died the following year without seeing the completion of the parkway. The superintendent and the regional director also recognized J. Leonard Volz, who began work with the parkway in 1942. (NPS.)

When Byrnes was no longer able to serve as president, Jackson, Mississippi, attorney Ralph Landrum, who had served as association secretary since 1934, stepped up to lead the organization. (Courtesy of Dot Ward.)

Four

A National Bicentennial Project

"Finish the Trace" 1970–2005

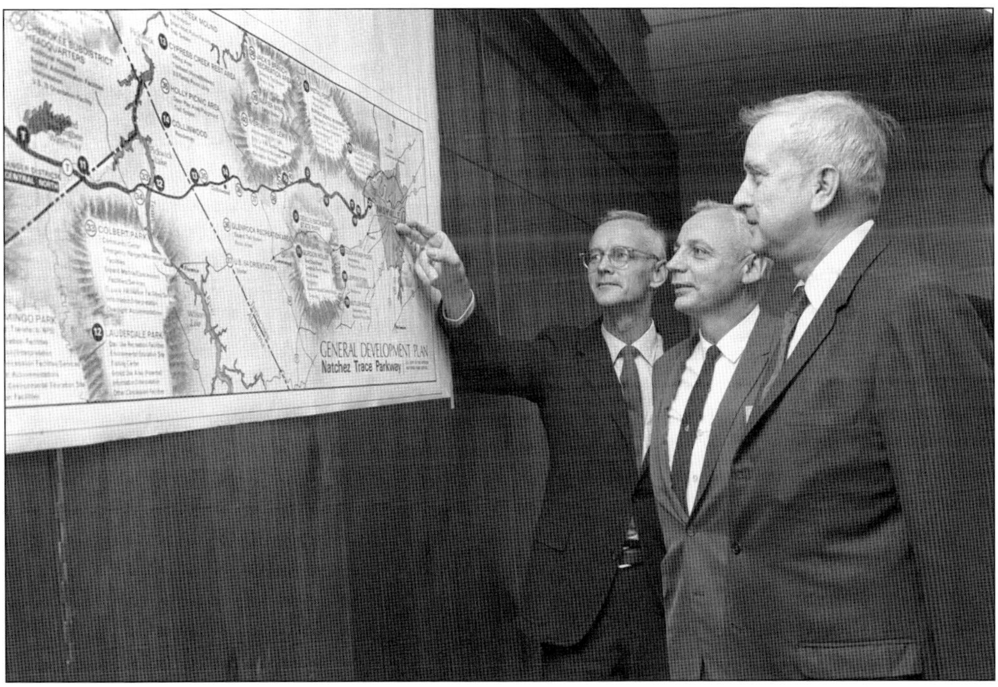

The National Park Service held public meetings along the parkway in 1970 to discuss a plan for completion, possibly in time for the national bicentennial, though no additional funds were appropriated. Association president Ralph Landrum was quoted as stating that the parkway had been "treated as a stepchild" and that it was time for it to be completed. Visitation reached 20 million by 1971. Superintendent Robert Haraden is pictured in the center. (Nashville Public Library, Special Collections.)

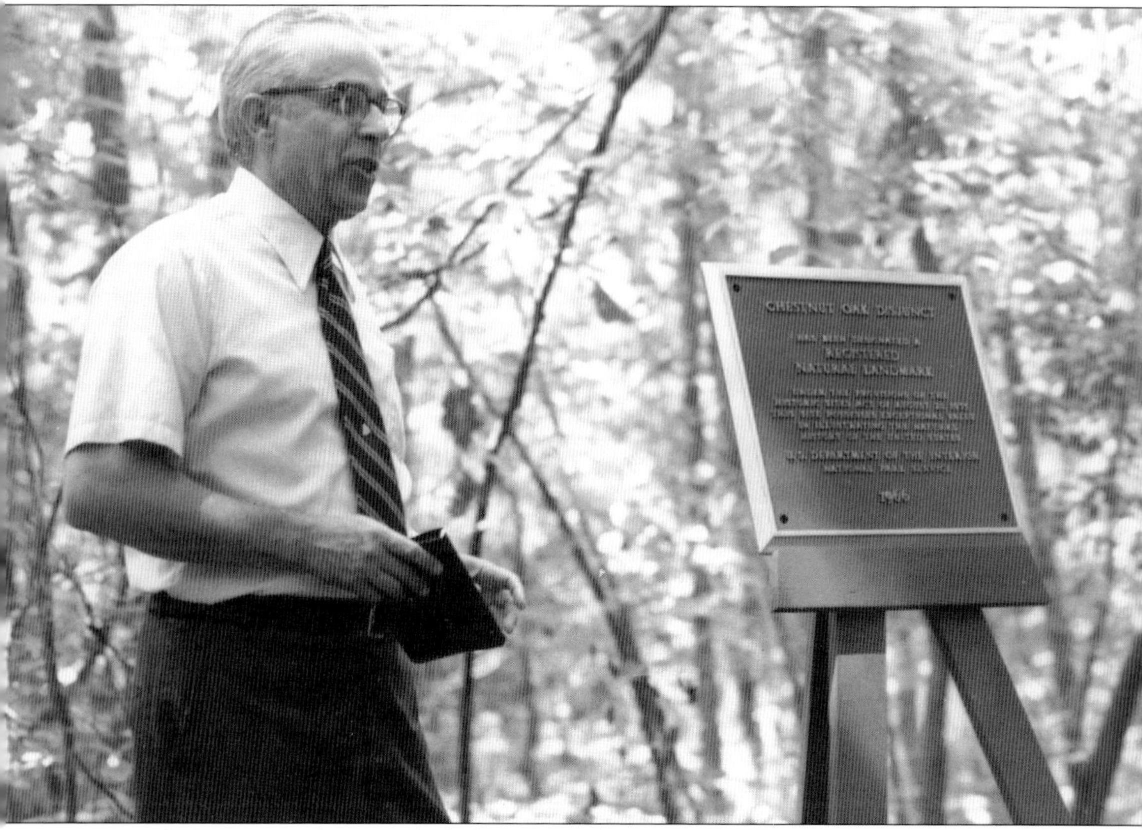

As the bicentennial approached, the nation's attention turned back to its heritage. Pres. Gerald Ford announced that the parkway would become a national bicentennial project. Not only would the bicentennial project provide new construction funding, but emphasis could also be returned to preservation of the history of the Trace. The route of the old Natchez Trace was listed in the National Register of Historic Places. Regional director David Thompson presented the dedication, as he also presented the natural landmark dedication to a grove of chestnut oak, shown above. (NPS.)

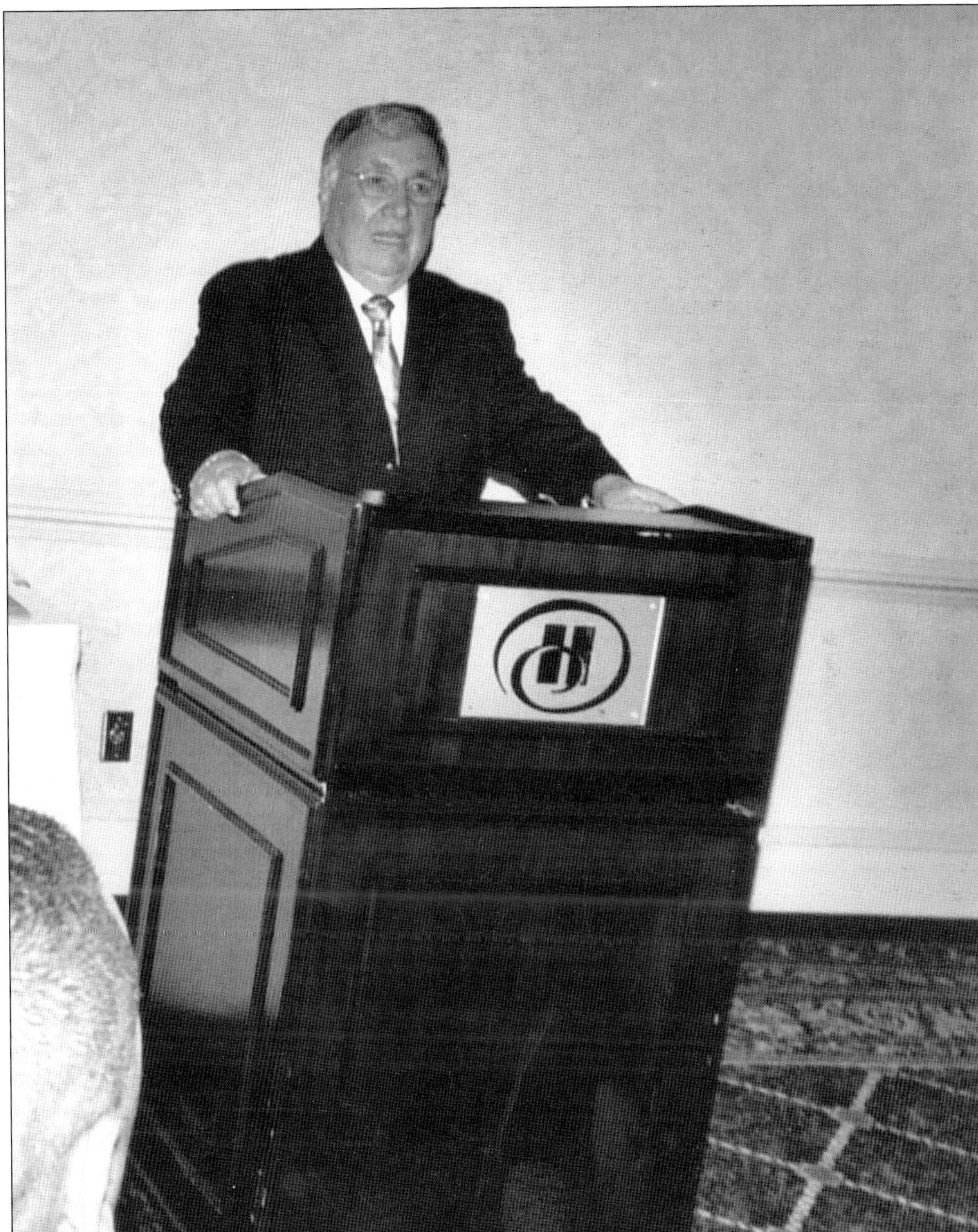

Harry Martin, director of the Community Development Foundation of Tupelo, Mississippi, saw the parkway as an opportunity to encourage economic development in the three states, and he began to work behind the scenes to assume the spearhead role the late Mrs. Byrnes had held. In 1971, he hosted a delegation including the chair of the House appropriations committee and the secretary of the interior in Tupelo to discuss the future of the parkway. (Courtesy of Williamson County Chamber of Commerce.)

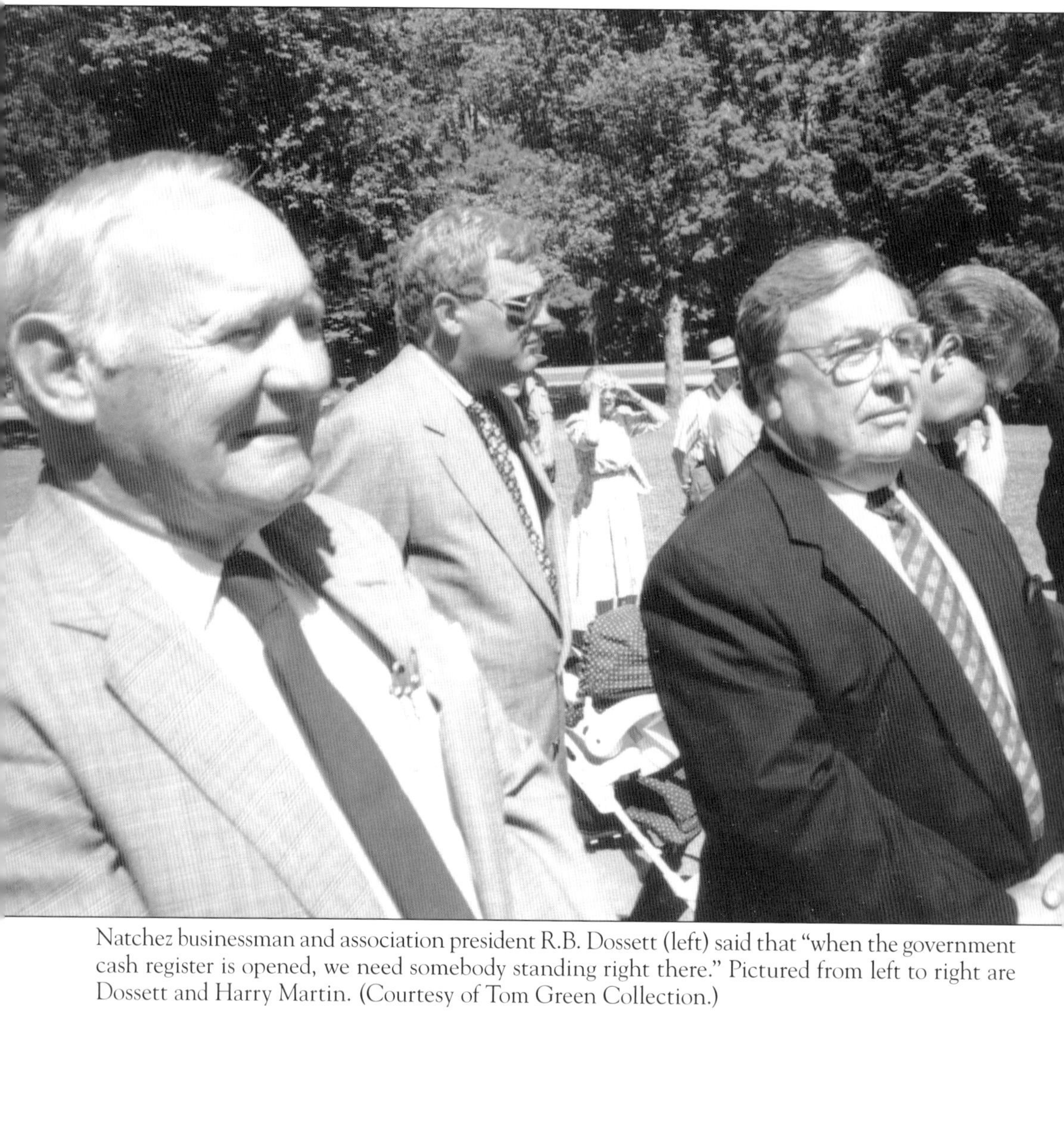

Natchez businessman and association president R.B. Dossett (left) said that "when the government cash register is opened, we need somebody standing right there." Pictured from left to right are Dossett and Harry Martin. (Courtesy of Tom Green Collection.)

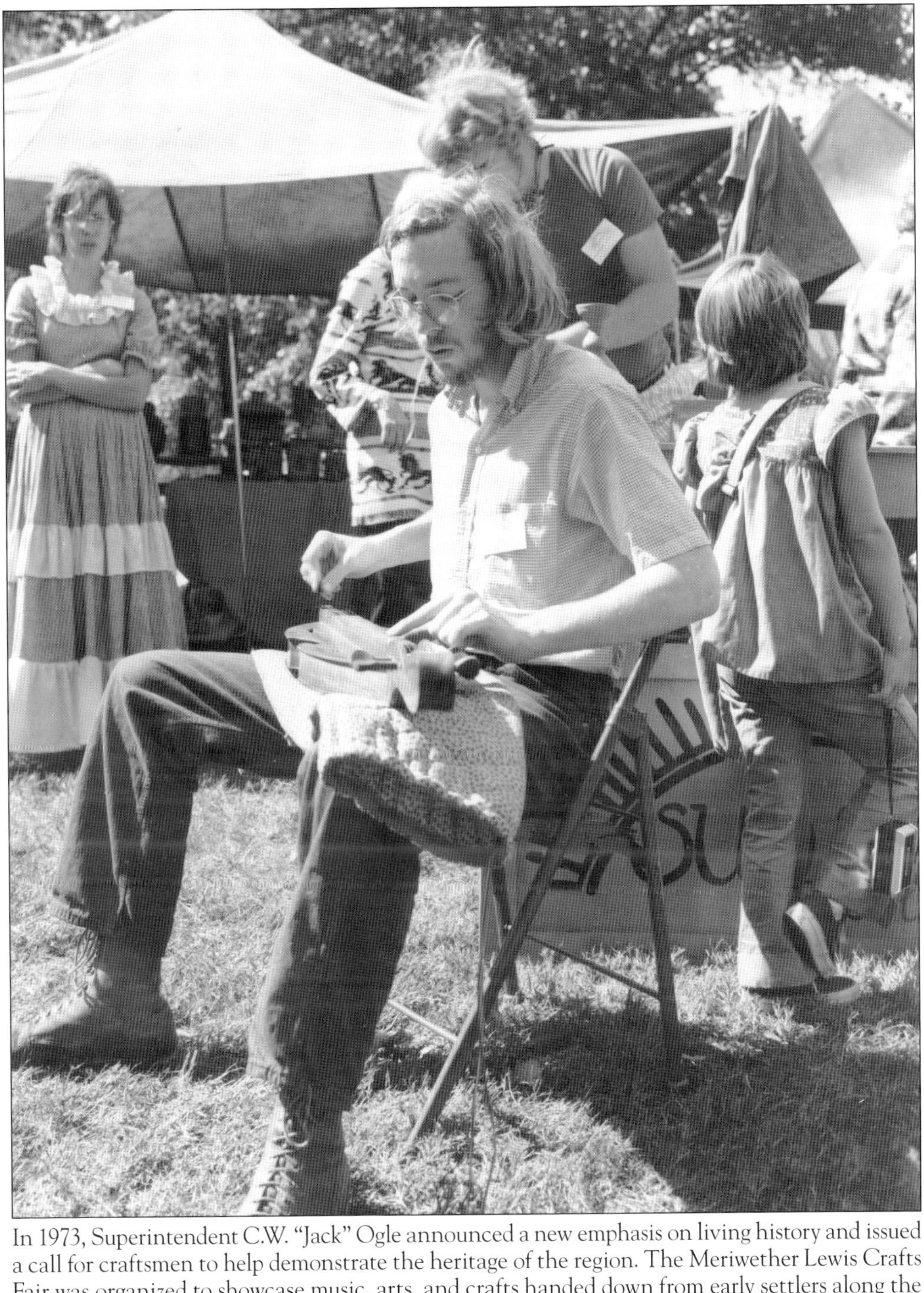

In 1973, Superintendent C.W. "Jack" Ogle announced a new emphasis on living history and issued a call for craftsmen to help demonstrate the heritage of the region. The Meriwether Lewis Crafts Fair was organized to showcase music, arts, and crafts handed down from early settlers along the Trace. The fair consistently drew over 10,000 visitors a year. This photograph shows a demonstration of an early musical instrument, like those that may have been carried by travelers on the Trace. The special activities brought the old Natchez Trace history and culture to life. (NPS.)

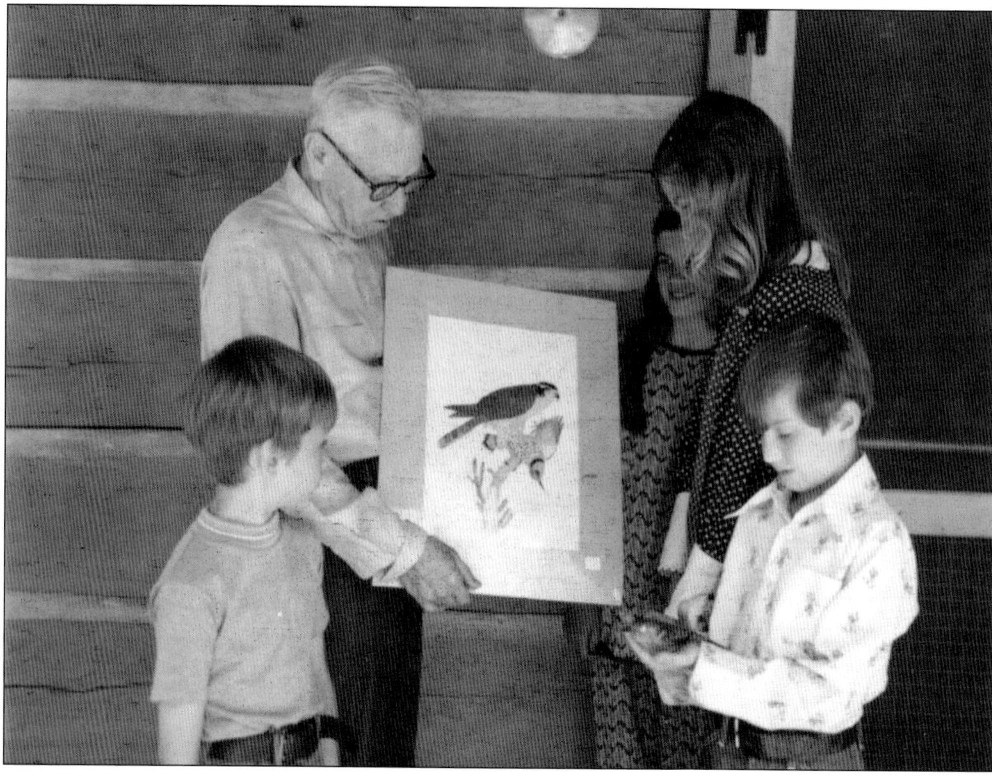

Dick Quin discusses his nature illustrations with unidentified young visitors at Ridgeland. (NPS.)

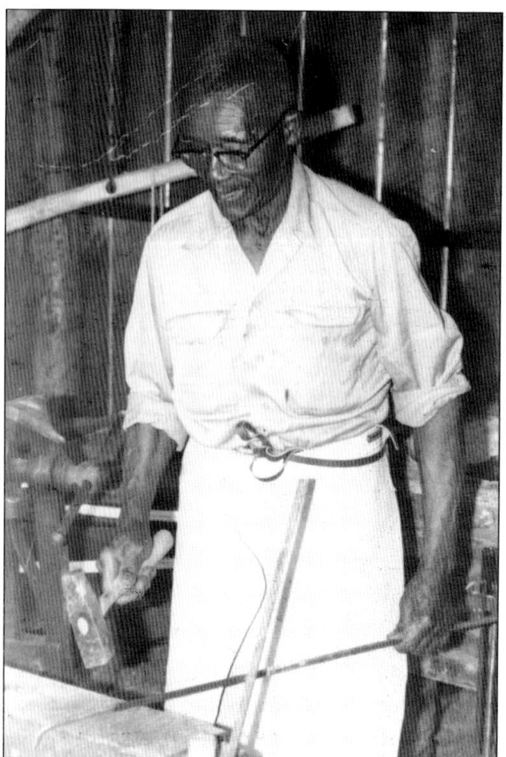

Ned Weatherby from Meadville, Mississippi, demonstrates the craft of blacksmithing by making an iron hinge during a living history event at Mount Locust. Blacksmiths set up shop along the old Natchez Trace to provide horseshoes and equipment needed by travelers—similar to today's automobile repair shops. (NPS.)

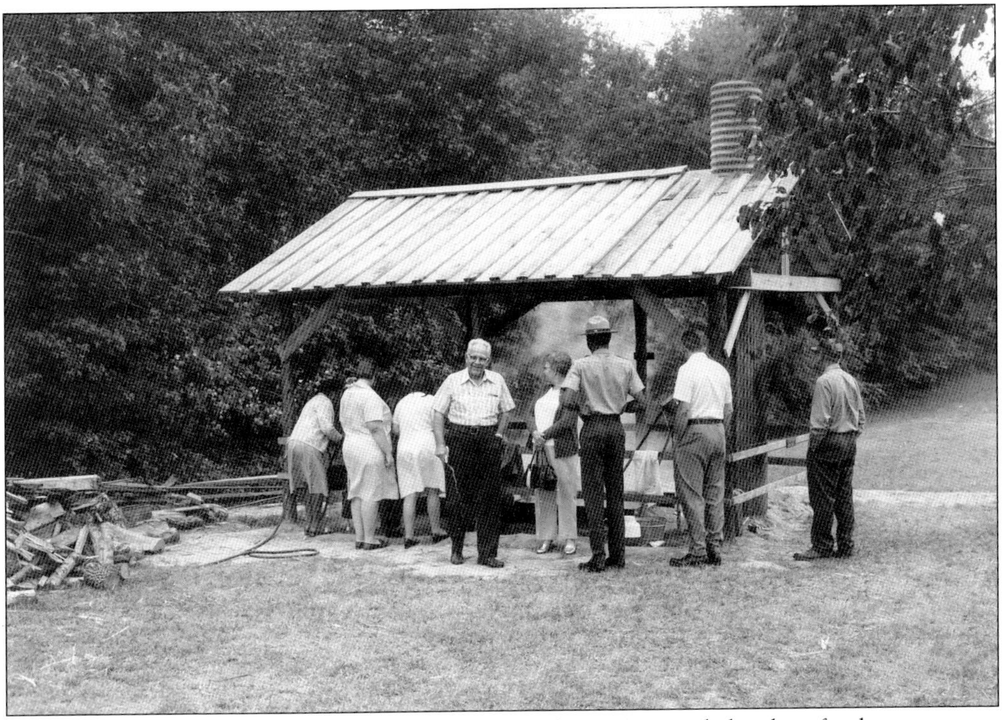

An outdoor shed built at the visitor center in the early 1970s provided a place for demonstrators to show how early settlers cooked and made necessities on the old Natchez Trace. (NPS.)

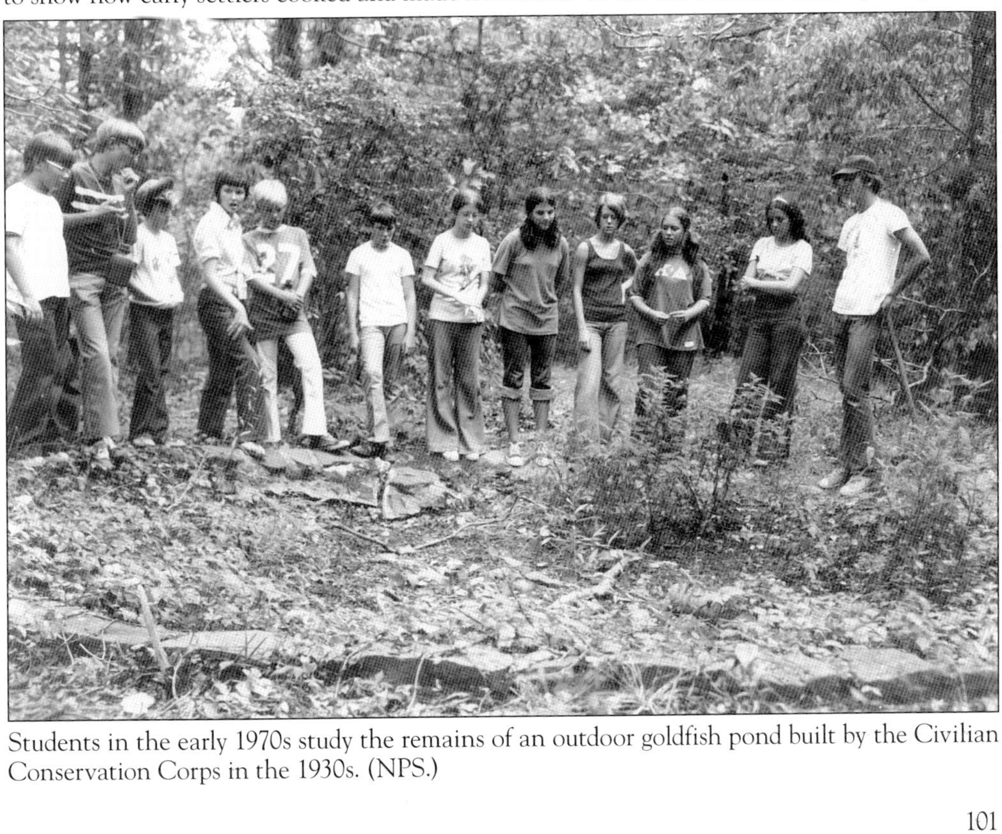

Students in the early 1970s study the remains of an outdoor goldfish pond built by the Civilian Conservation Corps in the 1930s. (NPS.)

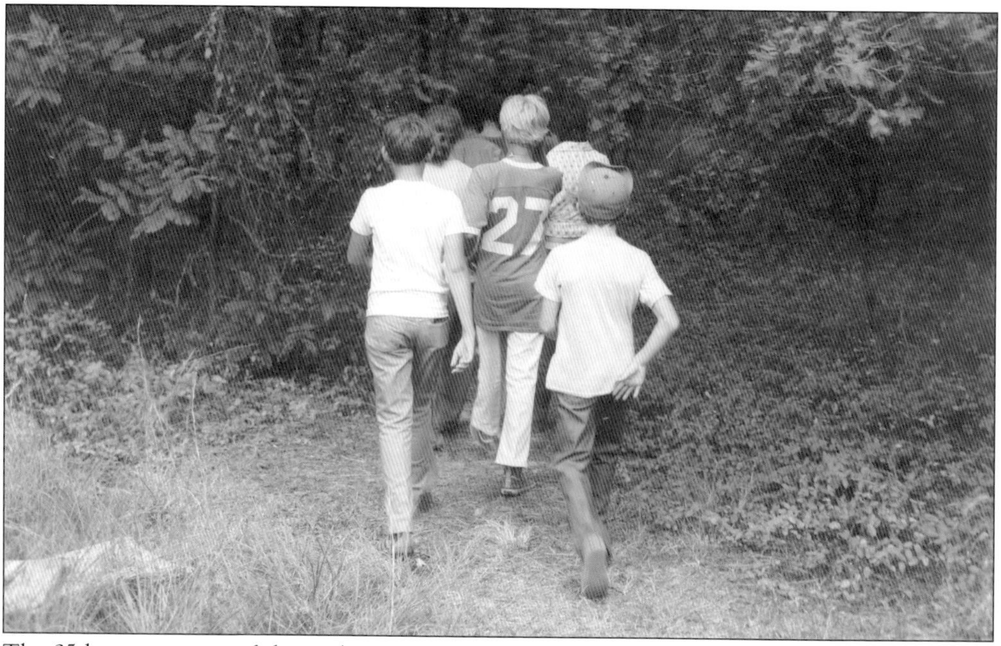

The 35th anniversary of the parkway was commemorated at headquarters with trail hikes and outdoor living history events. (NPS.)

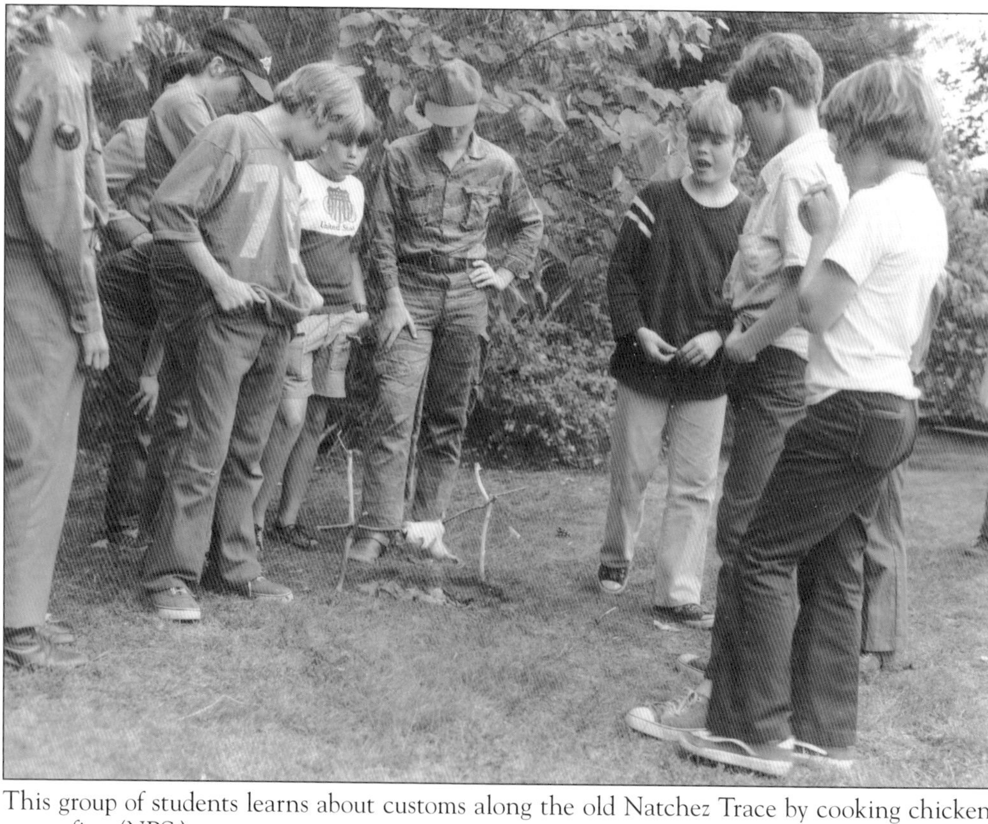

This group of students learns about customs along the old Natchez Trace by cooking chicken over a fire. (NPS.)

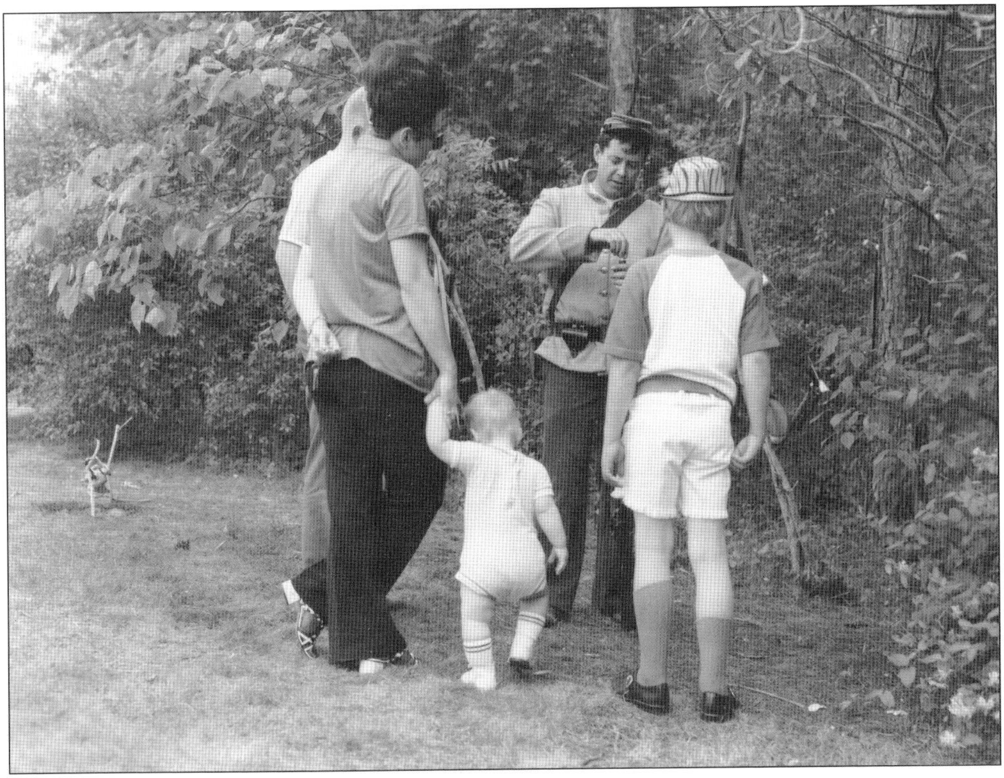

A Civil War reenactor explains camp life to a family in the 1970s. (NPS.)

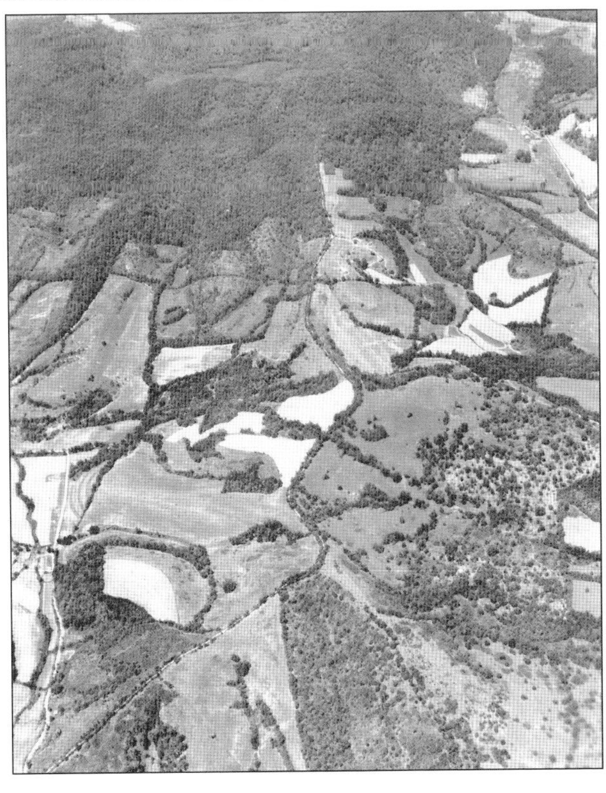

As construction moved northward into the hills of Middle Tennessee, shown in this aerial photograph, construction workers tied to ropes rappelled from the sides of hills to begin preliminary work. (NPS.)

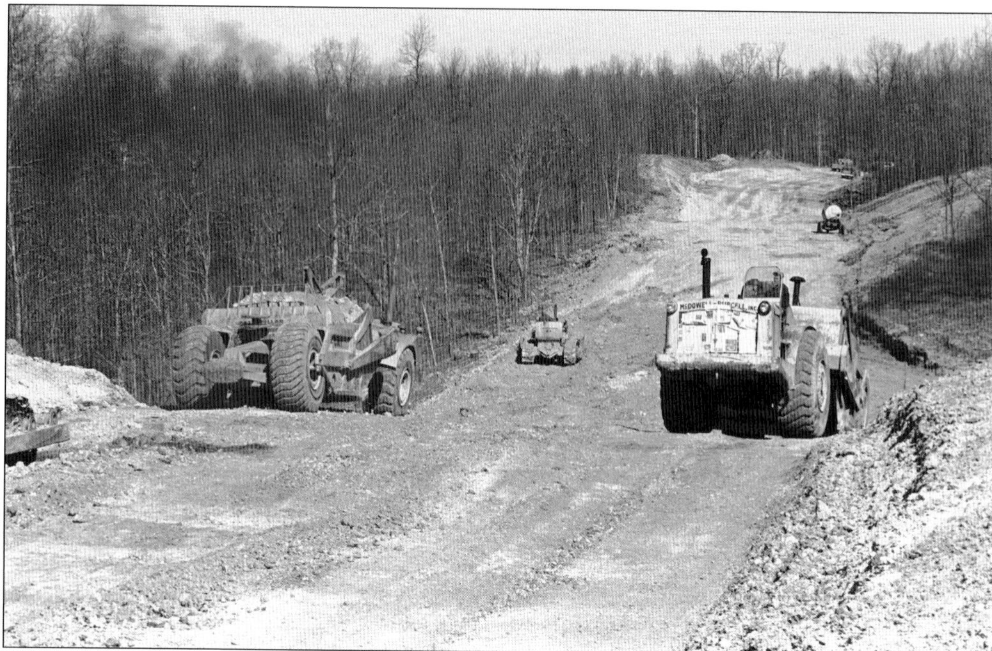

Advances in the design of earthmoving equipment sped the process of creating appropriate grades and curves through the hills. In this section, the old Natchez Trace is still marked as an identified county road and intersects the new parkway in a serpentine pattern. The old road is often visible from the new. (Nashville Public Library, Special Collections.)

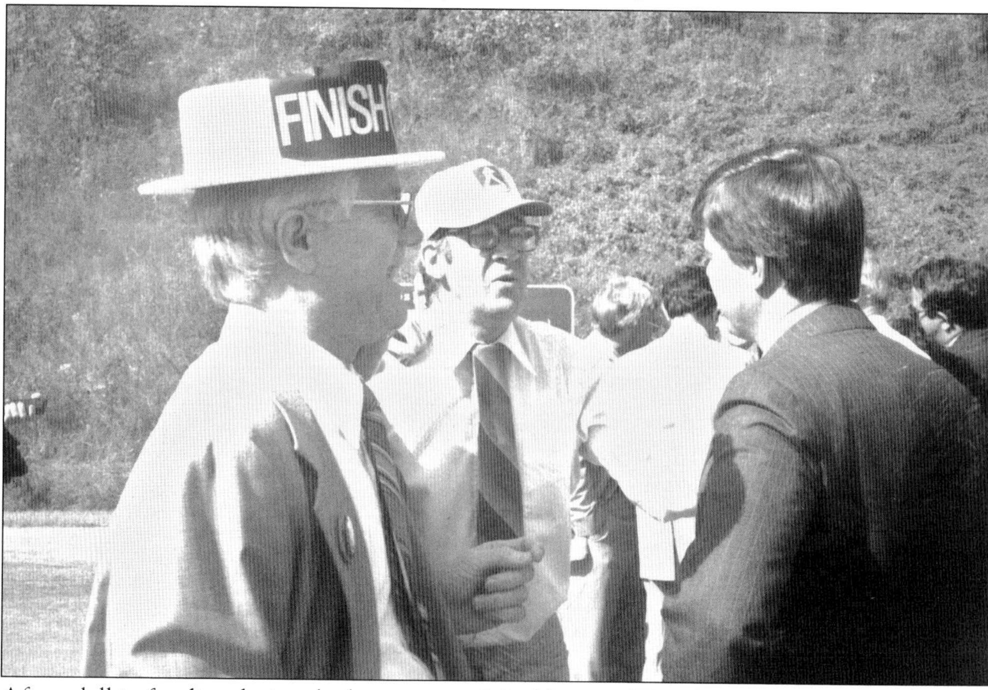

After a lull in funding during the later stages of the Vietnam War, the sight of new construction gave encouragement to efforts to renew the association. Members are shown here at the 1979 ground-breaking of the Jackson Falls, Tennessee, site. (Courtesy of Tom Green Collection.)

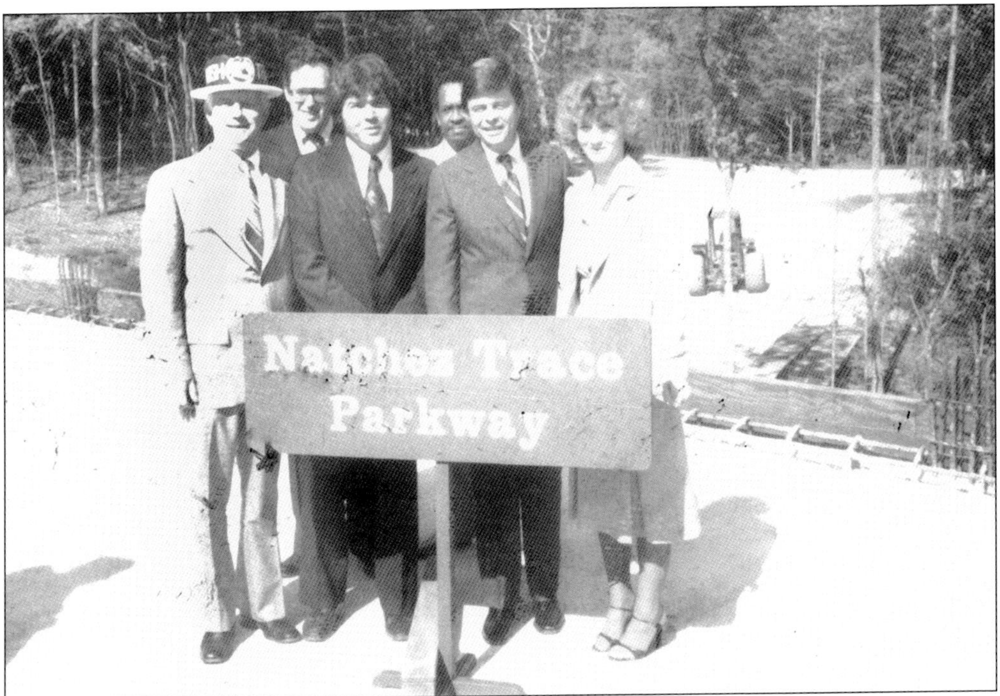

At an association meeting at the Loveless Café near the future northern terminus, Tom Green introduced the motto "Finish the Trace." Association members agreed to pool their efforts under a new organization structure for all three states with a focused mission to "Finish the Trace." (Courtesy of Tom Green Collection.)

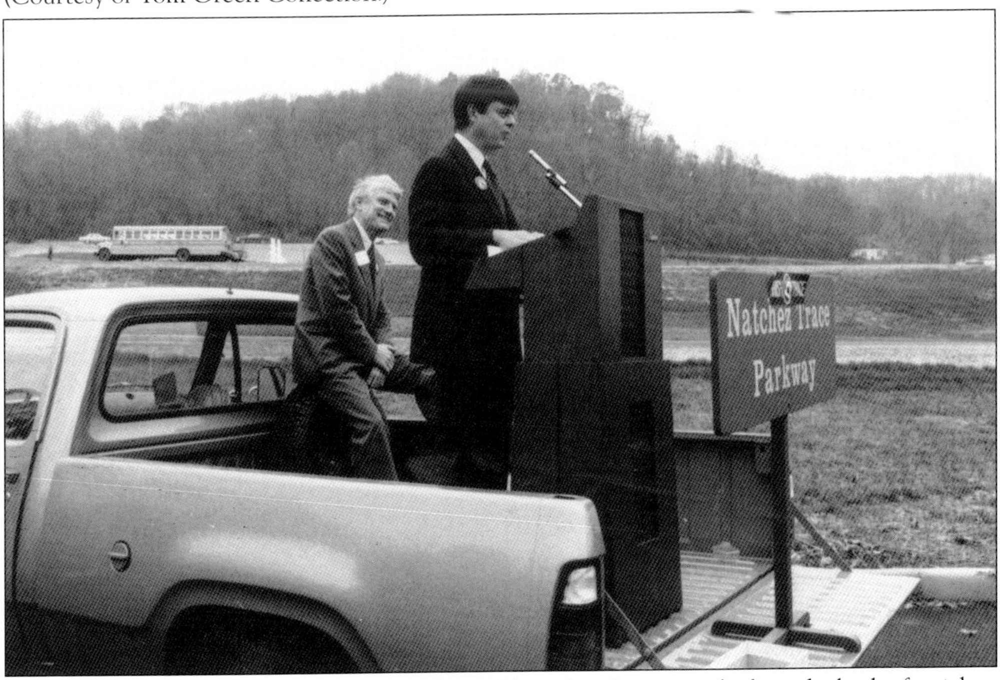

Tennessee senator and future US ambassador to China Jim Sasser speaks from the back of a pickup truck at the ribbon-cutting at Jackson Falls. (Courtesy of Tom Green Collection.)

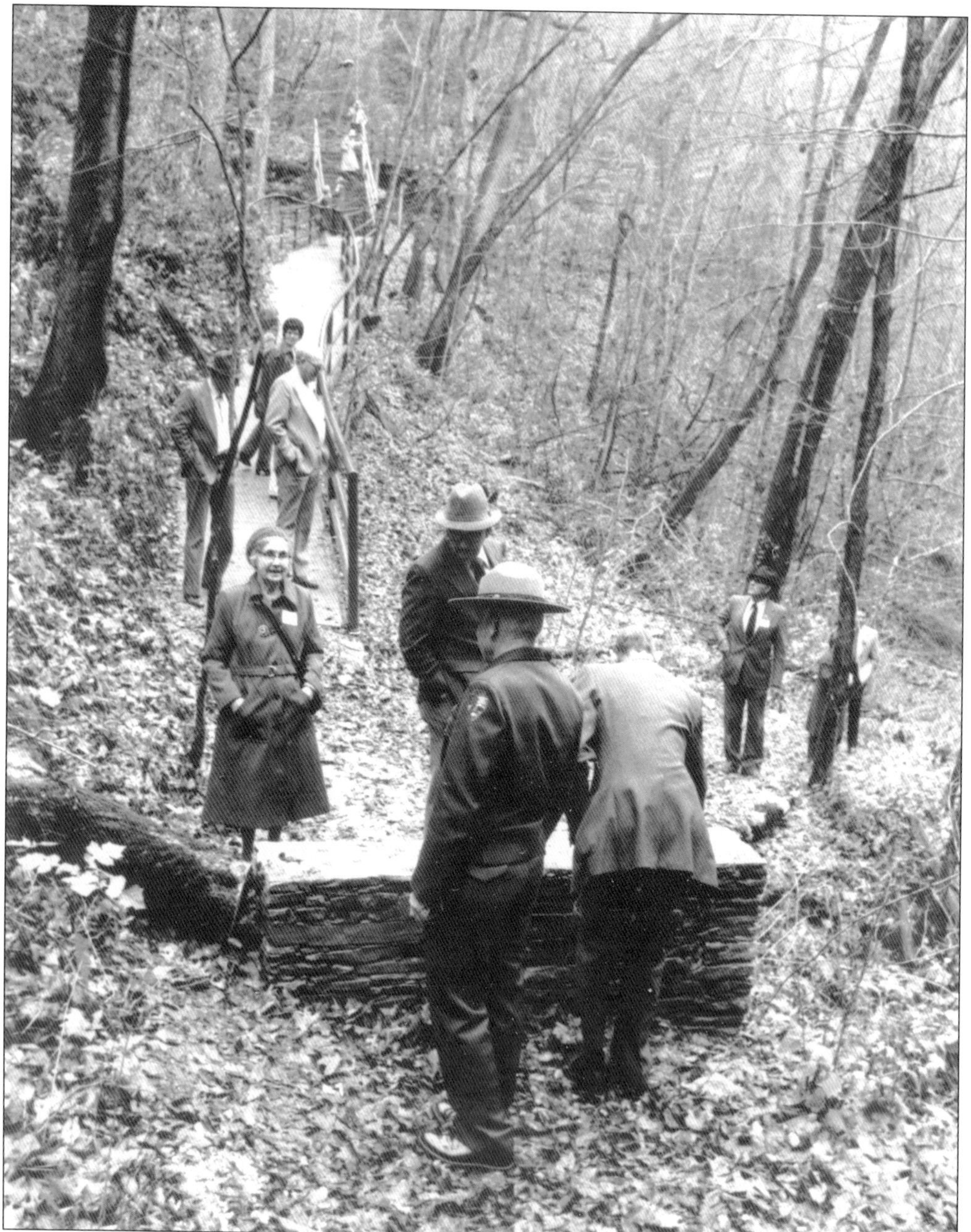

Following the opening of the Jackson Falls site, audience members were invited to walk the new trail to the base of the falls. The site takes its name from the local legend that General Jackson's troops drank water from the falls during their marches. Some troops marched past the falls near the Keg Springs Stand, and it is likely that the legend is true. (Courtesy of Tom Green Collection.)

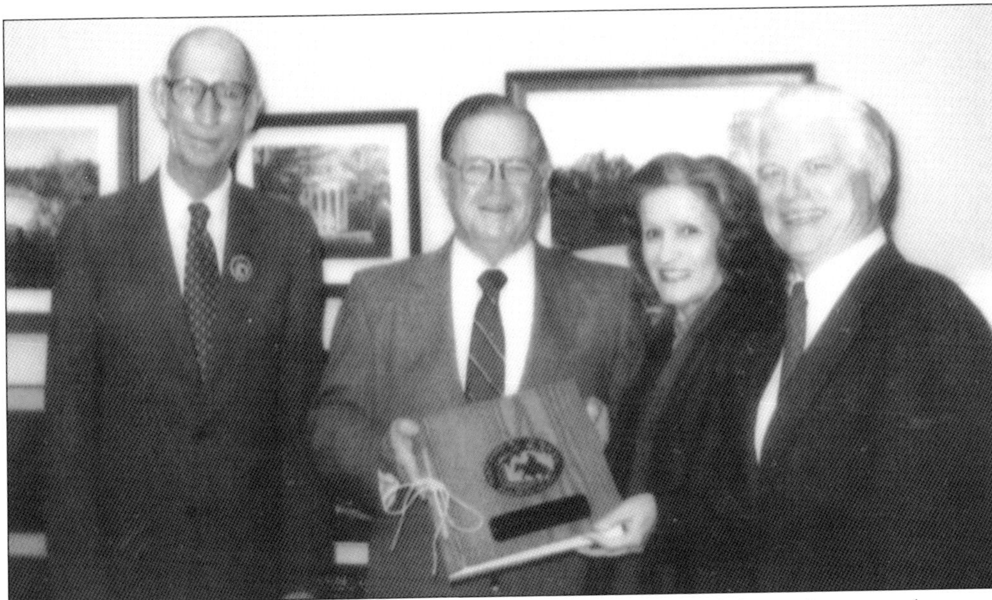

Mississippi congressman Jamie Whitten's support of completion of the parkway was honored by the naming of the Natchez Trace Bridge over the Tennessee-Tombigbee Waterway in 1984. Completion of the bridge linked the parkway from Jackson, Mississippi, to Jackson Falls in Tennessee. Association presidents P.O. Beard, Jean Ratliff, and Tom Green present the congressman with a souvenir Natchez Trace book. Pictured here are, from left to right, P.O. Beard, Jamie Whitten, Jean Ratliff, and Tom Green. (Courtesy of Tom Green Collection.)

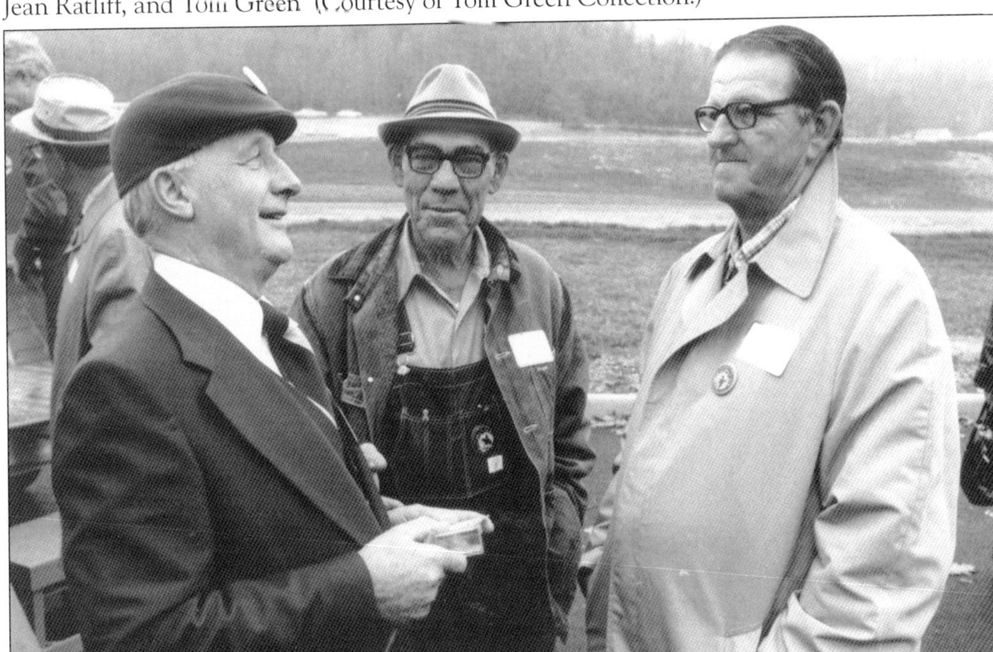

Politicians, farmers, and Natchez Trace enthusiasts all celebrated the opening of each new section. These visitors join in the opening of the section of the parkway to Highway 50 at the Gordon House in 1987, where it was announced that the Gordon House would be restored for living history. (Courtesy of Tom Green Collection.)

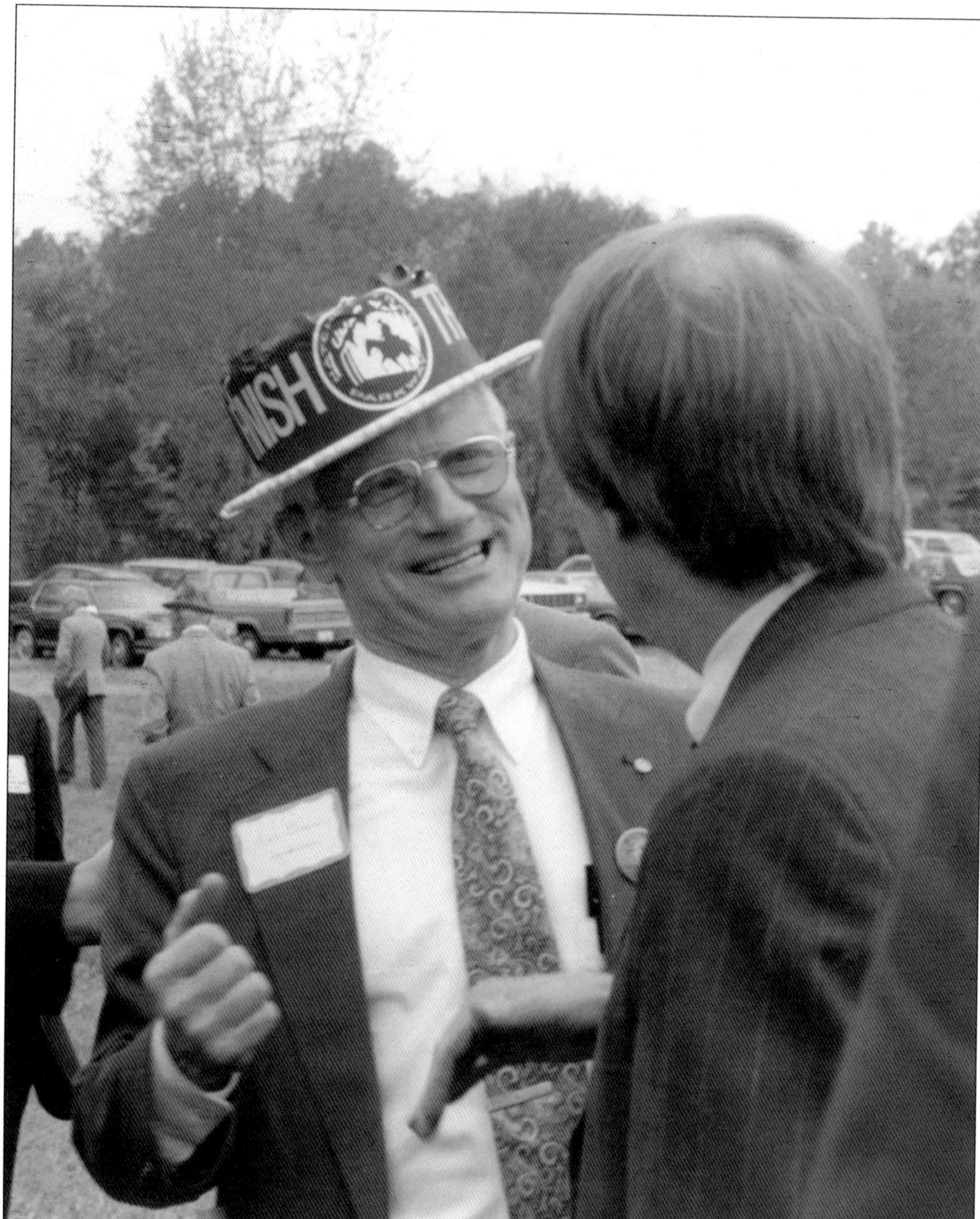

Association president Tom Green placed one of the "Finish the Trace" bumper stickers around the straw hat he wore to the ribbon-cutting ceremony. On a lark, he bit a chunk out of the hat to mark the completion of that section, and he kept up the tradition. Green was unable to attend the opening of the last section of road, but he sent the hat to complete the tradition. (Courtesy of Tom Green Collection.)

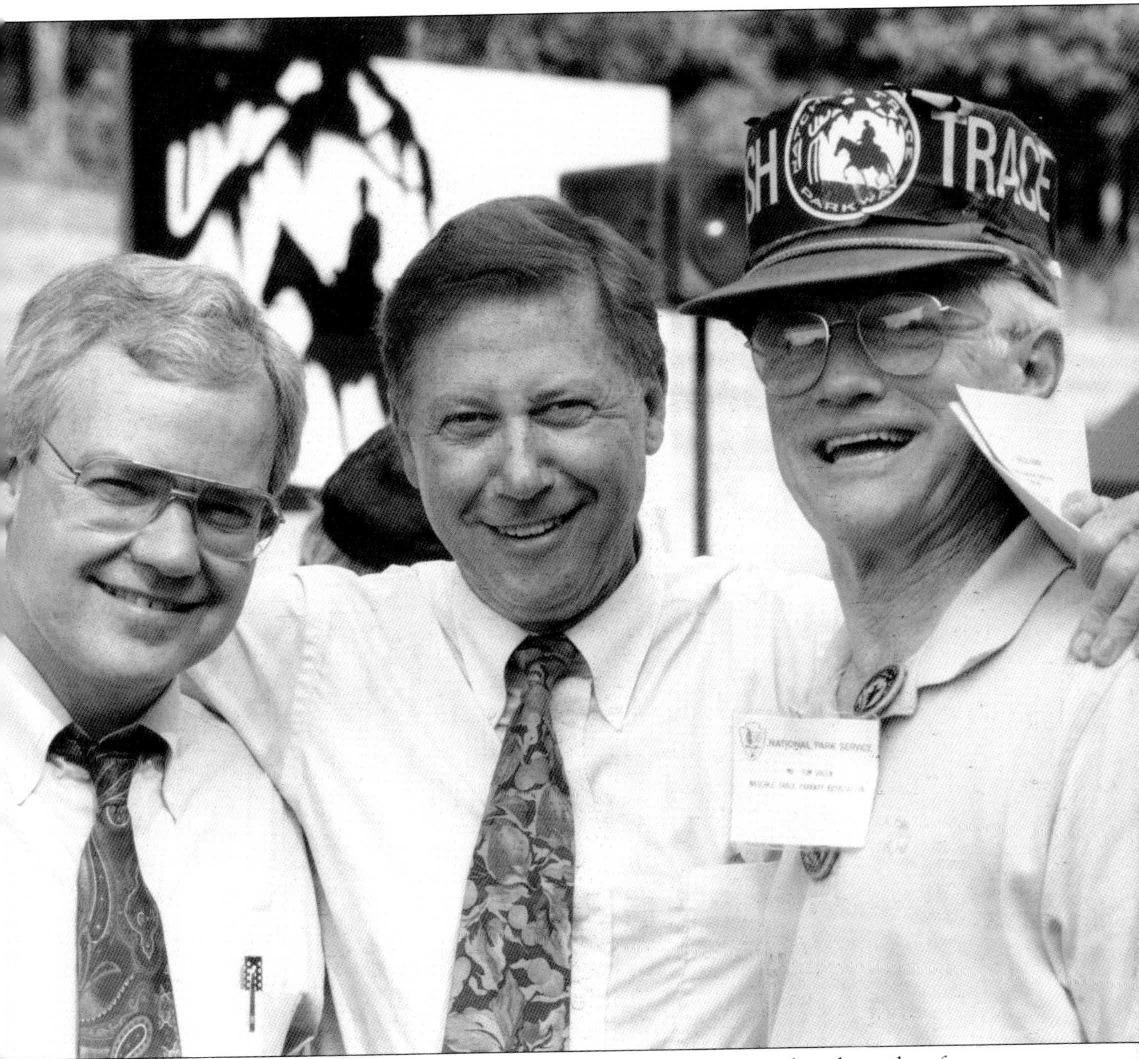

The roadway would never be finished unless a concentrated effort was made to lay miles of pavement. Counties, cities, chambers of commerce, and tourist sites were mobilized. Calvin Lehew urged members to work to "make the cash registers ring" down the parkway. Their voices were heard, and construction was renewed. Annual two-day membership meetings focused on construction progress reports and tourism development. Pictured, from left to right, are Congressman Bob Clement, Calvin Lehew, and Tom Green. (Courtesy of Tom Green Collection.)

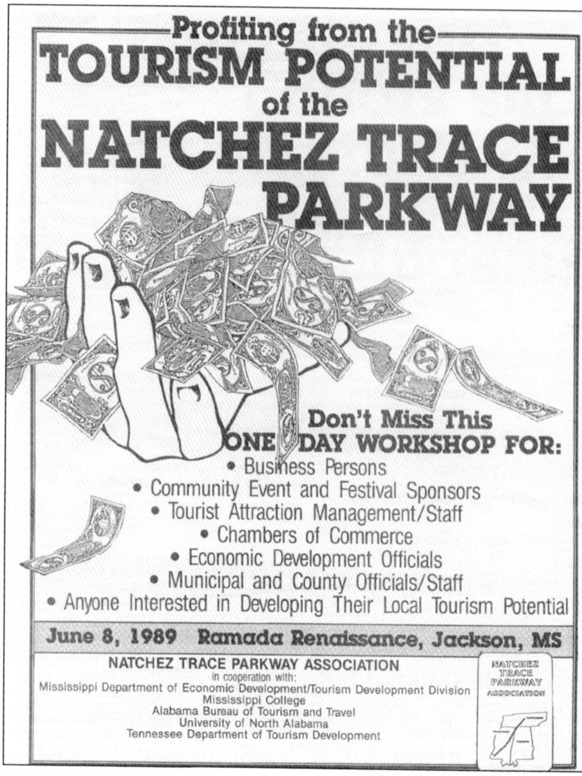

The parkway association encouraged tourism to stimulate additional interest in completing the road. A marketing plan was developed, and *Trace Travels* was published in a magazine format in time for the 50th anniversary of the parkway. *Forbes* magazine publisher Malcolm Forbes aided the effort by riding his motorcycle the length of the Trace to draw public attention to the national park. When asked if he had an ulterior motive, Forbes said, "the fun of doing it." (Courtesy of Tom Green Collection.)

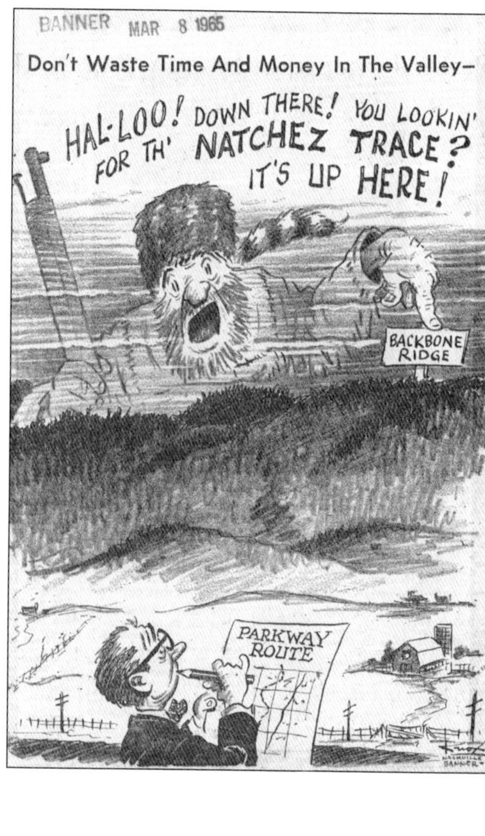

Work on the northern end slowed when a dispute arose over the route the parkway should take through Leiper's Fork, Tennessee. Plans at first called for the road to follow the original route through the town. Businessmen and farmers whose property would be taken argued for a route along an undeveloped area of the ridge. The route was moved, and work resumed. (Nashville Public Library, Special Collections.)

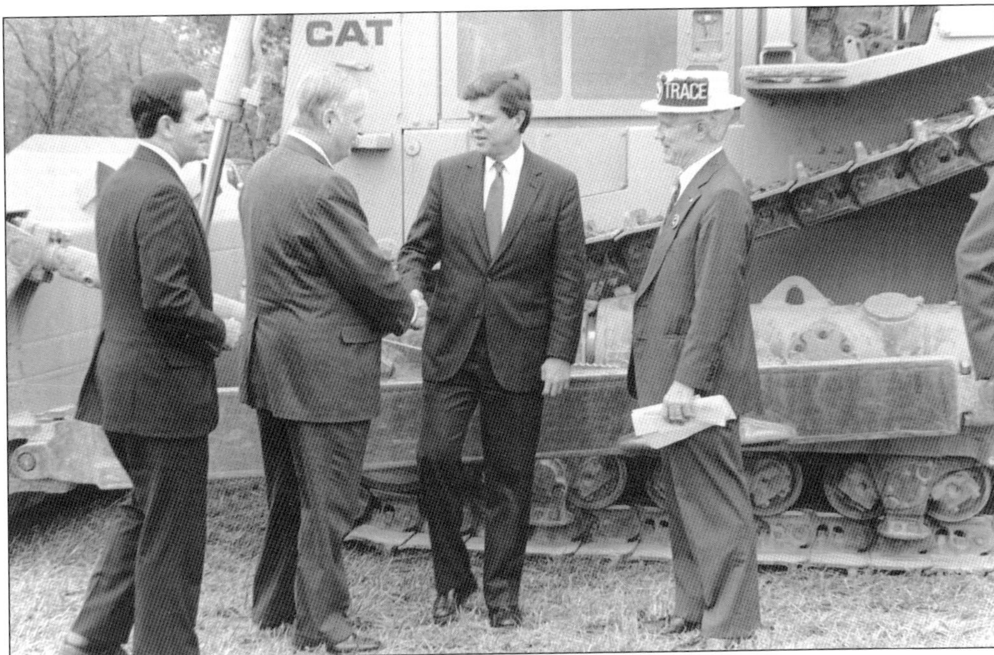

The ground-breaking ceremony at the northern terminus in 1988 was a psychological milestone in the effort to build the parkway. For years, Nashville residents had driven by an abandoned house and a cedar-woodworking store on Highway 100 and pointed out that someday the Natchez Trace would end there. When large bulldozers removed the structures, the end was in sight. (Courtesy of Tom Green Collection.)

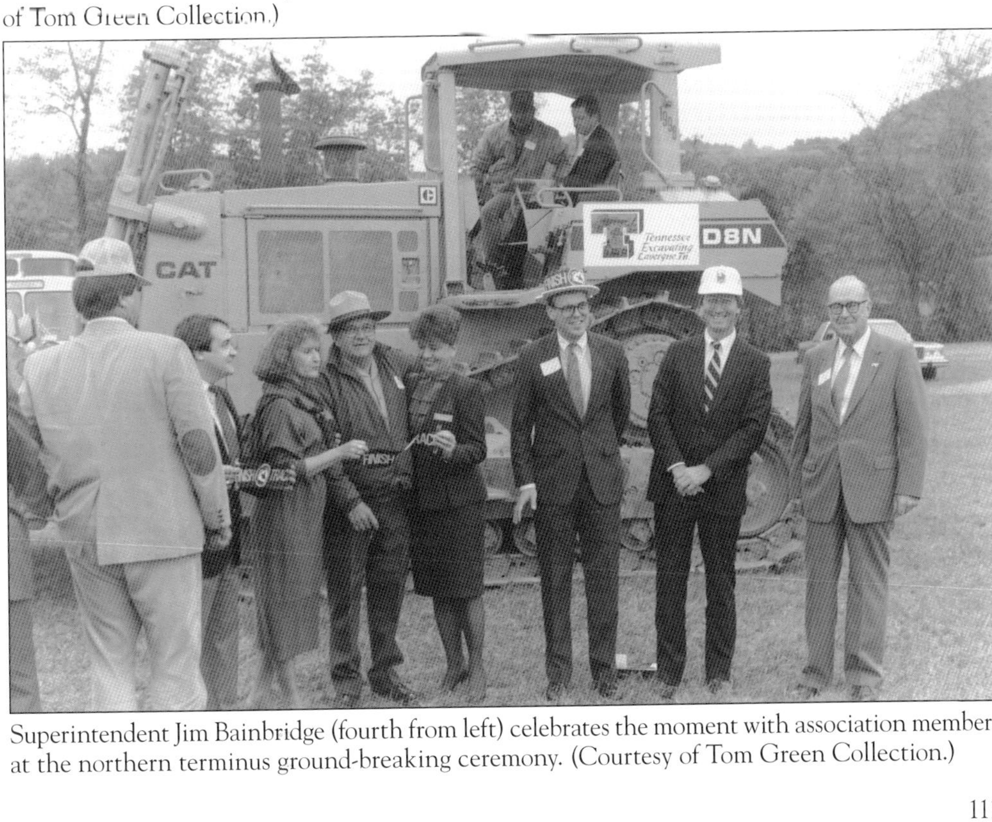

Superintendent Jim Bainbridge (fourth from left) celebrates the moment with association members at the northern terminus ground-breaking ceremony. (Courtesy of Tom Green Collection.)

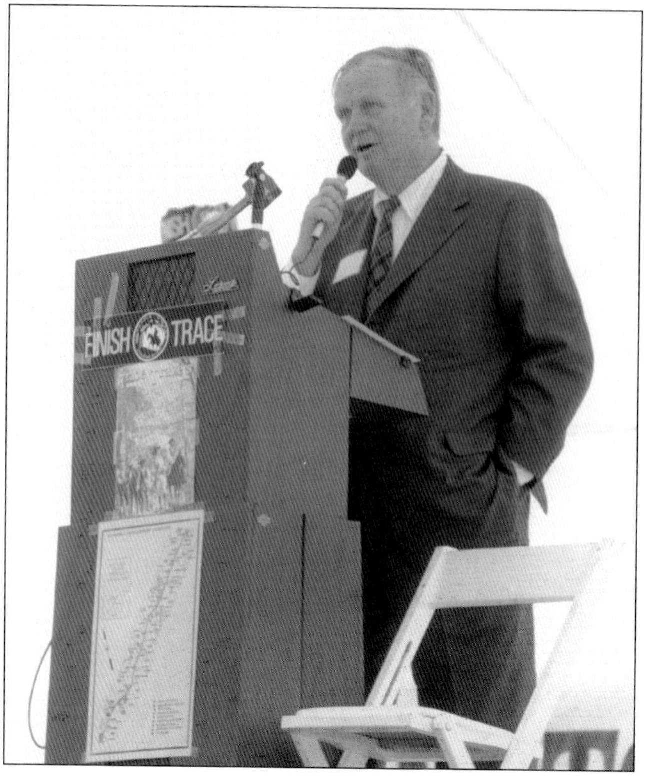

Nashville state senator Douglas Henry, a longtime supporter of the Natchez Trace Parkway, speaks at the northern terminus ground-breaking. (Courtesy of Tom Green Collection.)

The 50th anniversary celebration of the parkway was held at parkway headquarters in Tupelo, Mississippi. Pictured in the center are association president Calvin Lehew and future association president Buel Springer. Festivities included Choctaw dancers, stickball demonstrations, folk demonstrations, and a parade of antique cars. (Courtesy of Calvin Lehew.)

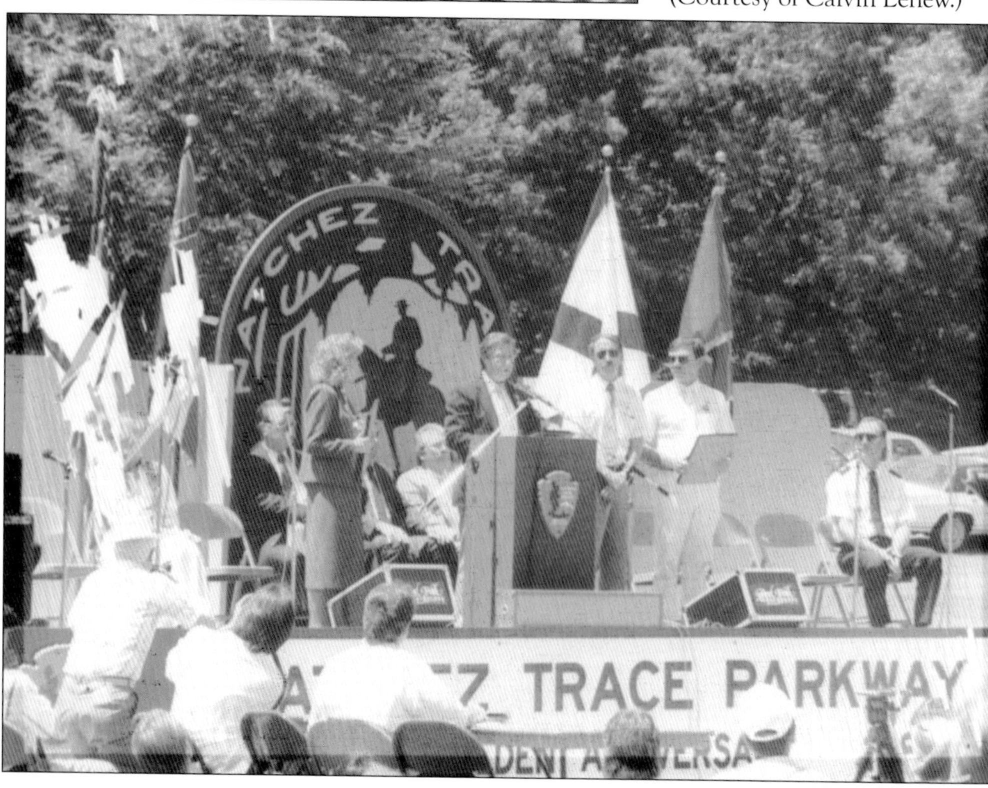

Tupelo CDF secretary Betty Scott maintained the organizational duties of the association for almost two decades, assuming much of the role Ralph Landrum had served. (Courtesy of Tom Green Collection.)

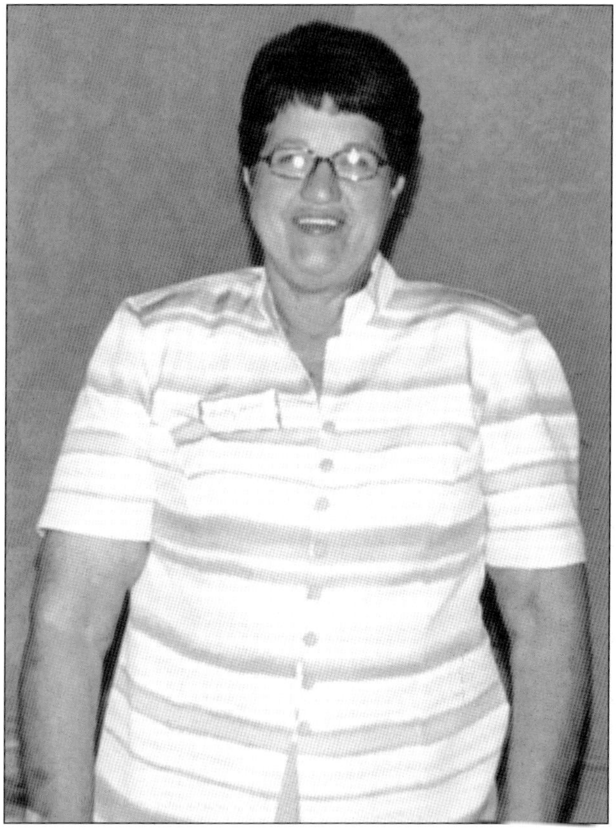

Superintendent Dan Brown oversaw completion of the road on the northern end. On July 3, 1991, more than 400 people attended a ceremony to open 13 miles of parkway at Garrison Road, at mile marker 428. Pictured here are, from left to right, superintendent Dan Brown, Sen. Jim Sasser's representative Harold Totty, Tony Turnbow, former president Calvin Lehew, and Tennessee state senator Keith Jordan. In addition to those cutting the ribbon, speakers included Herbert Harper, director of the Tennessee Historical Commission. (Courtesy of Williamson County Chamber of Commerce.)

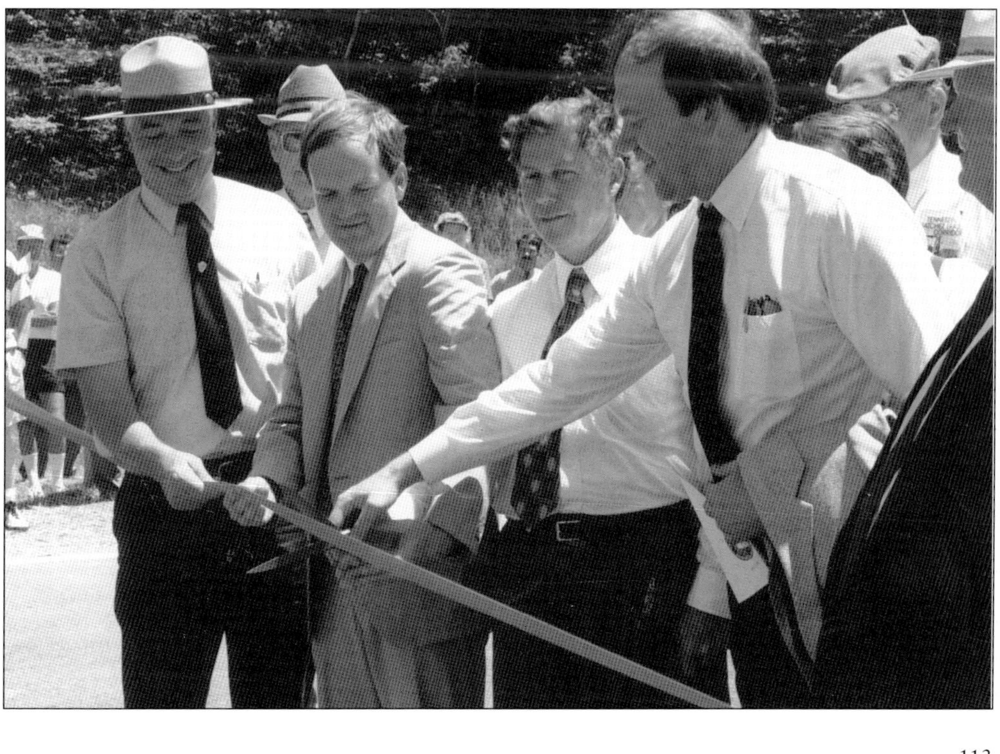

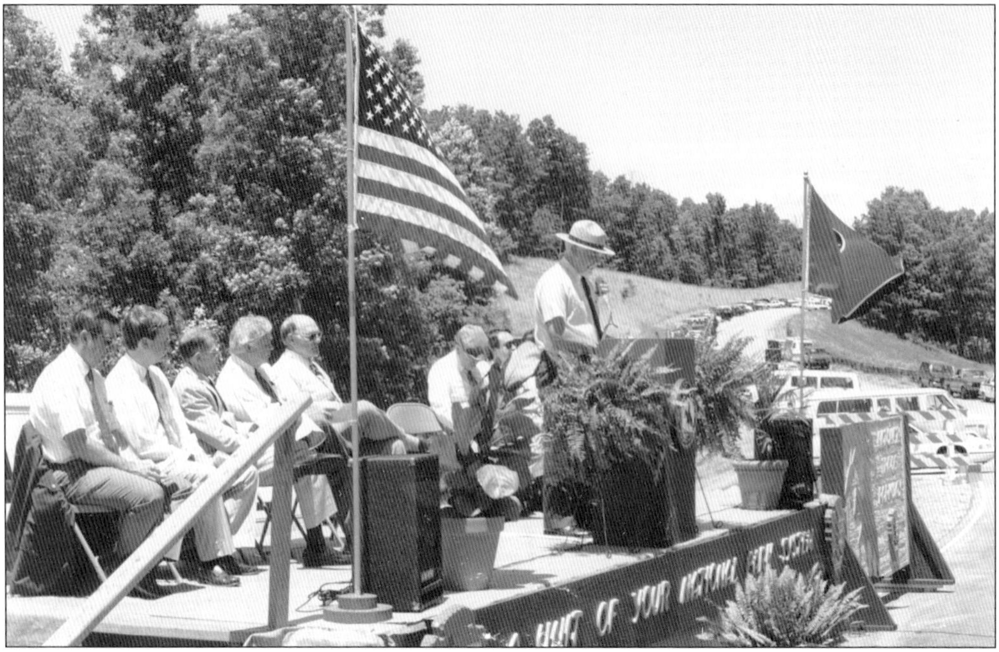

Participation in Tennessee increased as the completion of the northern end appeared to be a real possibility. The Garrison Creek site is near the original location of one of the forts that defended early Nashville. Soon after the opening, volunteers built a 20-mile horseback-riding trail from Garrison Road south to the Gordon House. This trail is now part of the Natchez Trace National Scenic Trail. (Courtesy of Dan Brown.)

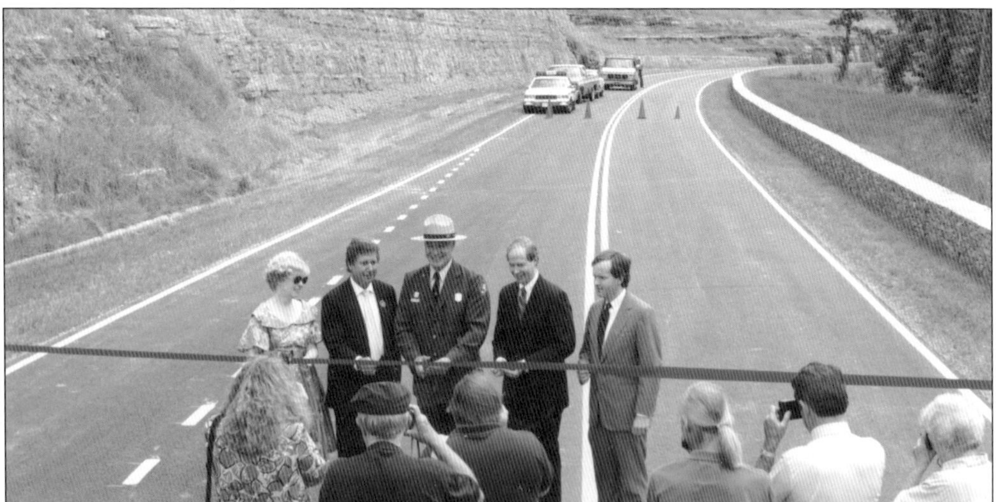

The pace of construction increased. Just two years after the opening of the Garrison Road segment, another 13 miles of parkway were opened at Leiper's Fork, Tennessee, on June 21, 1993, for the next segment to Tennessee Highway 96. Superintendent Brown told the 200 people who attended that if all went well, the Tennessee portion would be complete in about two years. Pictured here are, from left to right, Ilene Cornwell, Calvin Lehew, Superintendent Brown, Congressman Bart Gordon's representative Kent Syler, and Tony Turnbow. (Courtesy of Williamson County Chamber of Commerce.)

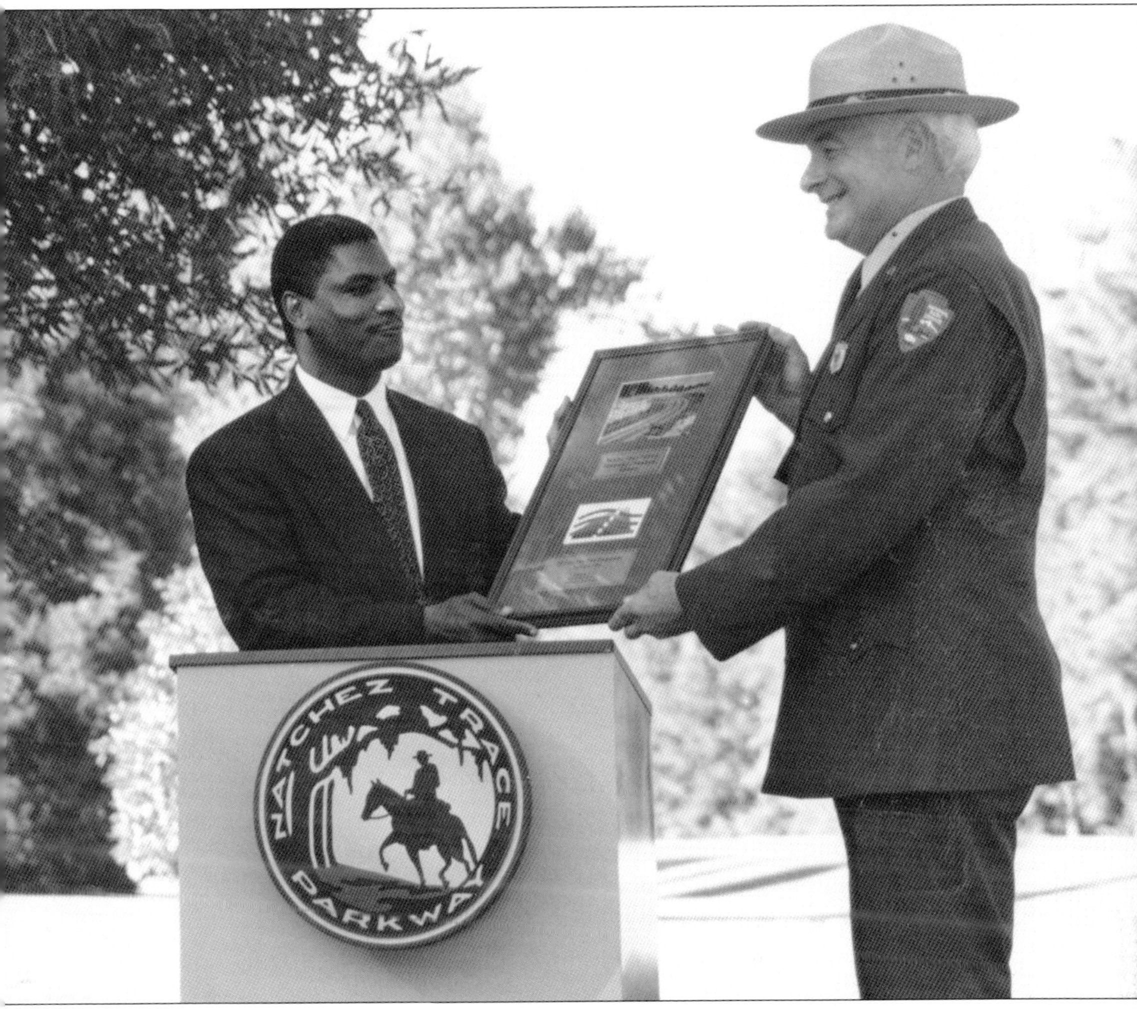

At a ceremony at the visitor center on September 26, 1993, Federal Highway Administration director Rodney Slater presents a plaque to Superintendent Brown acknowledging that the Natchez Trace Parkway has been designated an "All American Road"— a National Scenic Byways certification that travelers will have "an exceptional traveling experience" based solely upon the scenic beauty. It is the National Scenic Byways Program's highest honor. (NPS.)

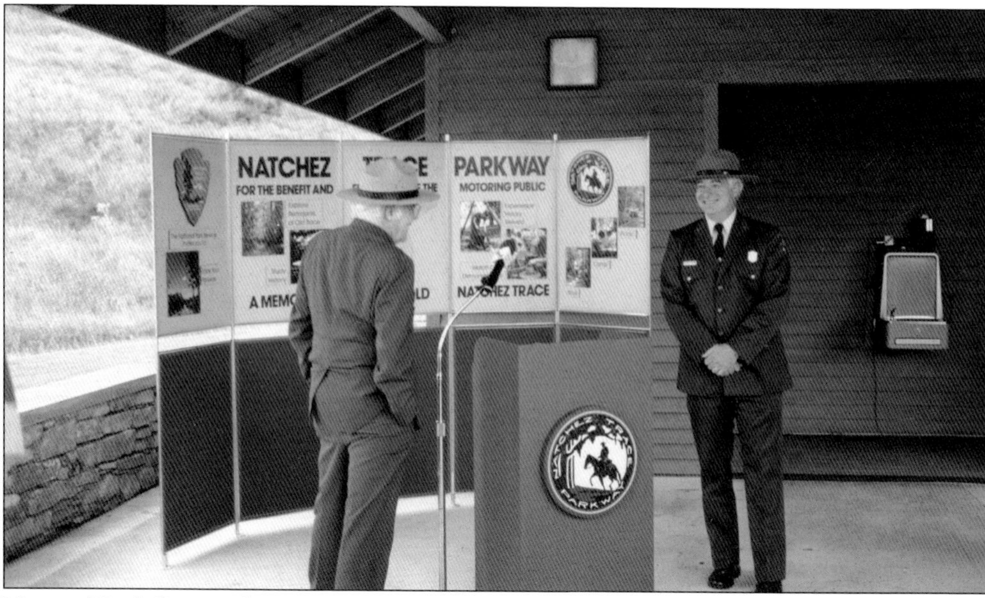

National Park Service director Roger Kennedy toured the parkway in the mid-1990s to view the progress. Kennedy, a former NBC correspondent and historian, also wrote about prehistoric tribes who lived in the Southeast. (Courtesy of Dan Brown.)

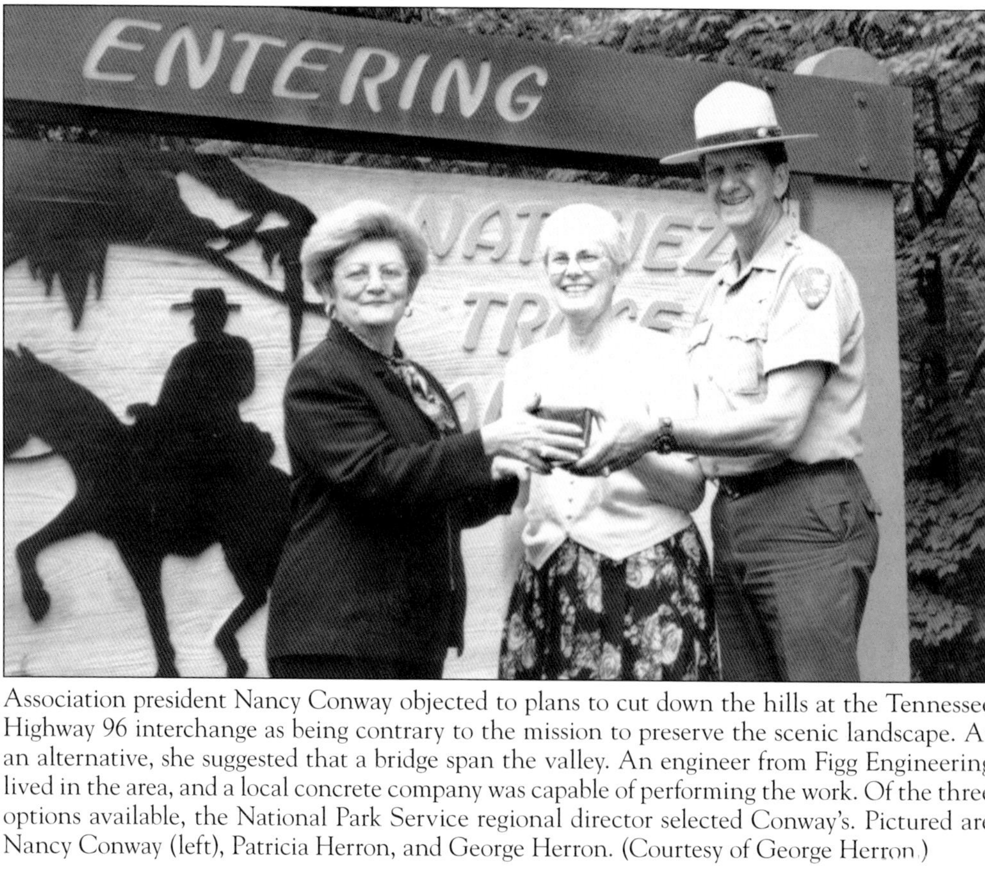

Association president Nancy Conway objected to plans to cut down the hills at the Tennessee Highway 96 interchange as being contrary to the mission to preserve the scenic landscape. As an alternative, she suggested that a bridge span the valley. An engineer from Figg Engineering lived in the area, and a local concrete company was capable of performing the work. Of the three options available, the National Park Service regional director selected Conway's. Pictured are Nancy Conway (left), Patricia Herron, and George Herron. (Courtesy of George Herron.)

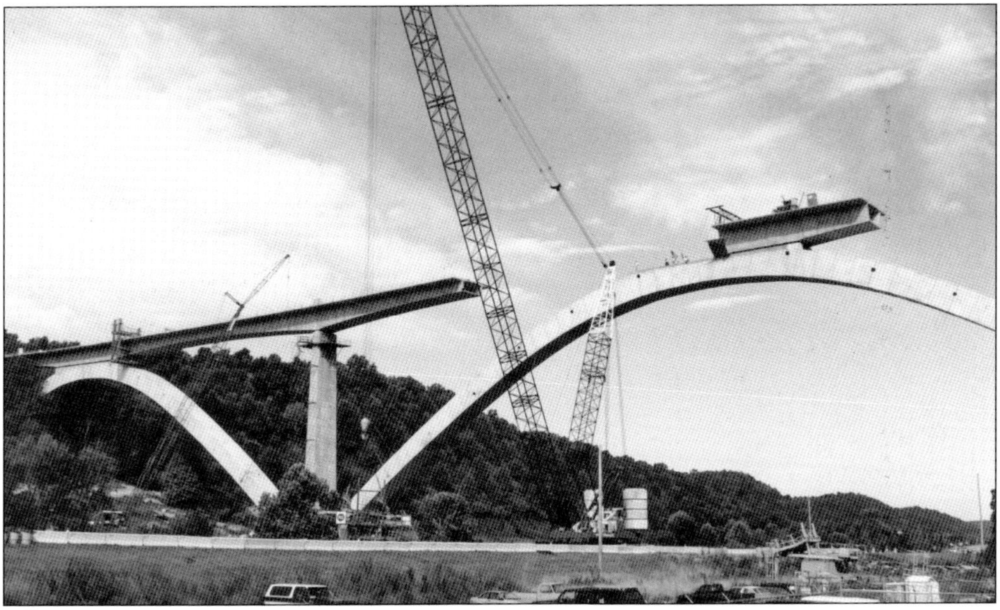

The Double Arch bridge across Birdsong Hollow was an engineering feat, the first of its kind in the United States. The designer told the audience at the ground-breaking ceremony that he thought his team had finally figured out a way to keep it from falling. Guests in the audience who did not appreciate the engineering humor commented that they did not want to be the first to cross the bridge. (Courtesy of George Herron.)

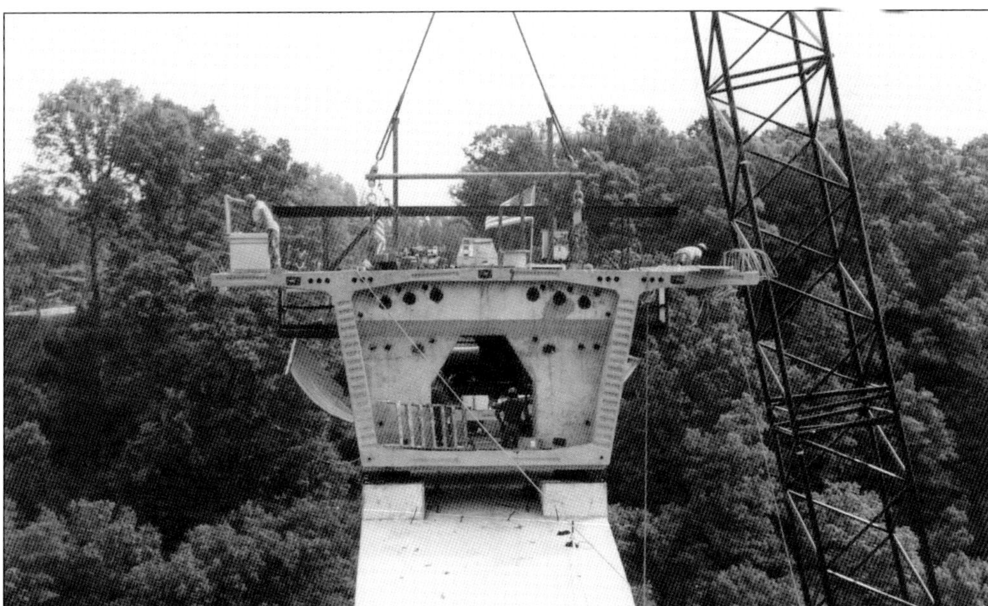

Pieces of the Double Arch Bridge were cast from concrete off-site at a local plant, assembled in place, and connected using heavy cables for support. The bridge would provide a bird's-eye view of the hollow, but it would also become one of the few locations on the parkway where attention would be drawn to the structural elements of the road. (Courtesy of George Herron.)

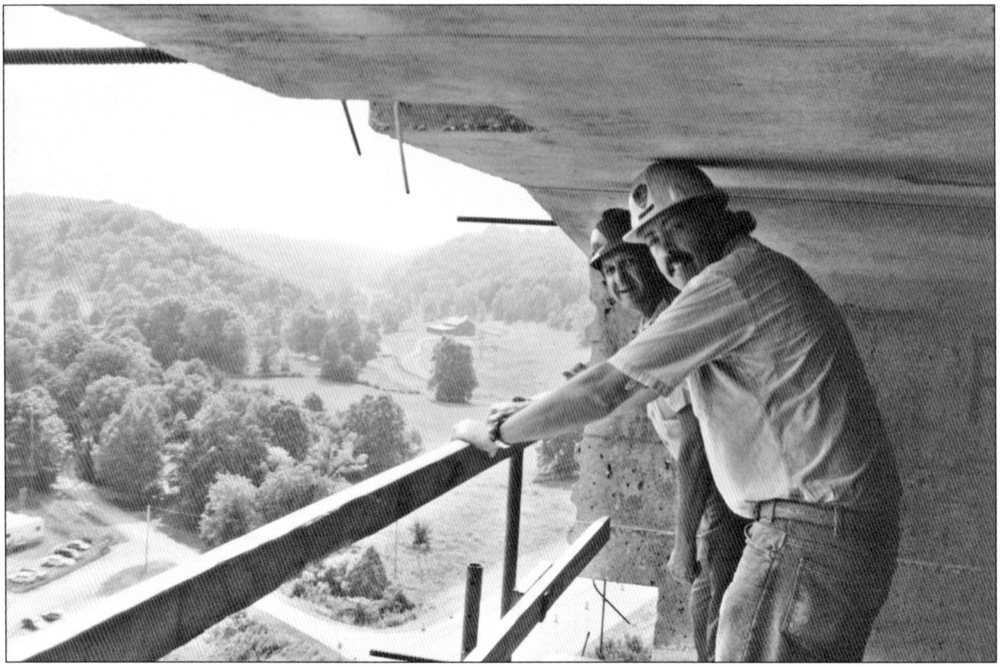

Northern District Ranger George Herron (left) and NPS Denver Project Supervisor Bob Felker inspect the bridge during construction. (Courtesy of George Herron.)

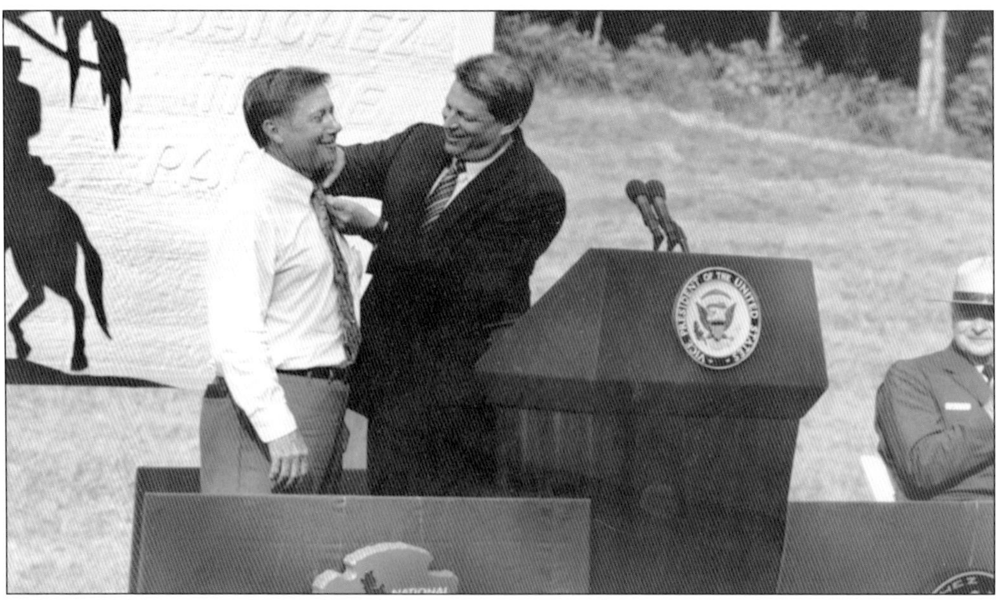

A farmer told young Calvin Lehew that the government planned to build a parkway, but the boy would never live long enough to see it. The farmer could not know that a teenage Lehew would work as babysitter for future vice president Al Gore and take up the challenge to "Finish the Trace" as association president. Lehew introduced the vice president at the northern terminus completion ceremony in Nashville on June 22, 1996. Here, Gore pins a Secret Service pin on Lehew as his "First Bodyguard." (Courtesy of Calvin Lehew.)

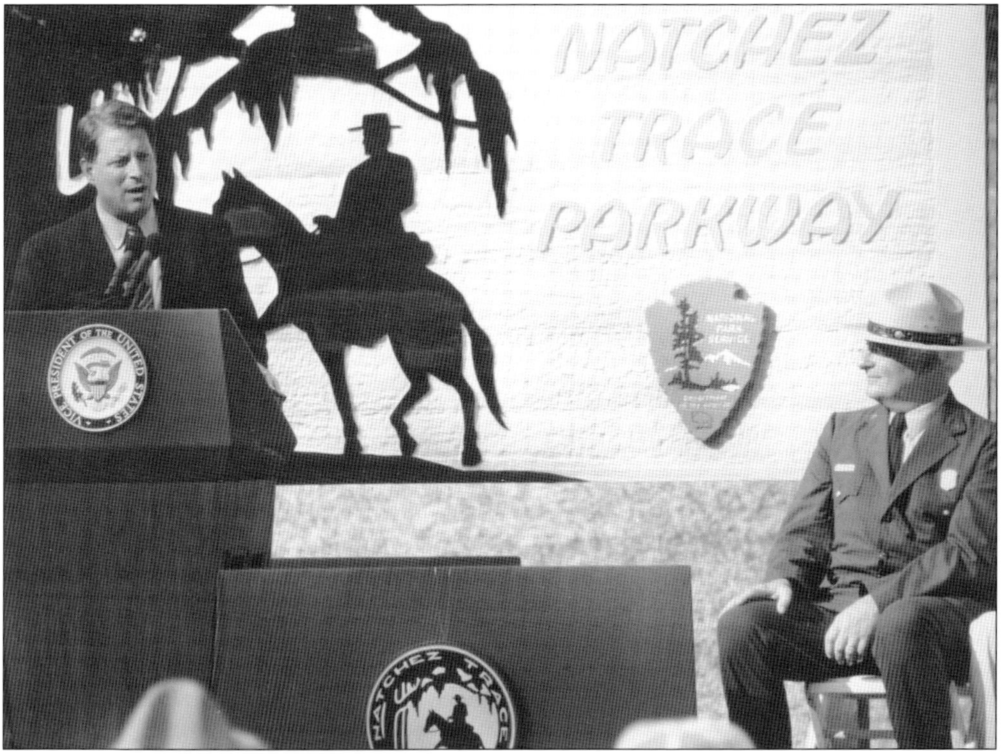

Vice President Gore told the crowd that cutting ribbons was the most exciting thing he got to do as vice president. (Above, courtesy of George Herron; below, courtesy of Dan Brown.)

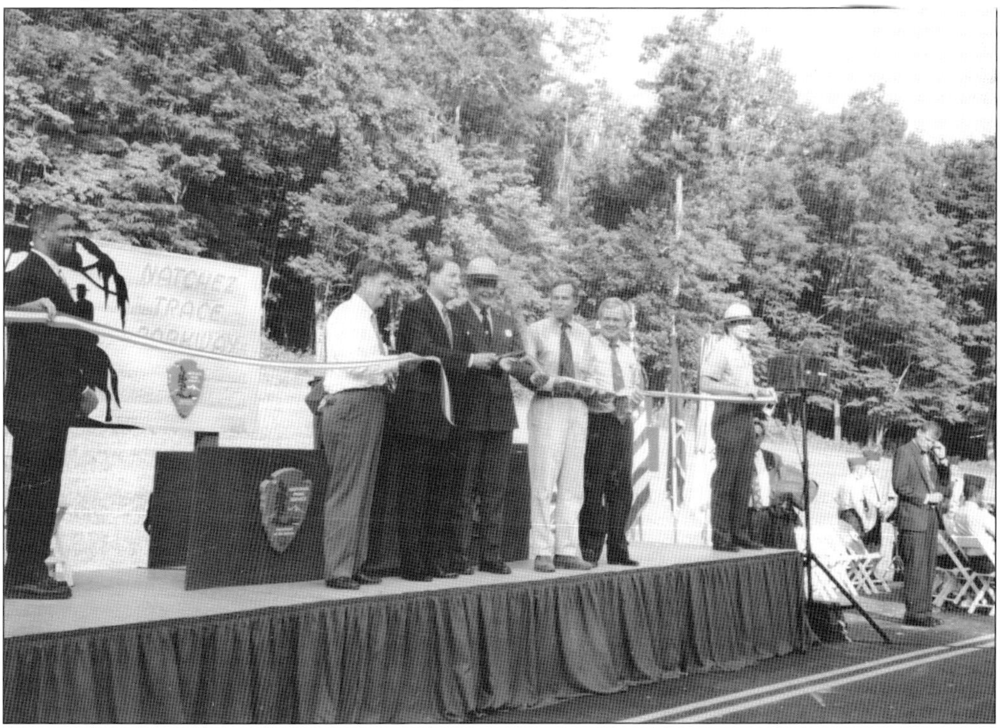

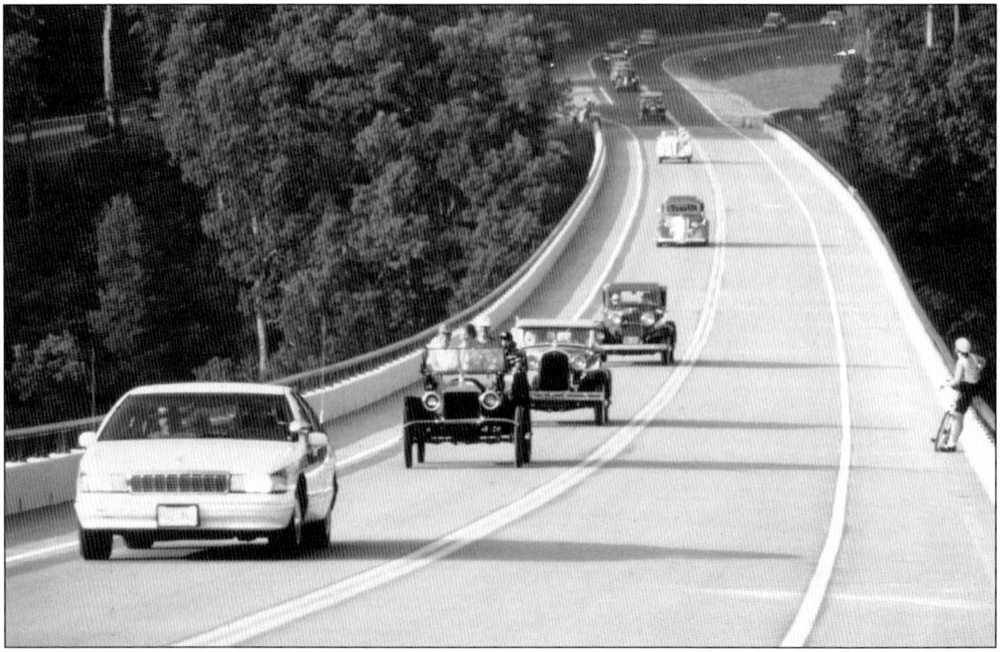

VIPs attending the ribbon-cutting at the northern terminus rode in cars representing various decades of travel. They formed a motorcade to become the first to travel south on the newly opened roadway from Nashville and across the Double Arch Bridge. (Courtesy of George Herron.)

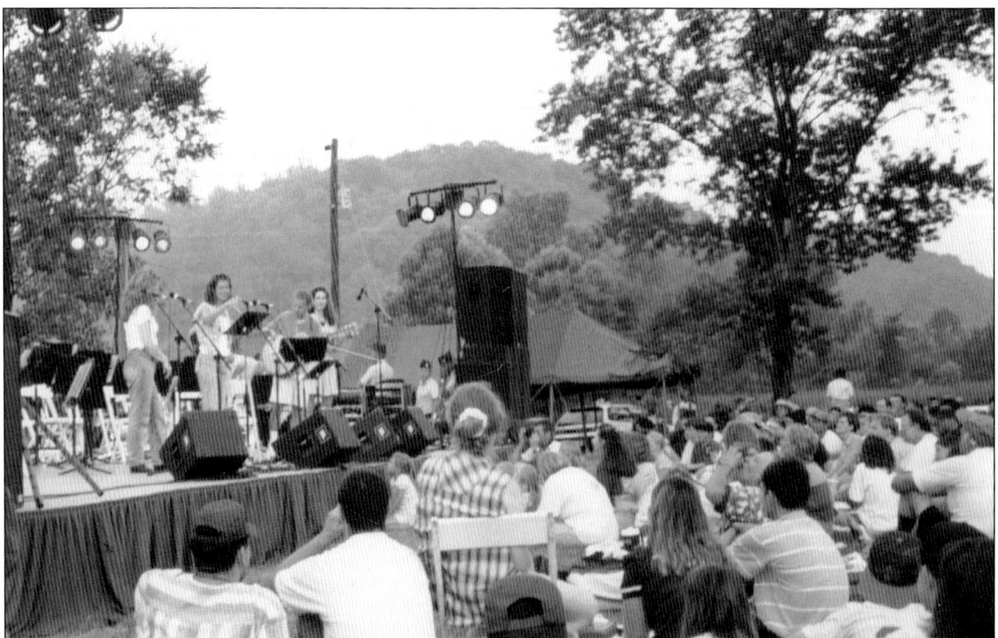

Following the ribbon-cutting at the northern terminus, recording artist Amy Grant and the 101st Airborne Infantry Orchestra performed as part of an evening concert in the shadow of the Natchez Trace Parkway bridge. The crowd enjoyed an ice-cream social on the warm summer's evening, listening to the music as the sun set behind the bridge. (Courtesy of Tom Green Collection.)

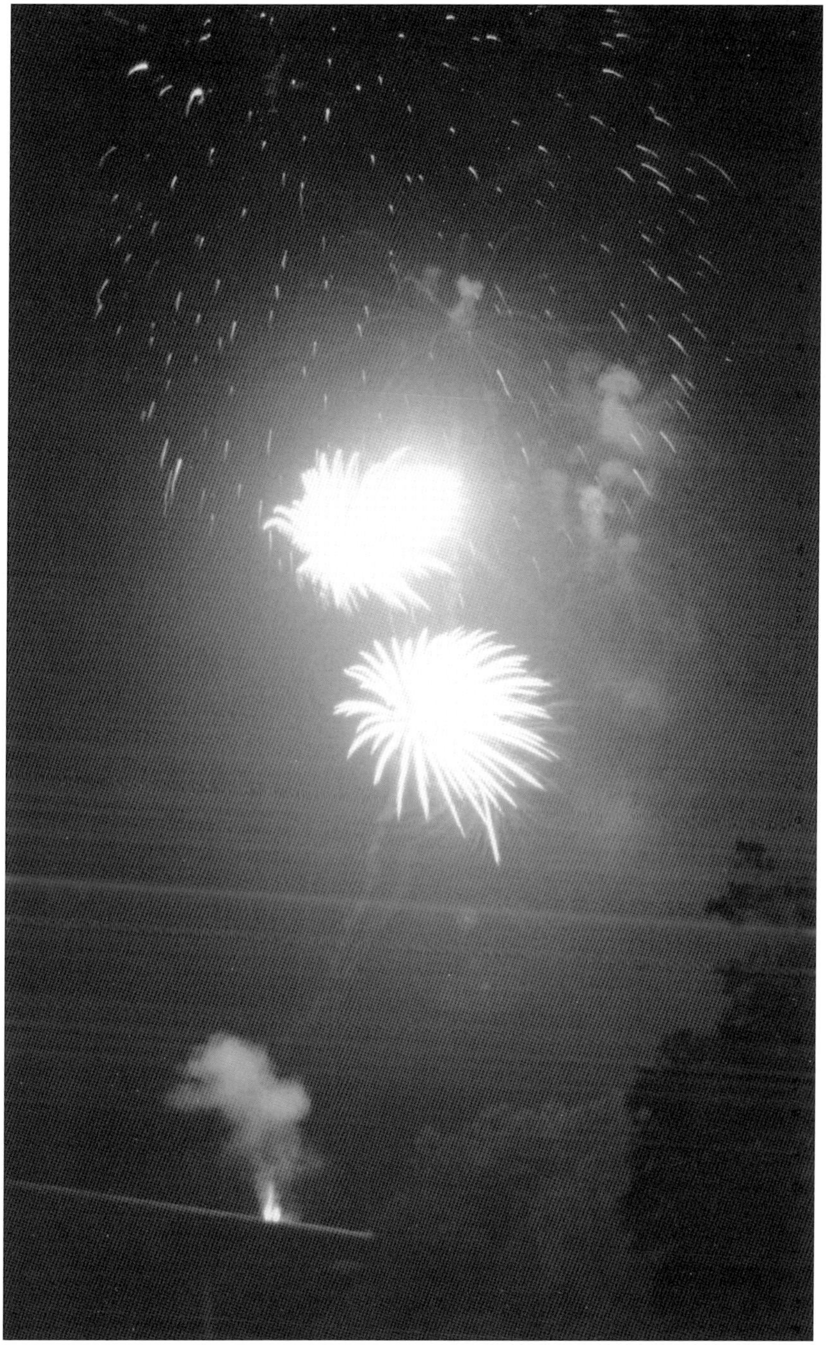

At dusk, as the orchestra played "Stars and Stripes Forever," fireworks silhouetted the new bridge spanning the valley. The brilliant colors reflected a justified moment of celebration. When rallies were held along the parkway 60 years earlier, the completion of the roadway into either Natchez or Nashville was a distant dream the earliest supporters would not live to see. Roane Fleming Byrnes was present in the minds of those she had recruited over the years to make the event possible. Her nickname, "Sweet Annie," was invoked often that day. (Courtesy of George Herron.)

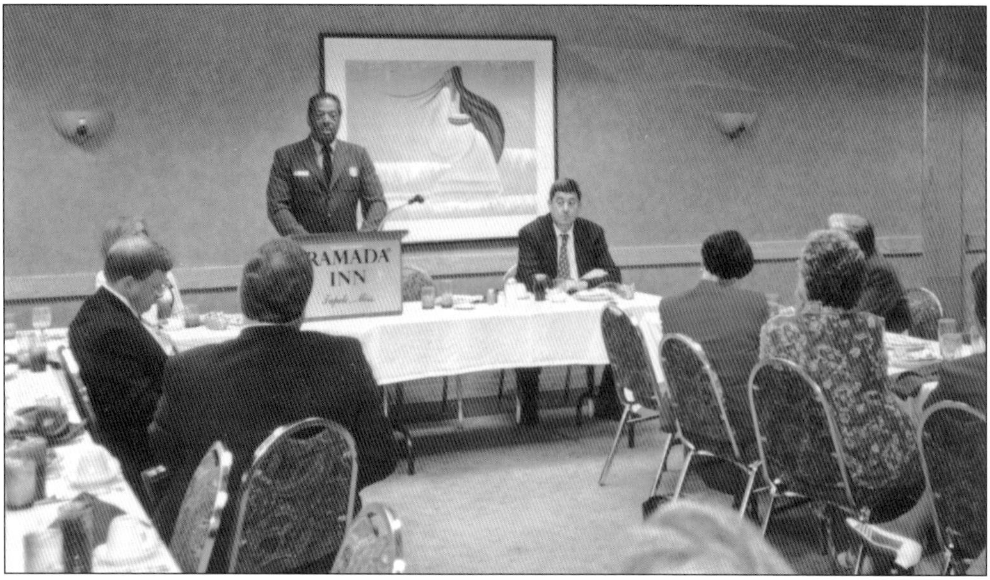

Executive director Jim Ballard, seated at the head of the table, and superintendent Wendell Simpson addressed the association meeting in Tupelo. Completing the road to the southern terminus was the focal point, but for the first time, the association looked beyond the completion of the road and began a serious discussion with the National Park Service about visitor amenities to be added to the list of priorities. Funds were soon sought for a multiuse trail at Ridgeland and assistance with a Chickasaw cultural center near Tupelo. (Courtesy of Tom Green Collection.)

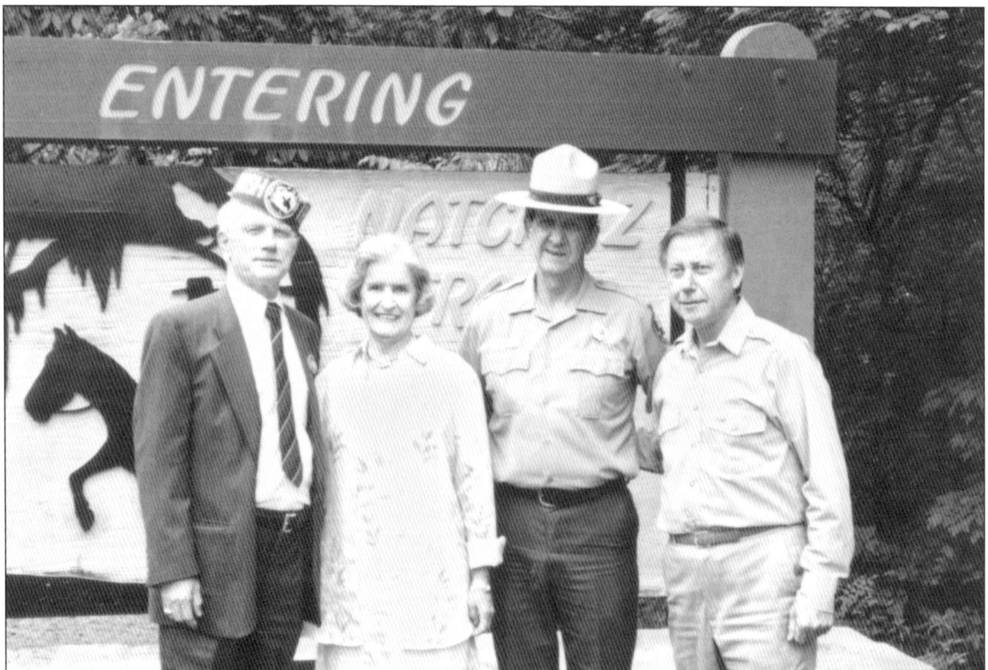

Former parkway association presidents, from left to right, Tom Green, Jean Nelson, and Calvin Lehew honored retiring District Ranger George Herron, who supervised the northern district. (Courtesy of Tom Green Collection.)

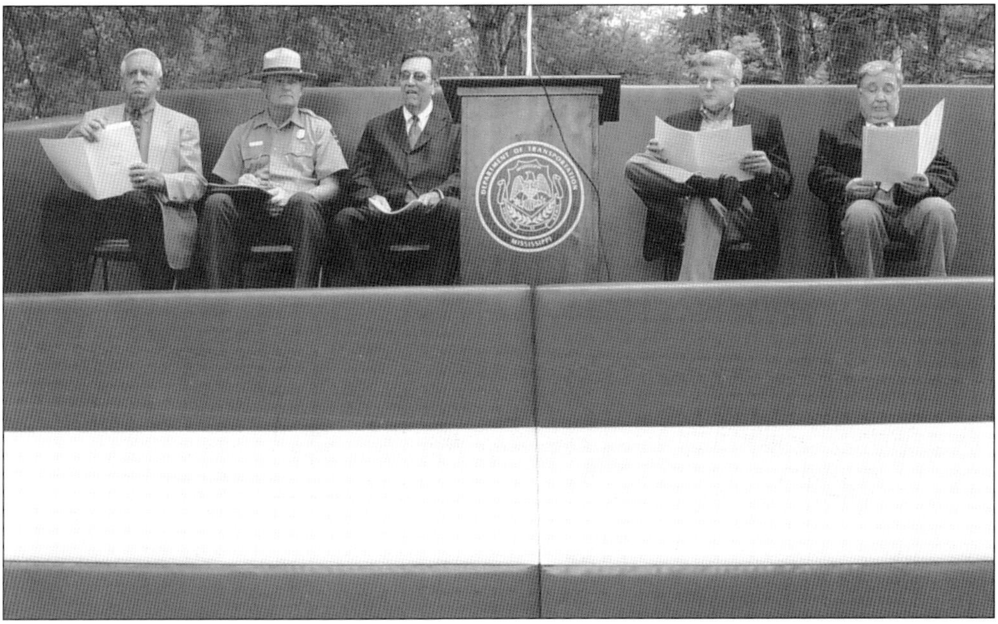

S.A. "Junior" Hancock served as association president in 1976, but more often, he worked as a director to push for parkway completion. The City of Tupelo honored Hancock's work by naming one of the parkway exchanges in his honor. Pictured here are, from left to right, North Mississippi highway commissioner Bill Minor; acting parkway superintendent Stennis Young; City of Tupelo mayor Ed Neelly; state senator Alan Nunnlee, and Harry Martin. (Courtesy of Harry Martin.)

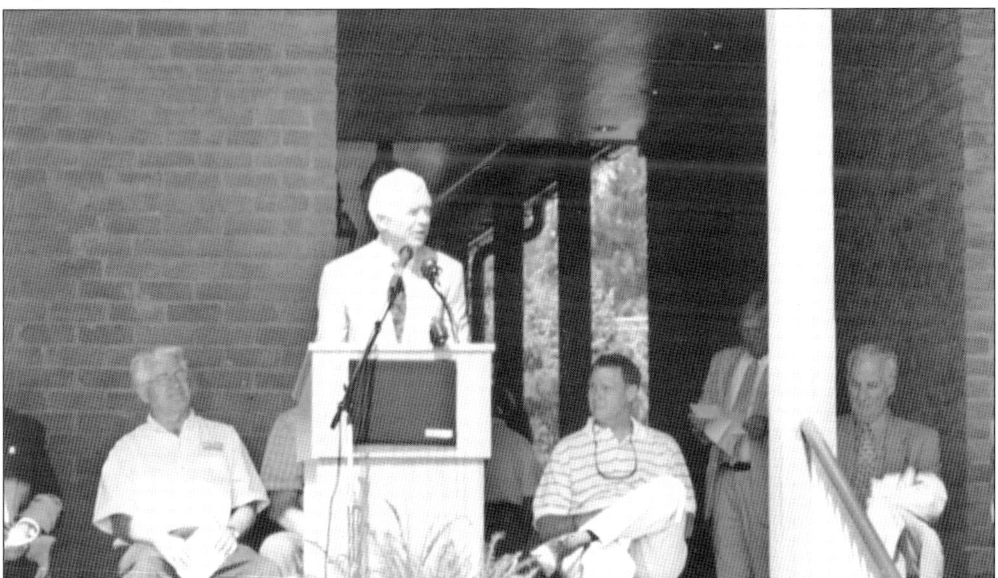

Sen. Thad Cochran speaks at the opening of the visitor center in Clinton, Mississippi. The center, like an earlier project in Kosciusko and a later one in Collinwood, was located off the parkway as a community project and represented new interest from adjoining communities in helping improve the visitor experience on the parkway and to reconnect their towns to parkway activity. Dignitaries then formed a motorcade of 61 cars, representing the 61 years it took to complete the road, for the drive to Natchez for the final opening ceremony. (Courtesy of Tom Green Collection.)

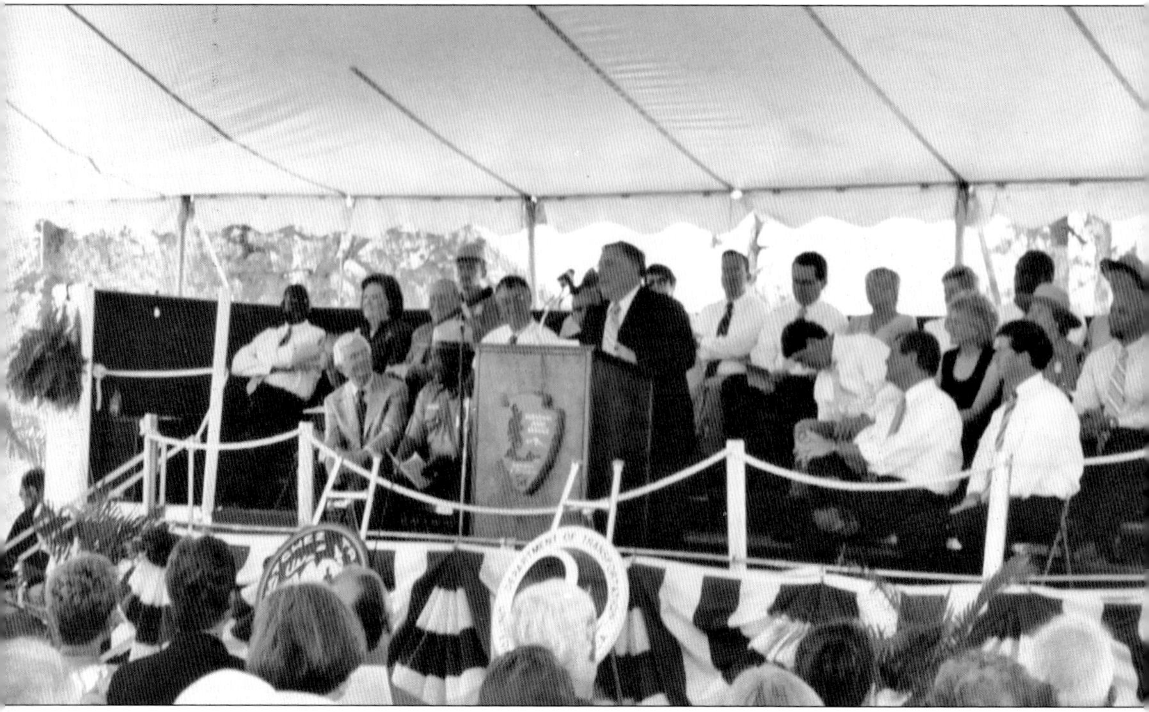

Set in motion in Natchez in 1937, events came full circle with the completion of the final section of roadway at mile marker 1 on May 21, 2005. Here, Harry Martin addresses the crowd assembled not far from Brandon Hall, where the inaugural celebration had been held in 1937. (Courtesy of Tom Green Collection.)

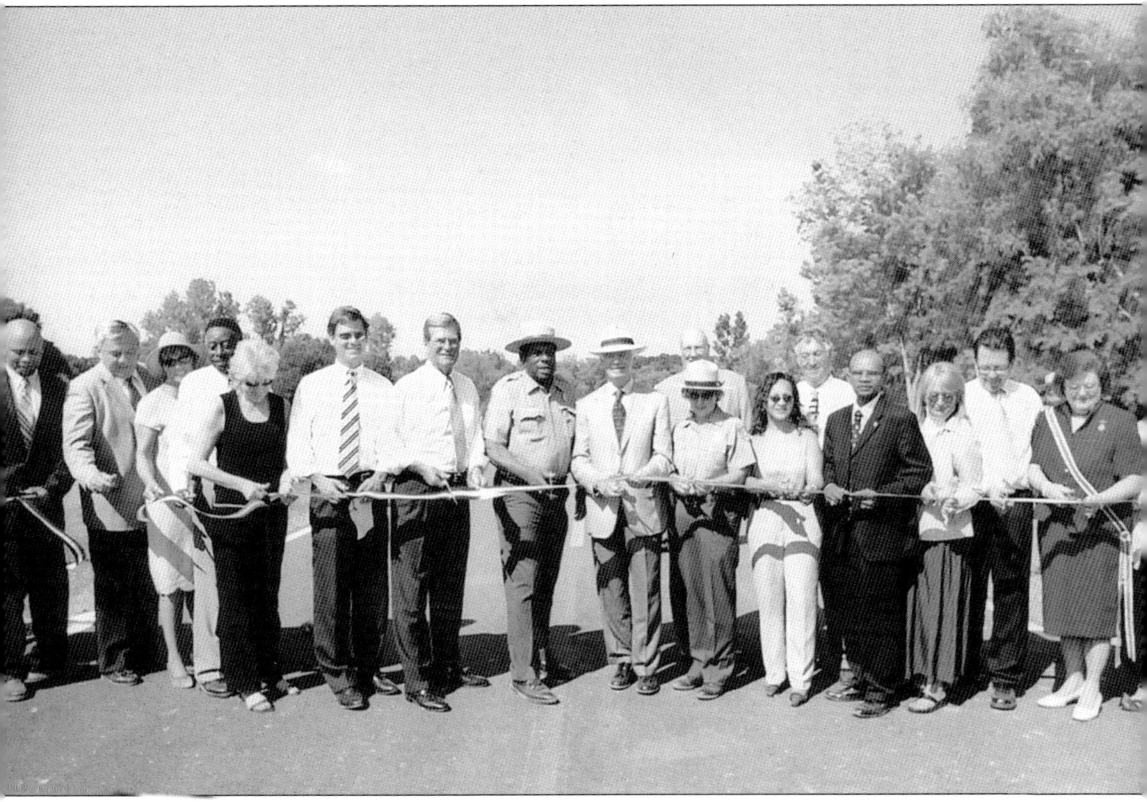

At the conclusion of the ceremony under the tent, dignitaries walked out to the parkway road to cut the ribbon to open the last segment. Identified are Harry Martin (far left), Rep. Chip Pickering (seventh from left), Sen. Trent Lott (eighth from left), parkway superintendent Wendell Simpson (ninth from left), Sen. Thad Cochran (tenth from left), National Park Service director Fran Mainella (eleventh from left), and regional director Patricia Hooks. Senator Cochran observed that the Romans had built the Appian Way in less time than it took the United States to complete the Natchez Trace Parkway motor road. (Courtesy of Dot Ward.)

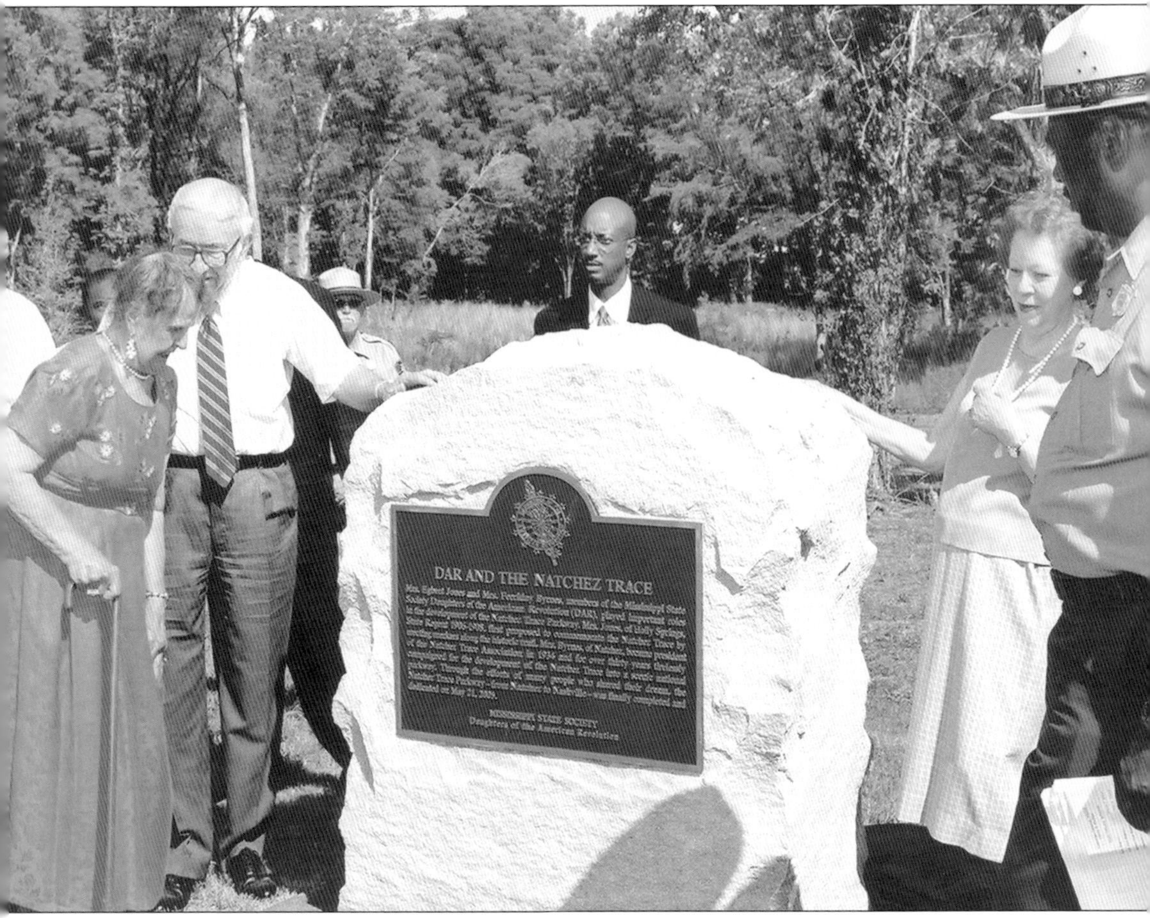

Once the ribbon was cut, descendants of early leaders in the movement were present for the dedication of the DAR monument at the southern terminus. Pictured in the foreground, from left to right, are Byrnes's niece Kate Don Green; Mrs. Egbert Jones's grandchildren Blanton Jones and Mrs. Edward B. Warren; and Superintendent Wendell Simpson. The marker honors the work of Elizabeth Jones and Roane Fleming Byrnes. A dinner at Rosalie, on the bluff of the Mississippi River, concluded the celebration. The man standing directly behind the monument is unidentified. (Courtesy of Dot Ward.)

About the Organization

A Modern-Day Path through American History

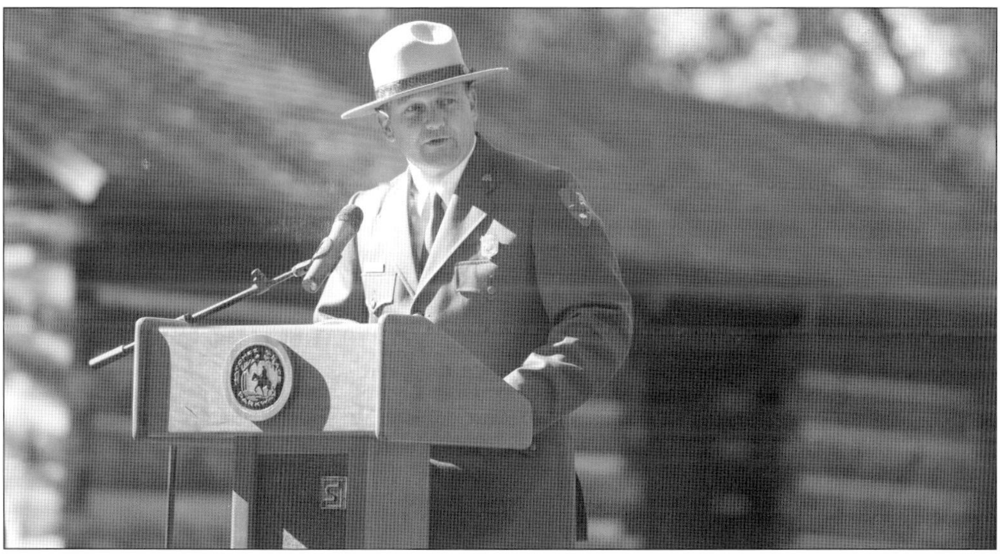

Superintendent Cam Sholly has worked to rehabilitate aging facilities and to "put the park in the parkway." He is shown in this photograph speaking at the 2009 national memorial service for Meriwether Lewis on the 200th anniversary of the explorer's death. Superintendent Sholly has overseen major rehabilitation of the Meriwether Lewis site. Now that the roadway has been completed, the last phase of development is to create amenities to help visitors to learn from, and fully appreciate, their experience of the parkway. The association now turns its focus to supporting the completion of the park portion of the Natchez Trace Parkway and finally achieving the original goal. (TN.)

The association is a nonprofit group that continues to work with the National Park Service to encourage the exploration of the park, promote the completion of the park, support parkway maintenance and programs, and protect the parkway and its scenic views. To become a member, visit the parkway association's web site www.natcheztrace.info